LIFE AFTER JOY

About the Author

Gary Cunningham is a writer, musician, inspirational speaker and author of *Joys of Joy: Finding Myself in an Irish Prison*. He keeps a regular blog which can be found at https:// garcunningham. wordpress.com.

LIFE AFTER JOY

A Prisoner No More

Gary Cunningham

The Liffey Press

Published by
The Liffey Press Ltd
'Clareville'
307 Clontarf Road
Dublin D03 PO46, Ireland
www.theliffeypress.com

A catalogue record of this book is
available from the British Library.

ISBN 978-0-9957927-5-3

Printed in Spain by GraphyCems.

Contents

Contents

Dedication

To the memory of my beautiful Megan. You will always and forever own a very special place in my heart. And to Lily and Annie. I would not be where I am today without the two of you. I love you both with all I've got.

PREFACE

'It must be an incredible feeling, Gary, freedom.' This was a statement I heard on many occasions after my release from prison. And yes, of course, it was fantastic being free after serving two years and nine months in Mountjoy Prison, and then Loughan House. And yet, incredibly, in the early days, at times I longed to be back...

My initial incarceration brought with it so much shame and regret. I had let down every single person who meant the world to me. I had let myself down. Therefore, I chose to use my time inside to radically change everything about myself, both inside and out, and that ended up being the best decision I have ever made. So, when the day of my eventual release finally arrived, I felt I was ready, ready to take this life by the scruff, ready to hit the ground running. How wrong I was.

I was to enter a world that not even the Irish Prison Service, and all the assistance they provided, could have prepared me for. A world of judgement, snide remarks and knock backs. In prison I was 'someone', I was accepted. But in the free world I felt like an outcast. Please don't think I am calling for the violins here. The only person to blame for my incarceration was me, and me alone. I was the fool who chose to go and collect a stupid amount of cannabis. I deserved everything I got. I am not a man that hides behind a plethora of excuses any more. I did before my incarceration, but not today. I believe that we should all own our mistakes and failings. Only then can people begin to forgive you, and can you begin to forgive yourself.

The story of my shameful stint in prison was documented in my first book, *Joys of Joy: Finding Myself in an Irish Prison*, a book whose success no one, including me, ever saw coming. No pressure with this book so! In the telling of that story, I tried to show that not every prisoner should be written off and that if you work hard, and have an honest yearning for change, you should be given the opportunity to prove yourself. And judging from the outpouring of positive comments I received from my peers, it seems I achieved this goal. But what happens once a prisoner is released? For me, this is when the hard work really began.

I had the daunting task of trying to fit back into a society that, unfortunately in some quarters, frowns upon ex-cons. I needed a job in order to try to sustain a 'normal' life. Alas, obtaining that job is a book in itself. The voice inside my head was so loud at this time, so overbearing, *What do you expect Gary? You messed up. It's all your own fault and your own doing.* I remember vividly the first two or three weeks of my release. I was engulfed in paranoia as I walked down the street, feeling like every person who passed by knew of my disgusting past. Silly, I know, and yet sadly I am not the only one with these thoughts. I have spoken to so many men and women who have also served time, and these feelings seem to be the common denominator. And those first couple of weeks of any person's release from prison are pivotal, as they are faced with the choice of whether to go forwards or backwards.

So I picked up my trusty Bic biro and decided to write the very book you now hold in your hands. This book could be viewed as *Joys of Joy, Part 2*, and for the people who loved that story I promise updates on how Fitzer (the man I traversed my sentence with and the first true friend I ever had), The Off#enders (the band Fitzer and I started behind the intimidating walls of Mountjoy Prison), and of course Antoinette (my beautiful partner and soul mate, whom I also met whilst she was on a visit in Mountjoy) are getting on. And for those who have not read *Joys of Joy*, don't worry. I will explain again who these people are and how they altered my life, not only in prison but as a free man too. But, of course, my hope and dream is that this book will stand on its own.

I was released on November 10th, 2014, and the journey I have been on since is one I could never have imagined. From humongous highs to lethal lows, this is my honest account of life after prison – a sometimes heartbreaking but most often amusing story of fitting in and being accepted, a story of getting knocked back and suffering seriously bad health, but mostly a story of never giving up. This is also a story written with as much positivity as I can muster. Of course there will be low points, but my ultimate goal is to show that anything is possible with the right mindset. Today, I live a life of gratitude and it really works for me. I tell everyone around me how grateful I am for having them in my life. From Antoinette to my family to Fitzer to friends I've made on Facebook. And I fervently hope that my story will help others who are struggling too.

So, is there a Life After Joy? Well, jump on in and find out...

Chapter 1

FREEDOM
(I WON'T LET YOU DOWN...)

'I'll see ya later ma,' I say over my shoulder as I head out the front door of the family home. 'And don't worry, I'm only gonna have a couple of pints.' I turn to look at my mam's face. Ah yes, my mam. Elizabeth Carmel Mary, although for most of her life she has gone by the name Lily. With her golden hair atop her head and her mischievous smile constantly on display, this lady is my hero. They say a mother's love never wavers and I can confirm this fact. Although I am now officially a free man, and my mam is elated to have her baby son home, her love is the same as the love and support she gave me during my incarceration. When I received three and a half years in prison for the possession of cannabis, not only had I destroyed my life, but I had ripped my mother's world wide open too. And yet, it seemed her love for me grew stronger as she did what all good 'Irish Mammies' do – she stood by her son, even if he was a complete gobshite. She never missed a visit while I was in prison – expect once when she was taken into hospital to get a new hip – and she never gave up on me. And in turn she became the first of two incredible women who were to become my inspiration to change.

My two brothers, Noel and Jason, had made the two and a half hour drive that morning to Loughan House Open

Prison in County Cavan to bring their little brother home. And as soon as we arrived, I made a beeline for the kitchen and embraced my mother in a way I never had before. 'Thank you mam,' I start, 'thank you, thank you, thank you.' And in that kitchen we sat and just allowed ourselves to be in the moment.

So, as I was heading out the door that evening and I turned to look at my mam, I could see the worry etched across her face. 'I promise mam, only a couple of pints. That alcoholic shithead I was before is gone. I can handle this. No problem ma.'

This seemed to work as she smiled at me in a way only Lily can. 'Okay, Gary, enjoy. Just be careful son,' she softly said to me.

'I will ma. And don't worry, I've got this.' And in all honesty, I genuinely thought I had.

And so out the door went myself and my brother Noel. The walk to Martins Pub from my home is a short one, and as the chill of a November evening in Dublin began nipping away at the two of us we kept it at bay by talking.

'So, The Fingal is gone buddy, what?' I laugh to Noel. Before my incarceration, The Fingal House Pub, which was across the road from Martins Pub, was my second home. In fact, if they had allowed me to sleep there it most probably would have become my permanent feckin' home.

'Yeah Gar, it's a bit mad not having it there anymore. Some of the lads are blaming you for it closing down if I'm honest.' Noel says this as a small grin begins to develop on his face.

'What do you mean?' I counter.

'Sure, when you went inside they lost out on a lot of money,' he laughs.

'Go and ask me arse,' says I as we both begin laughing.

Noel was approaching a milestone birthday – half a century. Yet the only clue to his age were the streaks of grey that flow through his dark hair. Standing just a little shorter than me, it has been said that we are very alike. I'll take that. He's a good-looking bloke, 'our Noel'. It's good that we can laugh about my drinking days, although Noel's concern for his baby brother is never far away. 'Are you sure you want to go down here Gar? We don't have to bud,' he says.

'I'm grand Noely,' I reply, 'stronger than I have ever been. I'll stick to having just four pints. I have no intention of going backwards. Onwards and upwards man.' And as I say these words to Noel, I really meant them.

We enter the lounge of Martins, with its low ceilings and snug ambience, and I am instantly stopped in my tracks. Standing in front of me are my nephews, Mark, Alan and Séan, my brother Jason, and a man who has always been like a father to me, Joe Tobin. Joe and his son Derek came to visit me in Mountjoy every Friday. Sometimes work would prevent Derek from coming, but Joe never missed a visit.

I make my way down the line of the men gathered in front of me and embrace each and every one of them. I thank them, well, for everything really. This beautiful moment was shattered by the shouting of my name.

'Gary Cunningham? Ahhh jaysis. Would ya look at this fella. Holy lantern Gar. Where the fuck is your belly gone?' It was the barman Archie, and he was making reference to the fact I was a much larger man when I got sent down. Archie was about the same age as myself, late thirties, a stocky lad with short black hair. The last time I saw him, he was tending the bar in my old home, The Fingal, and what an incredible barman he was. The importance of a good barman to an alcoholic whose main tipple was Guinness is paramount. A bad pint could spell disaster. Archie never served a bad pint. And he was always great at handling the shite that would come out of my mouth once I had consumed about half a barrel!

6

'Archie, ya aul' shite, how the hell are ya?' I ask smiling.

'Grand Gar,' he starts, 'so, are ya finished being a gobshite now, or did prison do nothin' for ya?'

'Prison did a lot for me pal,' says I, 'but it can't work miracles. I'm still a gobshite.' We both share a laugh and an awkward hug. 'So, you're working here now?' I ask.

'Yeah, almost all the barmen from The Fingal are working here now. It was a good move on the part of Ray and Ian (the two lads who run Martins) as all the crowd from The Fingal started coming here once it closed. So at least we know how to handle the saps like you Gar.' He starts laughing hard.

'Ah, ya won't know me buddy,' I say, 'them days are gone. Four pints, maybe five ... and that's me.'

I grab a pint and a stool and begin answering any questions that the nosey gathered have for me. My brother Jason takes me to one side and says, 'Look Gar, I know you have to go to the welfare to get your stuff sorted, and I know that can take a while, so I have a couple of days' work for you if ya like? I'd take you on full-time if I could Gar, but I'm barely keeping my head above water at the moment. This recession is a bloody killer.'

This act of kindness from my brother Jason, who ran his own painting company, blew me away, and yet I wasn't one bit surprised. Growing up Jason and I didn't always see eye to eye. This mainly stemmed from the fact that he was the baby in our family for eight years until one night, the TV in our home must have broken because nine months later yours truly came along. This put Jason's nose out of joint, but as the years passed, we became what we are today. Not just brothers, but solid friends too. A stocky lad with a shaved head and really cool glasses, Jason is more like my dad's side of the family in looks, whereas I have been told I'm more like my mam's side. 'Ah Jay, that is amazing. Thanks man.' Although Jason was not in a position to offer me full-time employment, he still gave me the opportunity to get out there and start working, albeit only for a couple of days. Obtaining a job was the one thing that kept me awake at night in the weeks leading up to my release. So, for now, Jason had put a band-aid over that problem.

The night was swinging as more people I knew arrived. But when I looked up and saw my big brother Gerry standing there, it caught me in the chest. The eldest in our family, with a full head of grey hair but a youthful face, Gerry was the super cool one in our family. He never gets worked up, and always has the right solution to a problem. He is the perfect big brother for me to look up to and admire.

'Welcome home, Gar,' he says as he embraced me in a bear hug which almost cut off my air supply. 'That's it now. You've done your time. Now you start moving forward, okay? That is all in the past now.' He says this with the perfect balance of love and warning.

'Thanks Ger. And thank you for everything you and Barbara (Gerry's beautiful wife) did for me,' I say.

'Would ya stop outta that,' counters Gerry, 'you're my brother.' Those who know me know I cry – a lot. So hearing these simple words from my big brother really meant the world to me as my tears began to flow. 'Oh, by the way,' says Gerry as I try to gather myself, 'I picked this fella up on the way here. Come out and say hello.' I look over Gerry's shoulder only to see a man appear from behind a pillar in the pub ... Cunny!

I couldn't believe my eyes. Cunny was the first lad I met on my first night in Mountjoy. We've known each other all our lives, and we both made horrendous life choices at the same time! And yet the support we gave each other on the inside could not be bought. 'Gar, ya aul' shite,' smiles Cunny. God, how I've missed that smile. His whole face lights up every time. Standing over six feet, and with muscles bulging from the (very tight) white T-shirt he was wearing, I have to say he was looking great. Cunny had been released almost a year earlier, and to see him looking so well and happy really invigorated me as I began life as a free man. He had faced so many personal demons whilst inside and I watched with such admiration as he seemed to conquer each and every one of them.

'Cunny, wow, you look amazing man. How are you getting on?' I ask.

'I'm doing great, Gar,' he says, 'myself and Ciara (Cunny's partner) are flying, and the kids (Leah and Cian) are just thriving. Life is great out here Gar, once you work hard at it. It's gonna be a little tough in the next couple of weeks for ya, but you're "The Voice" (my nickname in prison because (1) I spoke up for prisoners and (2) I am extremely loud), so it won't be a bother to ya. Oh, are ya havin' a pint, yeah?'

I can see the worry on Cunny's face. Inside prison, men like Cunny and Fitzer and The Little Fella and Sweeny-Todd and, well I think you get the picture, were my family. And I couldn't ask for a better bunch of men to lean on. Cunny, along with the rest of these lads, knew my fears about the drink, so his concern moves me. 'I'm grand man, it's all under control,' I reassured him.

The rest of the night went really well and continued until … well, until I heard Archie call for last orders. My total amount consumed? Oh, about eight, maybe nine pints. But sure, it's my first night home, so it's a one off, right?

Oh the next morning – my 'bleedin' head'! I have to admit, I hadn't missed hangovers. I peel my face off the soft cotton pillow in the amazingly comfortable bed I had slept in – in my clothes. Funnily enough, I found it quite hard to adapt to sleeping in a 'normal' bed again. I almost missed my blue plastic mattress and wafer-thin pillows from prison. How nuts was that?

My mam must be out as the house was empty. I showered, got dressed, and headed towards the Social Welfare office in order to make a claim. And I got so lucky this particular morning. The lady who was going to deal with my case informed me of what I needed to bring with me in order to make a claim. I, in turn, produced everything she required there and then. Having OCD can have its benefits as I always try to be prepared.

'Ah, good man Gary. It's just ... em, it says here you haven't made any contributions since 2012? Can you explain that?'

Shit, I thought to myself, *I'll have to tell her where I was. The shame. Fuck. Right, here it goes.* I sheepishly explain that I have just been released from prison. I don't know this lady's name, but if I did I would print it here so she could receive the praise she truly deserves. She showed me empathy and kindness, which I didn't expect. She explained how my claim would work, how long it would take to sort out and so on, and then provided me with as much information as she could obtain in the hope that I might find it useful. She was so good to me. The way this lady treated me also reminded me that you should never judge a book by its cover, the very judgement I was so fearful of people making about me. How ironic. She was the first stranger I had told about my shameful past, and she didn't look down her nose at me. If only more people could be like this lady.

Over the next week or so, while I waited for my claim to come through, I got up every morning and went to work with my brother Jason. It felt so good to be working and earning a living. I actually wished times had been different, as myself and Jason are a good team when we work together. And I felt so sorry for him, as I knew that he wanted to keep me in employment full time. Alas, the times were hard for everyone in 2014, so I reassured him that I completely understood. 'In any case Jay, I'll get a job, just you wait and see.' God. You have got to admire my optimism.

So, I was doing a bit of work, and having maybe two or three pints after a day's graft, my family and friends had welcomed me back with open arms and I had met a lady who showed me empathy when I least expected it. Yep, things were starting off okay. I think I'm really going to enjoy this 'freedom' malarkey. Just one thing was missing. I could do with a strong woman to keep me in check. A woman I could fall in love with and spend the rest of my life with...

Antoinette? Where art thou? I have something I need to ask you...

Chapter 2

ROAD TRIP TO LOUGHAN

A ntoinette Gahan. Even as I type her name I feel the butterflies begin to converge in my stomach. Standing just a bit shorter than me, with long, silky, coal-black hair and the most attractive face I have ever seen, this woman was the first time I ever experienced 'love at first sight'. I still remember so clearly the first time I laid my eyes upon her magnificence, although the place of our meeting was somewhat strange to say the least. It was in the visiting area of Mountjoy Prison as Antoinette had come to visit her friend BC, another man I 'did my whack' with. The universe was on my side that morning, as I too had a visit from my two friends, Joe and Derek.

BC wasn't worried about embarrassing me that morning as he called for me to meet this beautiful lady. And after some cringe-worthy words from myself, and a promise from Antoinette that if I write to her and make her laugh she might consider writing back, well, the rest is history. It was through those many letters that we began the task of getting to know each other. And with every letter I received, I found more and more reasons to fall for this woman. Her letters would splash colour into the drab cell I was housed in on C Wing, and I will never be able to fully thank her for that. She gave me another goal, another reason to change and become a better man. She took my breath away. As a result, on the morning of my release, my closest friend Fitzer pulled me to one side and told me to make sure I made contact with her as soon as I can. 'She's the one Gar me aul' flower,' he said to me. And, as always, Fitzer was right.

So, that's just what I did…

I'll never forget the first phone call I made to Antoinette as a free man. It was roughly two weeks after I was released. I needed to pluck up the courage! What if she told me to get stuffed? What if I was just some prisoner that she enjoyed writing to? Would she enjoy me in the physical form or was I more attractive on paper? Jesus, I was nervous. It was a Saturday evening, and I was standing on Westmoreland Street waiting for a bus to bring me home. I loved how busy this famous street was, something I will never take for granted again. One of the things that prison did was to make me appreciate the smallest things in life. It felt good to be standing in the world that evening as a rare November sun began to sink into the Liffey.

I had my phone in my hand, and Antoinette's number had been sitting on its screen daring me to press the call button. *I'll wait 'til I'm sitting on the bus. Yeah … then I'll ring,* I thought to myself. The universe must have been listening to these thoughts and was getting fed up with my dithering, so when I looked up my bus was pulling up to the stop. I paid my fare and made my way upstairs. I take a seat, stare at my phone again, and then I hit the call button. After a couple of rings I hear her voice. 'Hello? Gary?' she begins.

'Eh, em, howya Antoinette. Look, I'd love to bring you out for a drink later. Just to say thanks for all you did and that.' Great use of the English language there Gary.

Antoinette laughs and says, 'I'd love to Gary, sounds good.' What? *Really*? Well, that was easy wasn't it? Sadly, that was to be the only easy part of our eventual future together.

I arrived home, hugged my mam and said, 'Guess who has a date tonight, Lily?'

'Oh, very good. Just be careful Gary, won't you?' she says. My mam's care for her children never ceases to amaze me. Myself and my brothers may be grown-up, but we will forever be her babies.

'I will ma, don't worry,' I say. I thunder upstairs and I am almost naked as I reach the top step. I shower and then begin the daunting task of picking the right clothes. After more changes than Mariah Carey would complete during one of her shows, I settle on a white T-shirt and dark blue jeans. How very original. I say my goodbyes and then, in a very Irish way, I wink to my mam and tell her, 'Not to wait up.' What a gobshite.

As I arrive at the bar of our meeting, I see Antoinette standing outside. *My God*, I think to myself, *she is so beautiful. Don't mess this up Gary.* 'Howya missus,' I stutter.

'Heya Gar. You look great.'

Ya should've gone to bleedin' Specsavers I think. 'As do you,' I offer as a reply.

She smiles as she thanks me and I can feel myself begin to blush. Keep it together man! We make our way inside, I get the drinks, and then everything just seemed to fall into place. I couldn't take my eyes off her as she answered the millions of questions I was firing at her. We laughed, we sang, we even had a little dance. Well, Antoinette danced. Me? I looked like an amalgamation of every dad and uncle dancing at a wedding rolled into one. I can't dance to save my life, but Antoinette seemed to like this. As the night passed by, I found myself longing to embrace this beautiful vision, right up until she 'friend-zoned' me. Yep, I got the *I think we'd be better as friends* line. Ouch!

But there was a sadness attached to this quote from Antoinette. She was a tough cookie, so when I noticed she was upset, I worry a little. 'I have a wall around me Gary,' she says, 'and I just don't think I am ready for a relationship. The last thing I would ever do to you is lead you on. I really like you Gary. The timing is just off.'

I see how upset she was getting and so I quickly say, 'That is absolutely no problem Antoinette. In fact, I feel very lucky to call you my friend. So everyone is a winner.' If only I actually believed that! I was gutted. But I actually did feel very lucky to call this woman my friend. What she did for me while I was incarcerated is something I will never forget. I lean in for a hug, and although this brings a few more tears, soon Antoinette was feeling better. I walk her home, we hug again, and she promises to call me tomorrow. I say my goodbyes and head for home, a little deflated, but happy I had made an incredible friend.

And what a friend she became...

She would ring me almost daily asking if I needed a lift, or would I like to go for a KFC (another of life's luxuries I will never take for granted again), things like that. We became so close so very quickly, and although I was pining for her, I made sure not to make her feel uncomfortable as I didn't want to lose her as a friend. But I couldn't help telling her how beautiful she was. She has an attractiveness that drives me to distraction, though she would laugh as I would inform her of this.

'Go away outta that, ya headcase,' she'd say, 'remember, *we're just friends!*'

'Ah, I know Antoinette,' I'd say. 'It just so happens that my mate, that is you, is a bleedin' cracker.' Our bond began growing stronger by the day.

I told her one day that I was going back to Loughan House Open Centre to help Fitzer play a gig for the old folks. Antoinette very kindly offered me a lift. I contacted Chief Carrick, the lady who was like a mother to me during my stay in Loughan, and asked if it was okay for Antoinette to come and watch the performance too. Of course the Chief said yes. This woman encapsulates what it is to be a lady.

The gig was a follow up to the previous year when I was still a prisoner. In the surrounding area of Loughan House is a small town called Blacklion. There are quite a few older people living in the vicinity, and so the prisoners and staff of Loughan House set about organising a Christmas concert in their honour that would be held inside the open prison. Some of the lads worked tirelessly preparing a Christmas lunch, while myself and my bandmates, Fitzer, Cunny and Sweeny-Todd, or The Off#enders as we are known, set about constructing a set-list of songs to hopefully entertain them as their food settled. It was such a magical day, enjoyed by all.

After my release, I made the Chief a promise that I would come back and play this year's concert for her. Although I didn't need much persuasion as it meant I would get to spend some time with Fitzer.

Myself and Antoinette set out on the road to Loughan House early that morning. It's a long drive but we never stopped talking, or at least I didn't stop talking. I've been known to talk – a lot. It was such an enjoyable road trip filled with laughter, singing and a ton of innuendos coming from myself. Friends we might be, but I was finding it hard to contain how I really felt about this woman. Still, somehow, I managed to never cross the line.

We arrived at Loughan House and made our way towards the visiting area where our 'welcoming committee' had gathered. We walked into the brightly-lit visiting room that has a few tables and plastic chairs strewn about the place, and instantly I was faced with an onslaught of slagging.

'Would ya look at this fella,' says KG, a tall, slender man with a completely shaved head whom I admire so much. He has his past, his demons, and yet he amazed me by having the strength to banish them for good. He was also the man I did the 'Insanity' workout with (a crazy, cardio-based training video) every day whilst we were housed in Loughan. And by god was it insane.

'Alright KG, ya aul' shite. Are ya still balls rough or wha'?' I counter.

'Ahhhhh Gar ya big bollox,' I hear from behind me, and I know that voice ... Gaga! He is small in height but a larger than life character with grey streaks ripping through his black hair. You were always required to have your thick skin on once he began berating you. 'Who is this vision with ya? There's no way she's your moth,' says Gaga.

Jesus Gaga, I think to myself, *leave it out. I'm bleedin' scarlet.* 'This is Antoinette, Gaga, and we are just friends.'

'Yeah, that makes more sense all right,' laughs KG.

'Fuck you and the horse ya rode in on,' I laugh back. Then I see him, Fitzer. This man saved my life in prison in many, many ways. Saying goodbye to him when I was released was one of the hardest things I have ever done. The first real and true friend I have ever had, and I had to go to prison to meet him. Between his incredible singing voice and silky smooth bass licks I knew we had something special when we began jamming in Mountjoy – but that's a whole different book.

'There ya are Gar me aul' flower,' says Fitzer. I don't reply, instead I launch my arms around him and hug the life out of him.

'Get a fuckin' room lads,' laughs Sweeny-Todd as he enters the visiting room. Sweeny-Todd is another member of The Off#enders who I must introduce to you. He plays rhythm guitar and has an incredible singing voice too. A lad with a heart of gold, he also happens to be one of the nicest blokes you could ever meet. It feels so good seeing the lads again.

'Lads, this is my friend (it killed me saying that) Antoinette. Antoinette, this is the lads.'

Fitzer goes straight in. 'Howya Antoinette, you're a singer right? So you'll get up and sing a song for us today, yeah? Nice one.' He didn't allow her to reply, and it worked.

'Yeah, sure, why not?' says Antoinette. I didn't realise it at the time, but I would soon come to learn that Antoinette suffers from confidence issues about her singing. And yet, once you hear her sing you can't begin to imagine why. She is simply fantastic.

Soon, Chief Carrick enters in an immaculate grey suit, her short fair hair glistening in the sunlight from that particular day. She introduces herself to Antoinette, and then ushers us all into the main building of Loughan House, an old, tall, grey building with countless sash windows dotting its face. We make our way towards the magnificent auditorium located at the building's rear. This is the very room where The Off#enders played many a gig, the very room where we recorded our album. So many wonderful memories for me. I see that the walls have been brought to life with a splash of white paint, and some inspiring quotes and images have been stencilled on. The old teak wooden stage sits proudly at the top of the room, and it was all set out with mics and guitars and amps. This was going to be great.

And great it was. As the folks gathered and sat in the seats provided, The Off#enders took to the stage and performed some beautiful acoustic tracks, if I do say so myself. But it was Antoinette who stole the show. She took the lead as a choir of prisoners stood behind her to accompany her through the John Lennon classic, 'Happy Xmas (War Is Over)'. The chief, Fitzer, KG, everyone in attendance stood and applauded her at the song's end. What a wonderful thing for her to do, and in front of a load of prisoners too.

Fitzer grabs me at the end of the show. 'Fuckin' hell Gar. She has some voice. It's amazing listening to a professional isn't it? Wow, Gar. She's bleedin' deadly. Are ya with her now or wha'?' he laughs.

'We're just friends, buddy,' says I.

'Fuck that Gar,' insists Fitzer. 'Don't you dare give up on her pal. Maybe back off a bit. But don't give up. Another thing I must ask ya. Are ya drinking out there buddy?' Fitzer, from day one, has always bowled me over with his genuine concern for me.

'I'm just having the odd pint,' I lie. Why am I lying to Fitzer? Why do I feel ashamed?

'Just keep your eye on it pal, yeah? Remember what we talked about,' says Fitzer.

I had promised Fitzer I would hit the ground running upon my release. Maybe I just didn't want to worry him. Yeah. That's why I lied ... I didn't want to worry him.

And so, as the dust settled on yet another highly successful Christmas Concert in Loughan House, and as the gathered thanked us all for such a wonderful day, I now had the daunting task of saying goodbye to Fitzer again. He still had a bit of time left to serve at this stage.

'I'm always here for ya man. If you need anything done for Ash (his wife), just say the word,' I say.

'Ah fair play to ya me aul' mucker,' replies Fitzer through a beaming smile. We hug it out and then I turn to get into Antoinette's silver Ford Focus.

But as soon as Fitzer is out of sight, I'm sobbing in front of Antoinette. 'He just means the world to me, Antoinette. I know I'm being a sap. He is just my best friend and I'm really going to miss him.'

'I completely understand Gary. He is a lovely fella, they all are. I am amazed if I'm honest. Thanks for bringing me here today and showing me that not all prisoners are, well, whatever I thought they were I suppose,' says Antoinette.

The drive home was somewhat sombre. I actually wanted to go back and stay there with the lads. I wanted to stay in a place where I had been made to feel like I belonged. But being with Antoinette made the drive home a bit brighter, and as we pulled up to my mam's she leaned over and gave me a big hug and a soft kiss on the cheek.

'I'm always here if you need me Gary. Thanks again for today.'

'Thank *you*,' I counter. And as I walk up the driveway of my home, I look over my shoulder to catch another glimpse of the one woman who has stolen my heart.

If we are to be 'just good friends' then I have gained the greatest friend that anyone could ask for. But I still longed to be her man. A longing I needed to keep to myself.

For now...

Chapter 3

I Just Called to Say...

'She is fantastic mam,' I explain to my mother one bright, cold December morning. We were sitting in the small, cheerful kitchen of my family home chatting about Antoinette, my mam drinking tea while I devoured a coffee. I never took the time to enjoy moments like this with my mam prior to my sentencing. She is such an easy woman to please. She doesn't demand anything from you. All she wants is some of your time. And I had honestly forgotten how enjoyable it was to spend time with her.

'She sounds great Gary, and wasn't that a lovely thing she did driving you to Loughan House? I know how long a drive that is, so fair play to her,' says my mam.

'Ah, I know ma, and all the lads loved her,' I reply.

'But look Gary, don't rush into anything here, okay? You know what you're like,' laughs Lily.

And she was right. I was a complete disaster when it came to relationships. In fact, how I ever got lucky to find myself in a relationship at all is quite something. Physically, I wasn't exactly an Adonis before my incarceration. I was an eighteen and a half stone man with a Persian rug of body hair covering my torso. I was, in all honesty, extremely unattractive. But I found the gym while in Mountjoy, and I instantly fell in love with the whole idea of bettering yourself through exercise.

There is a saying amongst the men in Mountjoy regarding the gym, *It's great for the aul' head.* And I can honestly say it truly is. In fact, one of the first things I did after my release was to secure a membership in a gym, and every morning I would go there and continue trying as hard as I could to feel better about myself. Overweight Gary would forever be a distant memory. Now, all I needed to do was save up for plastic surgery so I could sort out the feckin' head on me. The gym can do a lot, but it can't do everything. And I'm still lightyears away from being an Adonis!

'Ah, we're just friends mam,' I say with sadness in my voice.

'Well,' my mam says, 'some of the best relationships begin with people being just friends. Remember, Gary, what's for you will never pass you by.' She knows her stuff my ma.

I was struggling a lot at this time, but I was keeping it to myself. I had tried to obtain work, but I was getting knocked back every time. More about that later. I also had what I felt was a pretty amazing story about what happened to me in prison. How myself and Fitzer started The Off#enders and ended up 'touring' other jails in order to bring our sound to the ears of the captured. How I had almost finished a book ... a feckin' *book* ... that would explain all of this and so much more. And yet nobody seemed interested in hearing any of this. No one seemed to care. Even my own family seemed uninterested. 'Ah yeah, Gary, we know. But you're out of there now. It's time to start moving on,' they would say. At the time, this really hurt me. But today I completely understand why they found it hard to listen to these tales. As an alcoholic, I was prone to telling ridiculous and disgusting lies that caused devastating damage. 'The Drink' had truly addled my brain and even now, as I write this, I feel so much embarrassment and shame because of how deplorable I actually was.

But at this particular time, as I was trying to fit back in, it hurt me that no one seemed to care about my story. I never fully understood what it meant to be institutionalised, but it didn't take long for me to realise I was completely institutionalised. With every knock back I got, with every uninterested reaction to my story, I longed to be back inside where I felt accepted. Crazy, right? I actually missed the regime of being told when to get up, when to eat and when to sleep. And, of course, I really missed Fitzer. I could ring Loughan House and speak to him, and that was great. But it didn't stop me missing him.

I still possessed a determination that made me want to strive to be a better man, so I knuckled down and got on with things. And there was one person from my prison story who was very much in my daily life as a free man. A person who was really interested in all the mad stories and funny tales I had – Antoinette.

I certainly have had less attractive friends in my life than my newly obtained friend Antoinette. And I have spent less time with partners from my past than I was spending with Antoinette. And I was loving it. Although I was under no illusion that we were working towards being the next Posh and Becks, I would still find myself daydreaming of 'life as Antoinette's fella'. I would daily imagine what it would be like to slowly kiss her beautiful lips, or how amazing it would feel to hold her hand as we walked. But I kept these thoughts to myself – sometimes. I mean, I'm only human after all. And she is, hands-down, the most attractive woman I have ever laid my eyes upon. Her smile would make you remember those feelings you had as a teenager when the girl or boy you fancied was in your company. So I would regularly tell her she was 'a bleedin' cracker', but always made sure it came across light-hearted so as not to scare her away.

In that first month or so of my initial release, I spent as much time as I could with Antoinette and enjoyed finding out everything I could about her. She has got to be one of the funniest humans on this planet. Being in her company meant

I experienced a multitude of belly-busting laughs constantly. She was very funny indeed.

As a musician, I was captivated listening to her voice, and I would hang on her every word as she told me of the gigs she was doing with the wedding band she was in, and the karaoke duo she was a part of with her friend John. I would sometimes see her insecurities about singing in all their glory, and it saddened me. It is so true that every person has a story. To look at Antoinette, to hear her sing, you would almost feel annoyed that she didn't realise just how good she was. But we all have demons that prevent us from believing in ourselves. So, if it killed me, I would make sure that she felt great about herself.

I had known from the letters I received from Antoinette whilst I was in prison that she suffered from Perthes disease, a rare childhood condition that affects the hip. This was discovered when she was about the age of nine, so as a result she now had basically no hip on her right side as it was slowly eroding away. And yet she never let it define her. She found walking difficult. She was in constant pain and discomfort. But every day she would rise up out of bed smiling, and live her life as fully as she could. At one stage, she even flung herself out of a cable car in New Zealand to do one of the world's highest bungee jumps. Perthes disease would not prevent this woman from having a life, which I found so inspiring. Can you blame me for being crazy about this lady? I mean, *come on*.

I remember one evening sitting in Antoinette's car as we listened to the album myself and The Off#enders had recorded in prison. I enjoyed watching the look on her face when she heard Fitzer's voice, especially when he hits a particular note in the song 'Scream My Name' that he penned for his wife Ash.

'Wow, Gary. And to think you lads achieved all of this in a prison. Wow,' she says.

'Grand, isn't it?' I jokingly reply in a nonchalant manner.

'Go away out of that ya gobshite. Don't go fishing for compliments off me now.' Antoinette laughs as she says this. 'I'd say Fitzer is amazing live. God, last night at the gig I was doing, I had this guy trying his best to tell me how "amazing" he was at singing, so I asked him to prove it. He was shite Gary!' Her laughter fills the car, and I find I'm laughing too, right up until she said, 'He was just trying to get with me. He started telling me how beautiful I was and all that. But I have to say, thanks to you Gar, I am getting better at listening to these compliments.'

I know Antoinette meant no harm whatsoever with this statement, but it cut me to the bone. All of a sudden, I could picture her going on a date with some guy, and then telling me all about it the next day. Sure, isn't that what friends do? But this statement made me realise how crazy about this girl I actually was, and how much it would kill me to see her with another man. What a prick I was for thinking this. But I couldn't help how I felt about her.

Unfortunately, in the days that followed, these thoughts began to increase. I found I was getting upset about something that I knew was about to happen – Antoinette would meet someone. I knew I would not be able to handle this, so I took the coward's way out. I selfishly told Antoinette that I thought it would be best if we went our separate ways. I told her of my fears. I didn't tell her in the hope that she would 'all of a sudden' fall for me but because I don't lie anymore. She was upset, but being the woman she is, she told me she totally understood. I was heartbroken. Christmas was only around the corner, but it looked like Santa wouldn't be bringing me the one thing I really wanted.

In the week or so that followed, I became 'outside' what I never was when I was 'inside'. I became 'balls rough', which is prison slang for being down and deflated. My drive was slipping. It seemed the only bit of pleasure I was experiencing was at the bottom of a pint of Guinness down in the local pub. I really missed Antoinette. What had I done? And then, just to pile on some more misery, I got the deathly 'man flu'. That's right. I was struck down with the only strand of flu that is sexist. At one stage I croaked to my mam that maybe she should ring the local priest in order for me to receive the last rites. Oh, and I should also explain at this point that I am the worst patient you have ever met. I am a fucking 'aul' wan' if I'm brutally honest. But this dreadful dose I was experiencing was only making the fact I was missing Antoinette seem so much worse.

I'm lying in my bed, lost in an episode of *Fair City*, when my phone rings on the bedside locker beside me. It was Antoinette. 'Hello?' I croak. I was very sick I'll have you know.

'Hey Gary, look,' starts Antoinette, 'I have never done anything like this before, but I need to tell you something. Gary, I think I'm falling in love with you.'

I have tears in my eyes as I type this. I shot up in my bed and cried, '*What*?!?'

'Yeah,' continues Antoinette, 'I didn't realise it until you weren't in my life anymore. I can't stop thinking about you Gary. And I know I am falling in love with you.'

'Are you fuckin' drunk, or messing, or doing this for a bet?' I almost shout.

'No,' laughs Antoinette, 'I am out at a Christmas party all right, but I've only had two drinks. That's why I'm ringing now. Come in and meet me Gary. I want to see you. Only if you still feel the same way about me of course?'

Still feel the same? Was she mad? I was head over heels about the girl. 'Hang on,' I say as I start to drag myself from my bed. 'I'll be into you now in a...' and then the man-flu came up and punched me in the face. Nooooo! You have got to be kidding me. 'Antoinette? I can't. I really can't. I'm poxy smothering here,' I say deflated.

Antoinette laughs down the phone. 'Don't worry,' she starts, 'you do still feel the same way about me though, right?'

'Too bloody right I do Antoinette,' I reply.

'Well, we have forever to spend together, so don't worry about tonight,' she said. Wow.

We spoke for a short while on the phone that night, and agreed to go for dinner the next evening, which we did. And although this was officially our first date as a couple, I will always remember that date for the wrong reason. Antoinette didn't speak, at all, throughout the dinner. I mean, not a fuckin' word! *Ahh jaysis,* I thought to myself, *she regrets saying what she said last night. She doesn't want to hurt me now by telling me. Ahh jaysis.* I cannot stress this enough folks – not ... one ... word did she speak. It was so unnerving. But the reason behind her lack of communication was one that will tug at your heartstrings. She didn't feel good enough for me. For me, the ex-con. Well, I soon made sure she knew I was the one punching well above his weight. But that first date has got to go down as one of the strangest dates I have ever been on.

So the woman who gave me hope in prison, the woman who gave me her time upon my release, was now officially my girlfriend. The line from the song 'She', which I wrote about my mother while I was locked up, echoes through my mind, *If this is lost, I don't want to be found...*

And as for that first kiss? Perfection personified.

Chapter 4

THE SLIP

Into this world we're thrown
Like a dog without a bone
An actor out on loan
Riders on the storm
– The Doors, *Riders on the Storm*

And a storm was a-brewing...

Why do I always do it? Why, when things are going good for me, do I decide, *Yeah. I think I'll go and mess this up. Fuck it. And if I hurt people? So be it.* Before I served my sentence I was a nasty person. My drinking had taken over every aspect of my life. I hurt every single person close to me. I lost everything. From the love of a child and his beautiful family, to my own incredible family and all they had to offer. From partners to friends, I pushed them all away with my lies and my constant longing for a drink. But I confronted the alcoholic whilst in prison. I stared him down and told him, *never again will you control me,* and I honestly believed every word of that. But I didn't factor in how weak I truly was when it came to 'the drink'. Stupidly, I convinced myself that I would be able to become a 'normal' drinker, like the majority of people who enjoy a drink at social gatherings and the like. I reassured myself that I was a much stronger man nowadays, and that I could go and have just a few pints and leave early. How wrong I was.

I had completely underestimated the voracious stranglehold that comes with being an alcoholic. In prison, I had the encouragement and support of Fitzer. He listened to the tales from my past, and never judged me. This man should consider a career as a motivational speaker, as he would instil in me daily the strength I needed to succeed. And now, out here in the big bad world, I felt I needed him more than ever. Over six feet tall, with a stocky build and blondish, fair hair, Fitzer has the biggest heart I have ever seen in a man. So of course I really wished he was by my side during the time of 'the slip' that I found myself hurtling towards.

Myself and Antoinette were a few months into what I can only describe as the perfect relationship. At least for *me* it was perfect. For Antoinette? Not so much. There was one part of our relationship I am sure she would have liked to change – my drinking.

A common trait in my personal journey with 'the drink' was my insistence that I had everything under control. I was a functional alcoholic, if such a person truly exists. I would rise out of bed every morning and brush off the thumping headache and dry mouth. I would ready myself to tackle whatever that particular day had to throw at me, and in those early days of my release there was quite a lot. Job knock backs. Missing people I had hurt in the past who couldn't forgive me (which I don't blame them for). Feeling that I couldn't fit back in, that in some ways I was 'damaged goods'. So, in order to deal with these feelings of sadness, I did what old Gary always did. I self-medicated by consuming pints of Guinness. *It's okay Gar. You're only having a few. It's all under control*, I would foolishly think to myself. But it still shocks me today how quickly I was allowing myself to become the very gobshite I had worked so hard to eradicate.

I always viewed drink as a counsellor of sorts. When the demons of my past that haunted me before my incarceration would rear their ugly heads, I would go and have a drink and then ... whoosh ... all my problems would melt away. And now, as I began my life of freedom, I felt I had even more demons to deal with. I was, amongst other things, wracked with guilt and shame for the amount of pain I had inflicted on others with the life choices I had made that led to my incarceration. These feelings, coupled with the demons from my past, all combined to give me the excuses I needed to go on the drink. But who was I kidding? If the fucking temperature outside was a degree above or below what I wanted, I would use that as an excuse to drink! I was weak and foolish. I had around me an abundance of support from Antoinette and my family. I had what some people who suffer from addiction never have the luxury of enjoying – love, support and care. I was becoming a selfish bastard again. I was slipping.

I remember my poor mam would sit up in the living room of our family home, waiting for me to come home from the pub. I would always be in great form, and would usually try to soften the blow of the fact I was jarred with the offering of a bag of chips for her from the local chipper. But I could see how concerned she was. I had put this woman through so much before my time in prison. From lying and confrontations to hurtful words and moody demeanours. You would think that would be enough for me to realise I was messing up again. But the voice of the alcoholic, the selfish side of me that I detest so much, would reassure me that everything was okay. I honestly didn't realise at the time how far from okay things truly were.

I slowly began to feel worthless again. The drink chips away at you so subtly. Before you know it, you find yourself back at square one. And then the battle of your mind begins:

Strong Gary: Am I falling back into my old ways?

Alcoholic Gary: Not at all pal. Sure, you're only having the odd pint, here and there.

Strong Gary: But I'm drinking every night.

Alcoholic Gary: And how else are you meant to deal with shit? You will be grand pal, don't worry about it.

And shockingly, I didn't worry. Instead I started to morph back into the bar fly that I had promised myself was gone forever. Yet again, I was greedy and selfish. Please don't think I am labelling all people who suffer from addiction as greedy or selfish. I just want to be brutally honest about my own story. Antoinette and my mam were the only people in my life at this time who came close to making me realise what a fool I was being. But I took my chances with the drink anyway. *You're grand Gary. Sure, aren't you a great laugh when you have a drink on ya? You and Antoinette always have a laugh,* I would think to myself. I wonder if Antoinette would have agreed?

As the days turned into weeks, I started to panic. The guilt I had hated so much from my past was very prevalent at this time. And soon it was too late – I had slipped. Four pints became eight or nine, with maybe a 'small one' thrown in for good measure. I was great at being a caricature of the real me. When I was in the pub, I was always quick with a joke, and my fellow drinkers thought I was 'great craic altogether'. It's just a pity everyone else in my life thought I was a fool.

Antoinette, somehow, was still so supportive of me around this time. But neither of us realised what was coming. And the start of this downward spiral of disaster happened with me doing something I honestly never thought I would do...

Chapter 5

SHUTTING OUT FITZER

When I first decided to write this account of my life after prison, my publisher asked me to send him the chapter outlines so he could get a feel for what I was trying to achieve. And as I laid out the chapters for him, and explained briefly what each one would contain, I remember thinking to myself that this particular chapter would be extremely difficult for me to write. But it was also a chapter that I *had* to write.

Firstly, for those who haven't read my first book, who exactly is this guy Fitzer? In a nutshell, he is the greatest friend I have ever had. After our first meeting in Mountjoy back in 2012, he instantly became a massive part of my life. As you traverse this life you come across certain people who impress you, and Fitzer simply impressed me. He never looked for anything from me. He would always go above and beyond to make sure all around him were okay. He has the biggest heart and the softest shoulder for times when you need to talk. And he is a fucking headcase, if I'm honest! But this trait of his brought so much positivity into our prison world, a world that almost demanded negativity.

He is also the guy I started The Off#enders with, and together we wrote ourselves into the Irish Prison Service history books as the first band created inside a prison that was transferred to other prisons in order to play gigs. They were amazing days I can tell you. Fitzer learned how to play the bass from the music teacher in Mountjoy, Paul Byrne, and he quickly became the most accomplished and polished bass player I have ever had the pleasure to jam with. We recorded an album in Loughan House with Cunny, a self-taught drummer, and Sweeny-Todd on vocals and rhythm guitar, which he too learned to play in prison. I made up this band of misfits by playing lead guitar and singing on some of the tracks as well. Not only did Fitzer play the bass beautifully on this album, but his voice was incredible too. When he sang live, you could hear a pin drop – and trust me, keeping prisoners' attention for long periods of time can be quite challenging.

So, as I'm sure is quite clear, Fitzer was the most important person to me during my shameful incarceration. He became my best friend and allowed me access to his private life. He introduced me to his beautiful wife Ash, who quickly became one of my closest friends too. I even had the honour of meeting their son Cian, a bright and beautiful young lad. Just like his 'aul' fella' I suppose. Yep, Fitzer was the bee's knees.

So why did I shut him out of my life?

At the time when my release date was nearing, Fitzer made sure I was prepared for the outside. 'You've got this Gar, me aul' mucker,' he would say to me regularly. 'Grab this life by the scruff and live it, okay pal? You've done your whack and just look at the changes in ya. Look at what you have achieved during your stay. Fuckin' Andy Dufresne wouldn't have a patch on ya pal,' he'd laugh while making reference to Stephen King's character from *The Shawshank Redemption*. But he really believed in me, and I wasn't used to that.

I remember quite clearly the day of my release trying so very hard to keep it together, as Fitzer doesn't go for 'all that soppy shite'. But, with me being the emotional wreckage I am, I burst into tears as we said goodbye. I knew how much I was going to miss him. *I will make him so proud of me,* I thought to myself as I drove away from him that day. Sadly, it was that very thought that led to me shutting him out.

We rang each other every day and I would listen as he told a usually hilarious story about something that had just happened in Loughan House. I made sure to keep in contact with his wife Ash, and reassured Fitzer that if he needed me to do anything on the outside for her or Cian that I most certainly would. Everything was great. And then 'the slip' started to manifest. All the promises I had made this man started to slowly unravel. The alcoholic voice became so loud in my head. A disgusting, self-pitying voice that I was shockingly allowing to regain control. All reasonable thoughts go out the window, and soon you start believing the shite that the alcoholic in you throws at you daily.

You're a gobshite Gary. Ohhh, I promise Fitzer, I won't drink again Fitzer. Yeah right. You are pathetic, do ya know that? Why the fuck would he want a leech and a drunk like you as a friend? I stupidly began to believe these thoughts. It started with me lying to him on the phone about drinking, *so as not to worry him*, I'd think. Then the guilt of lying would start to consume me ... argghhh ... what was I doing? So, I again took the coward's way out, and this act of cowardly behavior was even worse. I didn't have the balls to ring Fitzer and tell him I needed some time to myself as I felt I was letting him down. No. Instead I rang his wife and asked her to tell him. What a prick I was. Of course, she was great about the whole thing. At first she didn't get it – in fact, I think she was a little annoyed with me, and who could blame her? But she told me not to worry, that everything will be okay, and that, quote, 'We will always be here for ya Gar, always. We love ya pal.' Fuck! Yet again I find that I have to ask myself the same poxy question that was coming up too frequently since my release, *What have I done?*

But I still went ahead and did it. At the time I blamed 'the drink' and the hold it had on me. But as I write this, I feel I need to be more honest and not hide behind an excuse. I feel Fitzer deserves that. I chose drink over my best friend. Plain and simple. I am sobbing as I type this. Had I just lost the greatest friend I have ever had? I had left him at a time when he really needed me the most. The man who went above and beyond for me in jail to make sure I was okay. The man who saved my life. But, shockingly, I made it all okay in my head. I reassured myself that he would understand. How in the hell would he understand his mate turning his back on him? How could I admit to him I was weak after I promised to be strong? I needed help, fast. I needed to stop feeling fucking sorry for myself and beg this man for forgiveness. I needed support, love and care. I needed Antoinette. But would I eventually push her away too?

And when I would think about my best friend in Loughan House, missing his family and friends but never ceasing to smile and be upbeat, that same horrid question would flash to the front of my mind:

What have you done, Gary?

Chapter 6

A DIVINE INTERVENTION, PART 1

It's such a negative cycle being caught up in an addiction. I would start my day with the greatest of intentions and would make good on them for the majority of the day. Then, something disagreeable would happen and soon I'd find myself propped up on a bar stool, milling pints of Guinness and solving the world's problems with anyone who happened to be in my company. Around this time, I somehow was still able to convince myself that I was okay and everything was under control. I remember one day sitting in Martins and listening to 'Dave the Eye'. Dave is a sound aul' fella and everyone loved him, but he can be a bit of a nuisance after a few drinks. His nickname stems from the fact that he only has one eye in his head, the other being a false one that he would pop out every now and then in order to freak people out. I remember once in The Fingal House Dave took out his eye and placed it beside a ball on the pool table while two people were trying to have a game. 'I have me eye on that ball lads, yeah?' he'd say as he headed out the back for a smoke. Mad fecker.

On this particular day in Martins, Dave was having a rant about our Government and their lack of ... well, I'm not sure what Dave thought they lacked, as he never finished his sentence. Instead, he jumped between his hatred for the Government and his love for the horses.

'I'm tellin' ya, they couldn't organise a piss up in a brewery those TDs. And another thing...' He stops talking and turns his good eye to a horse race that was being beamed on the portable telly above his head. 'Go on, ya beauty. Ahh jaysis move ya poxy bleedin' horse ya. Ohh, go onnn... *Yessss*,' he cries as his horse's nose crossed the finish line ahead of its closest rival. For Dave, this was an everyday event.

You would think I'd have had the wherewithal to realise that the only way I'd know that this was Dave's daily routine was if I saw him every day. Which I did, in fuckin' Martins pub. But on this day I actually had the audacity to think to myself, *That will never be me. I'll never end up pissed every day like that.* I had no right passing judgment on this harmless man for whom I actually have so much admiration. His mother and my father passed away only days apart in the same hospital. I remember standing outside the Mater with my brother Noel having a smoke, when we both copped Dave. We got to see such a different side to him, a side etched in sadness.

'Howya boys,' he says, 'sorry to hear about your aul' fella lads. Me own mother is on her way out too. Heartbroken so I am. That's me on me own now boys.' Like I said earlier, everyone has a story. Annoying as this man could become after consuming a few pints, he also found refuge and acceptance in that bar. I had some neck thinking I'd never end up like him. Dave has a heart of gold that is so rare nowadays.

'Can I buy ya a pint, Gar?' Dave asks after his horse wins.

'No Davey, I'm grand, the missus is coming up to my ma's to collect me shortly. Actually, hang on,' I replied. I pulled out my phone and sent Antoinette a quick text. *Hey ... can you collect me in Martins?* I hit send, and before I received a reply, I turned back to Dave. 'Yeah, go on buddy. I'll have one for the road.' Good man Gary. Squeeze in one more pint.

Drinking became a big part in the early days of my relationship with Antoinette. She wasn't ready to meet my mam and family, nor was I ready to meet hers. Antoinette would suggest plenty of things we could do, like the cinema or bowling, or playing pool, the latter of which I never enjoyed if I'm honest. To say Antoinette is competitive is the greatest understatement of all time. She has to win. And she is a bona fide pool shark too, which didn't help. She would wipe the feckin' floor with me, which was not good for my male ego. But no matter what activity we took part in, I always managed to get us into a pub before our date ended. And this was when the trouble really started.

You would think I would do everything in my power to ensure a long and happy life with Antoinette. But I was letting the drink get in the way. I have always had a problem with my anger, and alcohol only made this anger worse. I am sure my anger stemmed from incidents in my past that I had never dealt with, like losing my precious daughter when she sadly passed away. Not dealing with these feelings in a proper manner was my own fault. Instead of seeking help, I found solace in alcohol. But the more I drank, the more my anger would rise to the surface. And who was the one person you will always take your crap out on? That's right – the one you love. And I had fallen in love hard with Antoinette.

A pattern began to form. We'd meet up, usually with Antoinette collecting me from the pub, go out and do something fun together, then head for a drink. And as I became more comfortable in her company, the gobshite I was from my past began to appear more and more. I would start to become angry. *Never* in a violent way, but in a way that can be viewed as almost as bad. I would orchestrate a stupid row about something ridiculous and then become loud and extremely animated. I would say horrible things to this woman I absolutely adored. She would never engage me. She would never engage with the shite I was spouting. Instead, she would just pick up her coat and leave. And as hard as these words are for me to write, I need to show just how bad I was becoming, and how quickly after my release it was happening.

I remember a turning point one night in our relationship – if you could even call it that. We had just spent a fantastic night in a bar in town, and there was a sexual tension between us that was driving us both wild.

'My sister is away for the weekend if you'd like to come home with me,' whispered Antoinette into my ear. At this time, Antoinette lived with her sister Angela.

'Yeah, hic, I'd love that,' I slurred.

But in the back of my mind I was starting to panic. It had been a long time since I had been intimate with a woman. Prison will do that to you. Added to that was the fear I had about my 'performance' as I had just had a truckload of pints. So that sinister voice, the angry, selfish drunk inside me, started to pipe up in my mind as we snuggled in the backseat of the taxi that was bringing us to Antoinette's. *Who are you fooling, ya sap? She's gonna see what a total failure you really are now.*

And sadly, true to form, as soon as we got to Antoinette's I became a complete bastard. I started a row over something ridiculous that I honestly cannot remember now, although I can tell you it was complete claptrap. When I am drunk, the anger spewing out of me can be quite intimidating. But Antoinette was having none of it.

'Get the fuck out,' she yelled.

'With fuckin' pleasure,' I slurred back.

And, after slamming the door, because I am a dickhead, I stormed off into the night. Then karma did what she does best. She booted me up the arse. I put my hand in my pocket and realised I had no money. The walk home would take about an hour. Great. As I walked home, I amazingly continued the row over the phone. Thank God that Antoinette is one of the strongest women I know. She swatted away my shite with ease. But strong or not, she didn't deserve the way I was speaking to her. As I made the long walk home, I started to sober up a little. And that's when what always happens happened yet again. I became overcome with guilt. I cried my eyes out as I trudged home. I sent text after text begging for forgiveness, telling her how sorry I truly was. She never replied.

And can you blame her?

The next morning, as the hangover from hell was toying with my emotions, I received a text from Antoinette. 'I think we need to talk,' was all it said. *Good man Gar, another chance at happiness destroyed because of your drinking and your issues. A big pat on the fucking back for you, ya gobshite*, I thought. Not only had I pushed Fitzer away, I now assumed I had pushed away the woman who had shown so much faith in me. Or had I? At the time, I hadn't factored in Antoinette's strength and resilience.

We met and had a chat. Well, Antoinette talked while I listened. 'Look, that shite is completely unacceptable Gary. I don't do drama, not at all. But I can see these projections of anger from you have absolutely nothing to do with me. They are issues that you need to deal with if you want a chance at a happy life.' She was speaking so softly, and what an incredibly strong thing to say. She knew I had no problems with her per se, but I *did* have massive problems. I collapsed into tears.

'Gary,' she continues, 'you can't take your shite out on me. I won't stand for it. But I see so much good in you. I see so much talent and so much love. I see a future with you. But not if you keep going on like that.' I was preparing myself for Antoinette to offer me the ultimatum I selfishly feared – 'me or the drink Gary' – but Antoinette is not made like that. Instead, what she did was something for which I will forever be in her debt. She used the most subtle methods to show me

I had a drinking problem. Some (weak) men the world over complain that when a woman gets their hands on them, the first thing they do is change them to better suit themselves. I thought this was what Antoinette was going to do to me, but she didn't. She never once told me to stop drinking. She didn't end our relationship as a result of the scumbag I was the night before. Instead, she went out of her way to subtly show me how much the drink had a hold on me. And she started by talking about text messages!

Around this time, our text messages to each other were something we both loved. I would use these texts to send her poems and the like, whereas Antoinette would use them to be more affectionate towards me, as her wall was still preventing her from fully letting go. On this particular morning of our talk, as I felt the walls of the coffee shop close in on me, Antoinette suddenly changed tack.

'I love looking back at our texts Gary. I love how sweet you are. You make me feel so good about myself. But then something struck me. Look and tell me do you notice anything.'

She handed me her phone, and as I began trawling through our texts to each other I instantly saw it. 'I am always asking you to collect me from the pub, or to meet you in the pub, or asking you if you would like to go to the pub.'

This might sound surprising, but this was a massive kick in the face for me. I looked at Antoinette and she was smiling, smiling after all I had put her through. 'Look Gary. You are not always like the way you were last night. If you were, I'd be long gone. I have so much faith in you. I believe in you, and I want to be in a relationship with you, so maybe when we are together, you can try not drinking. I'm not asking you to stop outright, just maybe give it a go when you are with me.'

I couldn't believe it. After all I had done, Antoinette was still willing to give me a chance. That conversation was one of the most important talks I have ever had with anyone in my entire life. I was crazy about this woman. I was in love. And she was still willing to give our relationship a go. I had one of the most powerful penny drop moments of my life. If I didn't change, I would lose the best thing that ever happened to me. But Antoinette wasn't finished just yet.

'I need to tell you that I too have faults, Gary. I have demons that can prevent me from being happy. Demons that can give people the wrong impression about me, that I am rude and what have ya. But these feelings are all linked to my "wall". I don't ever feel good enough. But with you, I feel something changing in me. I can see a future with you, if you can get to grips with the things that are holding you back.' She then leaned into me, and as a single tear began the lonely decent down her face, she said, 'Don't give up Gary. Once I see that you are always willing to work on yourself, then I'll always be here. And as regards to me and my demons? Well, I'm asking you not to give up on me either. Although my wall is high, I have a good feeling that you will burst through it.' She then said the most perfect thing to me: 'I promise you Gary, once you're in, I'll never give you a reason to want out.'

I am crying as I write this. Yet again, just like when I was in prison, Antoinette had given me something to strive for. On that fateful day, she opened my eyes to what a dickhead I truly was, without giving me an ultimatum. She simply showed me that the drink didn't suit me. She showed me that I actually *was* a good person beneath all the crap. And she reassured me that she wanted a life with me, once I was willing to never give up working on bettering myself and conquering my demons once and for all.

I knew what I had to do. I knew what changes needed to be made in order for us to have a life together. I was scared. I feared the addiction. But I had Antoinette, and with her by my side I knew I could achieve anything.

Chapter 7

STARTING FROM SCRATCH (AGAIN)

The chance of sober life was laid out before me. All I had to do was grab it. Easy, right? If only...

After my chat with Antoinette, I instantly banished alcohol from my life. But I was one of the lucky ones. I had support, love and care. I had everything I needed to succeed. Unfortunately, this didn't make the task any easier. I quickly realised that my whole social life revolved around the pub. From the watching of football matches to catching up with my friends, I did all of these activities whilst my bottom was firmly planted on a bar stool and my hand was gripped around a pint. Having Antoinette in my life made missing these activities a lot more bearable. And besides, I had done this before. I was sober for two years and nine months while I was in jail, although I realise I was forced into this sobriety due to the lack of alcohol available in prison. But I know how good life can be when you are free from your addiction, and Antoinette was showing me a life I had convinced myself I didn't deserve. But there was one burning question I hadn't asked myself: *Why (besides greed) do you always drink too much?*

If I had a problem in my past, and I had quite a few, some inflicted on me, but most self-inflicted, I would drink to erase them. The more I drank, the more my problems began to dissolve. But the issues I was drinking to forget would always come back the next day, and they would bring with them the mother of all hangovers. So the negative cycle would start again ... and again ... and again. Is that why I was an alcoholic? I'm not fully convinced if I'm honest. Don't get me wrong, it does go a long way to explaining things, but I have to own my problems too. I should have sought help at an earlier junction in my life. Maybe then I wouldn't have lost everything. Maybe then I wouldn't have ended up in prison, which in turn, hurt so many people. I needed to take responsibility for how my life turned out and not hide behind excuses.

Unfortunately, at this time a lot of these feelings of shame and regret that haunted my past were still lingering, plus I was still trying to find my way as a free man. I now had to deal with all these problems sober, and it was honestly one of the hardest things I have ever done. I had relied heavily on the false power of absolution that alcohol offered me so dealing with my problems sober was a huge struggle. I would become angry. I would lash out. I'd find myself crying at the drop of a hat. I was feeling sorry for myself, and I am not a fan of self-pity. I am filled with so much guilt as I relive this terrible time of my life, but I need to be as honest as I can about all of this in the hope that it might help someone in a similar situation.

I would have massive tantrums, similar to a vexed child. I would say horrible things in order to intentionally hurt the person in front of me. I was a complete moron. And, for reasons that escape me, I took the majority of these issues out on Antoinette, the woman who was doing everything in her power to give me a better life, the woman who was good enough to support me as I dealt with my addiction in the first place. Don't get me wrong. I wasn't acting like this in front of her all the time, but doing it once was one time too many.

And although we came very close to splitting up, Antoinette never lost faith in me.

'You're struggling Gary, I can see that. But at the same time, you're making progress as well,' she would say to me almost daily. At this time, I honestly didn't feel like I deserved this woman, but I told myself that I would do everything I could to better myself and offer her a life she truly warranted.

'I think you should go and talk to someone Gary,' says Antoinette one evening as we lay beside each other on my bed in my mam's house. Yep, I was 35 years of age and I was bringing my lady back to 'me ma's'. How very classy.

Antoinette's statement made me shiver. My experiences with counsellors in the past were not favourable ones. After my daughter passed away, I attended a few with dreadful outcomes. This had little to do with the counsellor and more to do with the fact that I didn't want to be there. But this time felt different for me. I was out of prison a few months at this stage, and I still possessed a huge yearning to show the world that I had changed and had learned from my mistakes. And yet, I was struggling to stay positive, so I knew what I had to do. I turned to look into Antoinette's beautiful green eyes and said, 'You're right Annie. I really do need to talk to someone.' I instantly took to Google and found I was drawn to one counsellor in particular. And she turned out to be exactly what I was looking for.

Obviously I won't disclose the talks that I had with this lady, a wonderful woman by the name of Lorraine. But she did so much for me in the short time I spent with her. I began seeing why certain things made me feel the way I did. I had someone who would listen to my shame and regret as it came flowing out of me, someone who didn't know me personally and so could give me an unbiased view. I never expected to feel that way as I spoke to a stranger about such personal issues. If you are reading this and unfortunately you feel you can relate to my story, I urge you to talk to someone about it. Talk to anyone. Please, don't suffer in silence.

If this were a movie, some inspirational, uplifting music would now burst from the speakers and you, the viewer, would be shown a montage displaying the great progress our leading actor was making as he struggled to improve. So as you read the final part of this chapter, I would love you to have the music from Rocky *swirling around your brain, as I chop wood and run pointlessly up some really steep steps.*

I began believing in myself again. I focused on how much I wanted to show the world I had changed. I worked so hard on myself. I adapted. An example of this would be giving up going to Dublin GAA matches, and I was a huge fan. I understood though that they were massive triggers with me when it came to drinking. So I enjoyed watching the games on the TV with Antoinette (Up the Dubs!). I started meeting my friends in coffee shops instead of bars, though we still tried with all our might to solve the world's problems. I was getting the spring back in my step. But I was also mindful that life can throw many things at you. I realised that it really was 'okay not to be okay'. For me, the trick to surviving these set backs was two-fold: (1) It *is* okay not to be okay, just don't unpack and live your life there; (2) Again, *never suffer in silence.* Talk to someone – anyone. Hell, talk to me if you feel it would help. But never suffer in silence and never give up.

My fight back had begun. All I needed now was a job that would aid me as I tried to build a life with Antoinette. But actually getting a job is a whole chapter in itself!

Chapter 8

NO EX-CONS NEED APPLY

I had been extremely lucky when it came to work before my incarceration. My late father had his own successful painting and decorating company, which I became an employee of after finishing my Junior Cert. In hindsight, I do wish I had stayed in school and completed my Leaving Cert, but I remain eternally grateful to my father for allowing me to earn a steady wage. Alas, on my CV I had only a basic education and my work experience was as a painter and decorator – that was it (although I enjoyed 'long walks', 'playing sports' and other fabrications that for some reason I thought would help me get a job). But this was 2014. I had spent the beginning of the global recession in prison, and I have to admit that I didn't fully understand just how hard times had become. One of the biggest industries affected by this recession was construction, which painters and decorators are very much a part of. So the task of finding a job, especially with my shameful past, was always going to be difficult.

What I did possess was a never-give-up attitude, the very attitude that was such a help as I kept the demon drink at bay. I was beginning to find life as a sober man so much more appealing. I fully immersed myself in the gym again, and having Antoinette in my life gave me someone who I constantly wanted to impress. But getting a job was paramount. I have never been afraid of hard work, and I really hoped this would stand to me.

My day would begin with me trawling through websites advertising jobs, but I quickly noted the lack of painting and decorating positions available. This terrified me, but not earning a wage terrified me a whole lot more. So I changed tack. Antoinette would say to me, 'One of the things I love about you is your drive. You have no fear putting yourself out there, so why not apply for a job outside of painting?' This was the kick up the arse I needed. I began applying for jobs I felt I had transferable skills in. I was always good with the customer as a painter, so I had 'great customer service skills'. I had been foreman for many of my father's jobs, so I displayed 'good organisational skills' and 'worked well either as a member of a team or left to my own devices'. Yes, these skills were like the aforementioned fabrications from my first CV, but I had to try something. I began applying for customer service jobs, ones that didn't require much experience, and one day I was shocked to receive an email inviting me to an interview. And I will never forget it.

The position was as a Customer Service Rep, manning the phones and dealing with the customers of this particular firm. In the days leading up to the interview, I made a point of finding out every little detail I could about this company. I really wanted this job. There was just one little factor I hadn't taken into account – my time spent inside.

On the morning of the interview, I donned the best white shirt I had, a black silk tie and a pair of black slacks I had purchased in Pennys (I was feckin' broke), and off I toddled. While sitting on the bus, I found the rain that was battering the window quite soothing, truth be known. I was extremely nervous. I went over all the facts I had garnered from this company's website and felt I was as prepared as I could be.

I strutted into the reception of this company, comparable to the walk that Conor McGregor has made so famous, and addressed the lady sitting behind the desk.

'Good morning. My name is Gary Cunningham and I'm here to interview for the position of Customer Service Rep,' I said with confidence.

'Good morning Mr. Cunningham ... em ... you're a bit early no?' came the confused reply from the brown-haired receptionist, her accent informing me she was possibly from central Europe. And she was right. I hate being late, but I will admit that I take this a bit too far sometimes. I was an hour early for God's sake!

'Ah, I'd rather be early than late now,' I laugh.

'Ah, it's no problem Mr. Cunningham. Please take a seat and Seán will be with you ... em ... in about an hour.'

We both shared a laugh, and it was very welcome as it calmed my nerves somewhat. I used the hour to brush up on when this company started, what their mission statement entailed, what the boss's cat's name was. I wanted to cover every angle. But I should not have bothered.

An hour or so later, Seán, a tall, slim man with jet-black hair and the most perfect grey suit I had ever seen, appeared. He smiled as he offered his hand to me, and then directs me into a brightly-lit boardroom with a large wooden desk sitting proudly in the room's centre. He seemed very welcoming and friendly, and I found this really helpful. Seán quickly got down to business.

'I see you don't have much experience with customer service in a phone centre environment, Gary, but we do offer full training here. So what can you tell me about what we do here?'

Result! It was like when a question appears on a test that you have studied your arse off for. I relayed every drop of information I had on the company, and I did all of this while using my 'posh voice'. Yep, I possess the ability to drop my 'Finglas tone' and replace it with one that would fool you into believing I might be from Dalkey.

'Wow, very impressive Gary. You know more than I do,' laughs Seán.

He then proceeded to fire questions at me that I think you would be asked no matter what job you were applying for. 'Where do you see yourself in five years, what are your salary expectations?' and so on. Luckily, I had also studied the 'correct' answers to these questions, and again this seemed to impress Seán.

'That is excellent Gary,' he said to me. *Why thank you kind sir*, I thought to myself. 'I feel this went very well Gary,' continues Seán. 'I am going to leave you with this form. Fill in what you can, and don't worry if you don't have all the information to hand right now. I'll come back in a few minutes and see how you are getting on.' He hands me a pen, an A4 sheet filled with about ten questions, and off he went.

You're doing well here Gar, I thought to myself, but I was then stopped in my tracks by the very first question I had to answer: *Q1. Have you ever been incarcerated?* My blood ran cold. The only thing I hadn't factored in was a question of this nature. I just didn't expect to be asked about my incarceration during the interview. I stared at this question for the entire five minutes Seán had left the boardroom, battling with whether I should be honest and up front or keep my shameful past to myself. But 'the truth will set you free', and I had spent way too long being deceitful before prison. So I chose to tell the truth.

Seán re-enters the room smiling. 'I really feel that went very well Gary. Are you currently employed or, if you were to be successful today, would you be available to start immediately?' he asked as he took the A4 sheet back off me.

Instantly, Seán's smile faded when he saw the single word I wrote in response to the first question, *'Yes'*.

'Oh,' says Seán, 'eh, right. So you have been in prison Gary? How long ago was that?'

'I was released last November,' I reply, and I note how deflated I sounded.

'Right, em ... okay,' replies Seán. I can see he was feeling uncomfortable, and I actually almost felt sorry for him. 'Gary, I'm sorry, but it is the policy of this company that we don't take on ex-offenders.' And that was that. The interview ended that abruptly.

I thanked Seán for his time, and sulked out the door feeling so ashamed and embarrassed. I trudged up the road with my phone in my hand that had a text message vying for my attention. It was from Antoinette. 'Well? How did it go baby? Ring me as soon as you can xxx.' But I couldn't bring myself to ring her at that time. I was feeling very low, and I was very worried. *How am I ever going to secure a job? Why the fuck did I have to be such a gobshite that ended up in prison? What am I going to do?* And as all these thoughts were running through my mind, I was oblivious to the small truck that was approaching me from behind. When I did cop on, it was too late to get myself out of the way of the massive puddle the driver was about to plough into. *Whoosh!* I was soaked to the skin. Great! My Penny's slacks were drenched, as were my boxer shorts, socks – every inch of me. Well, when it rains it pours...

This massive setback unfortunately became a repeating scenario. Once I informed any potential employer of my past, I wouldn't get any further in the interview. Please don't get me wrong, I 'get' why they responded that way. There were too many worries and fears for these employers. Could I be trusted? Aren't all ex-prisoners just bad people? But what each of these employers didn't realise was that if they *had* taken a chance with me, I would have repaid them tenfold. My desire for employment was so great that I would have instantly become one of their hardest workers.

Around this time, I was required by Social Welfare to attend Seetec Employment and Skills Ireland which was a Government-run scheme that delivered the Jobpath and Welcome to Work employability and skills programmes across Ireland. This turned out to be the best thing that could've happen to me at the time. I was assigned a case worker, Shane, and we instantly hit it off. I told him of my past, and he didn't judge me in the slightest. Such a welcome change from what I was experiencing from potential employers at that time. Shane was younger than me, with a goatee and chin-strap that lead to his tight, mousey-brown hair.

'I keep getting knocked back Shane,' I say one day, 'I can't give up ... I *won't* give up. But my confidence is taking quite a battering I have to say. I am beginning to think I should lie about my time spent in prison. I always do really well in all these interviews. I am always over-prepared. I would get the sense that they really liked me, and then "that" question would crop up and I'd find I'm being ushered out the door. I am beginning to see why some re-offend Shane, if I'm honest.'

Shane gave me the official line on how I should answer a question about having spent time in prison. 'Honesty, Gary, is truly the best policy. You must tell them the truth. But if they don't ask, you are not obliged to tell them.'

Shane had arranged an interview for me in a hotel in Dublin's city centre as a maintenance painter. The interview went the same as the one described earlier, except this time the guy who interviewed me actually told me how impressed he was with me. In fact, we ended up chatting about all things painting and decorating for about half an hour after the interview ended. But then I was handed a sheet with that same dreaded question sitting at the top. I really wanted this job, so I attached a handwritten note to the sheet, almost begging to be given a chance. Alas, a couple of days later I received a generic email informing me I 'wasn't successful at this time'.

Shane from Seetec was a bit perturbed by this, but part of his job was to get feedback from the people I was interviewed by to see if there was anything I could do to improve for my next interview. I witnessed the call he made to this hotel, and I am so glad I did. The man who interviewed me told Shane that if it was up to him, I'd have got the job there and then. 'Sadly, I must adhere to the company's policy,' he said, 'but he was a great lad, very friendly, and he had all the skills we were looking for. It's such a pity really.'

But these words gave me another boost of confidence. He liked me as a person, and felt I was qualified, and this put a bit of pep back into my step. I knew I needed to get back on the horse. I needed to learn and grow from every knock back I received, and I needed to have faith in myself. At the end of the day, this whole situation was all my own doing so no self-pity. Get up and get out there Gar. *Never give up.*

And soon, it paid off.

I was sitting at my computer one Sunday trawling through job sites when a rare advert grabbed my attention: *Painter and Decorator Required. Must Have Experience.* Well, I fit that bill. I immediately fired off my CV to this ad that was on Gumtree, and within a few minutes my phone began to ring, displaying a number I didn't recognise. 'Hello?' I answer, a little timidly if I'm honest.

'Howya, I just got your CV there. My name is Robbie. Are ya at the game (painting and decorating) long?' No long-winded interview here!

'Yeah, Robbie, I'm Gary by the way, em, yeah, I am painting all my working life. So I know my emulsion from my gloss if that helps?'

This makes Robbie laugh. 'Ah, good man,' he says, 'look, can you start tomorrow? I would be willing to give you a trial day to see how ya get on, see if you can actually paint.'

As the cool kids would say these days, my reaction was simply OMG! 'I will be wherever you want me to be at whatever time you want me there, Robbie. Wow. Thank you so very much.' I actually felt like I was going to burst out crying.

'Grand so,' says Robbie, 'I'll text you the address and I'll see you there at eight am.' And that was that. And the one question Robbie never asked? 'Where you ever in prison?' Shane from Seetec jumped into my head, *'if they don't ask, you're not obliged to tell them.'*

What happened next was just incredible. I never worked as hard in my life as I did for Robbie. I was going to make sure he knew how grateful I was for him taking a chance on me. We hit it off instantly, and Robbie was soon complimenting me on my work. This man had given me something I honestly thought I would never have again. A job. And so I promised myself that I would become his best employee. Although I did have some stiff competition. The crew Robbie had assembled were fantastic tradesmen, and really nice guys to boot. I felt like I had won the lotto. I had made my mam so proud. I had made Antoinette proud. It was just incredible. It really pays to never give up. I have honestly never enjoyed working as much as I did at that time, and I really appreciate Robbie and all he did for me.

As this chapter ends, I want to get something off my chest. As already stated, I understand why companies won't employ ex-prisoners, but how are ex-prisoners who have learned from their mistakes meant to show the world that they have changed? In prison you are encouraged to gain employment while you serve your sentence – jobs like being a cleaner, or a painter, or in my case a kitchen worker. There are also incredible individuals who come into our nation's prisons daily – the teaching staff. They work tirelessly to try to give you a better chance in life upon your release. And as you serve your sentence, or 'do your whack', and you learn from these remarkable teachers, or maybe learn a new skill or trade, you begin to fantasize that these new skills will aid you in gaining employment once you're released. But the reality is so very different.

I know from experience that if someone was to employ an ex-prisoner, one who has an honest desire to change and has learned from their mistakes, they would never regret it. That ex-prisoner will give you 110 per cent simply because you showed faith in him or her. Not every man and woman released from prison is a 'scumbag' or should be written off. So many, like myself, just want a fair chance to prove that their past should not define them.

This may be all too John Lennon for some, '*you may say, I'm a dreamer...*' but I truly believe that '*I'm not the only one...*'

Chapter 9

'ALL WE HEAR IS RADIO GAR-GAR'

I was loving every moment of being in employment, of being sober, of being in love. All my initial longing to show the world how much I had changed had returned. I felt I had a responsibility to show people that a person really can learn from the errors of their ways. I felt I owed this to the men I had been locked up with who possessed the same yearning for change as I did. And most of all, I felt I owed this to Fitzer, so that he could be prepared for life outside.

As my mood became more positive, it instilled in me the courage to ring Fitzer to tell him how truly sorry I was for being weak and for turning my back on him. I hope the following telephone conversation will give you an insight into why this man means so much to me:

Fitzer: 'Ah, *Jaysis* Gar, me aul' flower. Long time, no hear. How the hell are ya buddy?'

Nervous and ashamed Gary (crying): 'Eh ... em, howya pal. Fitzer, I'm so fuckin' sorry man. I'm so sorry I turned my back on ya. I was so embarrassed at how weak I had become, especially after all you did to help me. I felt like I was letting you down...'

Fitzer: 'Stop all that shite Gar. Aren't ya on the phone to me now? I've missed ya, ya bollox. Here, wait 'til ya hear *this...*'

And that was it. That was how long Fitzer lingered on the fact I was a complete bastard to him. He was so happy that I got in touch. And, true to form, he ended our chat with an abundance of love and care, of positive mantras and the knowledge that he believed in me.

'You're me mate, Gar. I know you struggled, but look at ya now. Onwards an' upwards me aul' flower. And it's great to have ya back.'

It was great to be back, Fitzer.

One day my boss Robbie sent me to work in the home of one of his regular clients, which needed a splash of paint here and there. 'This lady can be a bit fussy, Gar,' starts Robbie, 'but you are great with the clients, and your work is spot on, so I've no problem sending ya to her.'

And I will never forget this particular client...

I arrived early on the first morning and was met by a bubbly lady. I'm not sure of her age, but I know she looked much younger than her years. Her dark-red hair, cut into a bob, shone with a healthy glow as it danced on her shoulders, her smile so very welcoming. 'You must be Gary? Come in, come in, can I get you a cup of tea?' She said all of this in a wonderfully bright, albeit slightly posh, tone.

'I'm fine thanks, miss,' I reply, 'I'm just going to get cracking thanks' (prison had put manners on me, and addressing a lady by miss was one of my favourite ones). I began preparing for the day's work that was ahead of me. I had a cheap pair of earphones that I would attach to my phone and then place only one into my ear so I could listen to the radio (and take a call hands-free) without disturbing those around me. And as any tradesman will know, it is vital to have an aul' radio on while you work. I started in the guest bedroom of this lady's spectacular home, and began arranging the furniture in a way that would allow me access to both the ceiling and walls. She arrived at the bedroom door, impressed, but with a burning question, 'Why the earphones?' she asks.

I explained that I have the radio on and I didn't want to disturb her.

'Not at all, you silly sausage,' she countered, 'what station are you listening to?'

Slightly amused by being called a silly sausage, I say, '98FM miss...'

'It's Orla,' came her interruption.

'Sorry,' I continue, '98FM Orla. I love the talk show they have on, *Dublin Talks* with Adrian Kennedy and Jeremy Dixon. I then switch over to Classic Hits 4FM just in time to listen to another fantastic talk show hosted by Niall Boylan.'

'Oh, well that all sounds very interesting. I shall put 98FM on in the kitchen now, and we can change it to 4FM later,' smiled Orla.

'Ah, thanks so much Orla,' I say with a smile.

'Now, what time will you have a cup of tea Gary?' asks Orla.

I'd jaysis murder a coffee right bleedin' now Orla me aul' mucker, I thought. 'About 10.30 am, Orla, and I'll look after myself, so please don't put yourself out.'

With that, Orla skips down the stairs, turns the dial on her radio, and soon *Dublin Talks* is blaring through her spacious home.

I was applying the final roller-full of brilliant white matt emulsion to Orla's ceiling thinking, *I'm really looking forward to a coffee and a sambo*, when Jeremy Dixon (Adrian Kennedy was off on this particular day) told the listeners what the next topic was going to be: 'Do prisoners have it too easy?' Ah no!

I make my way into Orla's very large kitchen, just as brilliant beams of sunlight streak in through the Velux windows dotted across her wooden ceiling. 'Tea or coffee Gary?' asks Orla.

'Coffee would be great,' I say, just as the adverts stop on the radio and *Dublin Talks* resumes.

'Oh, do you hear this Gary? Bloody prisoners. They should be fed bread and water and left to rot,' says Orla in a very stern manner.

Ah shite, I think, *why did this have to be the topic?* 'Eh, I don't know about that Orla,' I start, 'people make mistakes every day. Sometimes people make absolutely horrific life choices, which ends with them seeing the inside of a prison cell.'

'Well, serves them bloody right in my book, Gary. What about their victims? And sure, they go in there and come out feckin' worse!' came her reply.

Shit. I couldn't argue with this woman for two reasons: (1) Because obviously her remark about the victims of crime is a valid and extremely important point. Embarrassingly, it took about three months inside Mountjoy for me to realise that my particular crime had its victims. I may have only been a 'mule', a courier of cannabis if you will, but the victims of my crime were the people who are daily affected by drugs and all the sorrow they bring. So, I had no argument there. And (2) I couldn't exactly be all, *Hang on there now, Orla, me aul' pal. It just so happens I'm an ex-prisoner, in fact I'm not long out...* I'm not sure that would have gone down too well. Plus, what if my boss Robbie found out and sacked me?

So I sat over that cup of coffee and listened to Orla tear lumps off anyone who is, or has ever been, inside a prison. Coupled with that was the onslaught of listeners ringing into the show echoing Orla's views. *Oh wow*, I began thinking, *is this really what society as a whole thinks of me because of my past?* I couldn't finish my sandwich. I made my excuses and headed back up to work. I was feeling so low, so deflated, and so ashamed. But the next thing I know, I am sending a text to 98FM, firstly confirming that I am actually not long released from prison, and secondly addressing the fact that there is, quote, 'fuck all easy about prison life, although it is as easy as you make it'. I then hit the 'send' button.

Almost instantly, my phone rang and Katie, the show's producer, was asking if I would go on-air. Don't ask me why, but I said 'yes'. And I am so very glad I did. The first thing I did was own up to why I was in prison in the first place. I didn't give Jeremy Dixon a bunch of excuses, instead I told him the truth. I was a selfish, disgusting, lying, sub-human. But then I said the words that were to eventually change my life forever – and I never meant them more than on that particular morning: 'Prison saved my life.'

There was a pause from the show's host. 'Can you explain this Gary?' he asked.

So I did. I told him what a mess I had been before my incarceration, but how with the help of like-minded prisoners and some great prison officers and teachers I began the process of rebuilding my life. I also drove home the point that I was not alone. I highlighted that there were an army of men and women like me who shared my longing for forgiveness. I did acknowledge that there were a lot of men and women who reoffended. But I also asked the question, 'Why is the reoffending rate in this country so high?'

The way Jeremy Dixon handled my call is something for which I will be forever grateful. I was nervous as hell, and he could have used the fact I was being so open and honest about a subject matter that is not usually shouted from the rooftops to stoke controversy. But he didn't. In fact, one caller came on air and labelled me a 'scumbag', which I thought was not surprising coming from such a narrow-minded person. But

Jeremy actually defended me, and again I am very grateful to him for that.

When I got off the phone to him, Katie then thanked me for being so honest, and told me of the incredibly positive feedback and reaction from the listeners. 'Maybe we could get in touch again if other similar stories come up?' she asked.

'Of course Katie, I'll answer the call and give you my honest opinion,' I reply.

And it wasn't too long after that day that I found myself on *The Niall Boylan Show* on 4FM speaking about almost the same thing. Niall handled me and my story in such a positive way too. He actually thanked me live on-air for my honesty. I was gobsmacked. I also began noticing that the amount of callers who wanted to label me a scumbag began to dwindle, and in their place were people supporting me and congratulating me on my blunt honesty. Helena and Garrett, who work behind the scenes on *The Niall Boylan Show*, also asked if they could ring me for all things 'prison-related', and of course I said yes.

And so I became somewhat of a regular on both shows. I noted that the more frank and honest I was, the more I refused to offer excuses as to how my life turned out, and how I never tried to play the 'poor prisoner's' card, all really stood to me. I was bearing my soul, talking about my doubts and fears as a free man. And incredibly, most people (obviously not all) seemed to appreciate this. This period in my life helped to wake the beast that's inside me today, the beast that will stop at nothing to try to help the reintegration of prisoners back into society.

Although, at times I do wish that my 'specialist subject', so to speak, was not 'life in prison'. I kind of wish I had told them I was an ex-porn star or a F1 driver!

And what about Orla?

I went back down at lunchtime that day for another cuppa and I was met with, 'Did you hear your man, the ex-prisoner, who came on there, Gary? He had the same name as you funnily enough. I have to say, he made a lot of sense actually. I suppose they're not all bad – maybe some can change.'

I agreed with her as I headed out to her back garden to take her washing off the line. No, this was not in my job title, but I knew it would make my boss happy. Like I said, he gave me a chance, so I would repay him tenfold.

'You're such a good young man, Gary,' says Orla, 'your mother must be very proud.'

That she is Orla, far more than you'll ever know, is the thought that sailed through my mind, *far more than you'll ever know.*

Chapter 10

The (Un)Usual Suspects...

I am fully aware that the general perception of men and women released from our jails is not usually a favourable one, and I get why. But, obviously, it still upsets me a little. Would I have been so upset had I never been incarcerated? My honest answer is I don't know. But I like to think I have a forgiving side to me that would be willing to give someone who had earned it a second chance, although you do have to earn it. Luckily, during my time in both Mountjoy and Loughan House, I surrounded myself with men who were doing everything they could to earn their second chance. Of course there are some 'bad eggs' inside our prisons, men and women who have no longing for change. But that doesn't go for all prisoners so it hurts me that the lads described in this chapter are tarnished with the same brush. And yet, these men were the very ones who encouraged me to believe in myself when I was going through my own change. What's so special about this bunch of lads? Let me try to describe them.

Cunny

Cunny is a man I have known and admired my whole life and the one I saw in Mountjoy on my first day there, who so very kindly let me sleep on his floor. Unfortunately, Cunny's addiction to cocaine led to his internal combustion and ultimately incarceration. Yet, from day one, he did everything in his power to change and become a better man. He also taught himself how to play the drums while in jail, and incredibly became the drummer in the The Off#enders, a feat made even more difficult due to his anxiety. But he finally started to believe in himself and the results were there for all to see.

I worried about him when he was released, but my worries were groundless. He hit the ground running and was able to go back to work for his old company. I remember bumping into Cunny one day, not long after my own release.

'The bleedin' head on you Gar,' laughed Cunny.

'You're one to talk, ya shitebag,' I respond, 'you look like a member of a boy band on steroids!' This last comment was actually my jealousy coming to the fore. Cunny is in fantastic shape and loves to look after himself, yet he has absolutely no ego.

'Ah, ask me arse Gar,' laughs Cunny.

'So, what's the story pal,' I inquire, 'does it get any easier, this whole "freedom" thing?'

'It's tough adjusting all right Gar, isn't it?' starts Cunny, 'and I suppose it's not made easy by how quickly some people will judge you. You've just got to hang on in there. You'll find a way man, I promise. Besides, look at all you did while we were in "the other place" (prison). Fuckin' hell Gar. It fills me with pride when I tell people what we did together. How mad is that? Filled with pride about being in prison. You taught me to always show remorse for my crime but to be proud of what I achieved while I was paying back my debt to society. So swallow your own medicine Gar ... ya bollox ya!' Cunny erupts with laughter.

But he was right. Of course he was ashamed of why he ended up in jail, but he allowed himself to feel proud of what he had achieved while in there. He worked so hard to fit back into his community, to earn back the love and respect of his kids, his partner and his family. Cunny is a shining example of reform, and one I was so glad to be dazzled by.

'We'll sort out a jam in the next few weeks man,' I say, 'Fitzer will be out soon, so we better get working on new tracks ... you know what he's like.' We both share a laugh as Cunny allows himself to daydream about getting the band back together. 'I'm gonna give Sweeny-Todd a ring,' I say to Cunny followed by, 'it's brilliant to see you doing so well buddy. It's nothing less than you deserve.'

'Right back at ya Gar,' responds Cunny, 'just hang on in there. It will get easier – I promise.'

Sweeny-Todd

Sweeny-Todd and myself didn't really connect until Loughan House, but I am so glad that we did. Slightly shorter than I am, with brown hair and, like Cunny, a voracious appetite for the gym, it could sometimes be quite hard to get more than two words out of him. He is a private man with his head firmly screwed on. As The Off#enders began taking off, we realised we needed another guitar player. Sweeny-Todd fit the bill perfectly. He also possesses an amazing singing voice, a fact which was made clear to me one day as we were recording our album in prison.

I had penned a song about my son and how much I missed him. When we played this song live, I would have no problem singing it, but when it came to trying to record the vocals for it I couldn't make it past the first couple of lines without breaking down. I was too attached. I told Fitzer that I wanted to take the song off the track-list, only for Sweeny-Todd to speak up and say, 'I'll give it a go, if ya like?' And by God am I glad he did. He sang it better than I ever could. Breathtaking. I also have Sweeny-Todd to thank for introducing me to the book *The Secret*, which I truly believe has helped me change my thinking.

In prison, I did something for Sweeny-Todd that I will keep private, but I didn't realise how much it meant to him. Upon his release, Sweeny-Todd amazed us all with his drive and determination. I rang him one day to see how he was.

'All's great Gary, and it's all great because I have chosen my life to go in this direction. Yes, I was constantly judged at first, but I refused to allow that negativity in. I'm running my own company now and things couldn't be better, in fact I have something for you.' That 'something' was a gift that, at the time, helped me more than this man will ever know. Sweeny-Todd explained that 'I'll never forget what you did for me inside, so this is just my way of saying thanks.'

Yet again, this man showed me I should never give up, no matter how judged I felt. He kept getting knocked back after his release, but he kept fighting back.

'Now Gar me aul' pal,' says Sweeny-Todd, 'are we jammin' again soon or what?'

'Soon as possible buddy,' I respond, 'sure Fitzer will be home soon, so we better get our arses in gear ... you know what he's like!'

Smithwhicks

Good Ol' Smithwhicks. What a friend. I first met this guy on D3 in the cell he was sharing with Fitzer. His smile would light up the darkest of rooms, and it daily illuminated the drab wings of Mountjoy. If you met this guy, you would struggle to believe he was ever in prison at all. Well educated, well spoken and immaculately presented, with a bald head and a goatee, he quickly became one of my closest friends, both in prison and on the outside. Although how we managed to never smash each other's face in is beyond me. You see, we both have massive OCD and let's just say we each had our own particular way of doing things. Luckily, our friendship meant more to us than who was better at cleaning our work area.

I really missed Smithwhicks when he was released so I did all I could to locate him when I eventually came home. And when first I met him on the outside, he was struggling.

'I can't get a job Gar,' were the words that sadly flowed from his mouth. 'As soon as they find out I was in "the other place", it's game over.' This saddened me so much, but then I thought of how the words from Cunny and Sweeny-Todd had helped me so I relayed them to Smithwhicks. It gives me great pleasure to report that he refused to give up and is currently working at his dream job. He pops over to me every other week for a coffee and a chat, and his friendship is worth its weight in gold to me.

The common thread running through these three stories is that even after all the knock backs, even after constantly hearing 'no', they refused to give up. We all know that the difficulties we were presented with were a direct result of how we messed up our lives, but all four of us have gone above and beyond to prove how much we have changed. Surely, if a person displays genuine sorrow for their actions, and backs this up by changing and not hiding behind a plethora of excuses, shouldn't they be given a chance?

And there are hundreds more just like us. Indeed, most would be surprised exactly how many are just like myself, Cunny, Sweeny-Todd, Smithwhicks and Fitzer, to name but a few.

Speaking of Fitzer, he will be home for good – soon. I better get cracking on some new songs. We all know what he's like...

Chapter 11

'I Miss Ya Man...'

'*Good mornin' Ted. Another bright and beautiful day in good ol' Mountjoy, wha'? Gerrup outta that buddy. Stick on your smile and let's do this!'*

I suppose that sums up what Fitzer is like in a nutshell. This was the welcome I received every morning in Mountjoy after the officer opened each of our cell doors in order for us to head off to the kitchen to begin work. And he would literally skip into work, humming or singing, every day. I was such a 'Negative Nelly' before my incarceration, and even more so in the early days I faced behind bars. But Fitzer soon banished that negativity from me. He would always say, 'It's no one else's fault you're here Gar me aul' mucker. You fucked up, so now you have to own it. No point in feeling sorry for yourself for breaking the law now is there? Pick yourself up, dust yourself down, and start making changes for the better.' Wise words indeed.

What we achieved in prison is something I shall remain proud of forever. From penning songs in cells on the wings of Mountjoy to forming The Off#enders, touring the Irish jails, writing an album, and performing for the Irish media in the school in Mountjoy. From helping as many lads as we could as they served their time to being there for each other when our own waters became unsettled.

So, I'm sure you can understand why I missed him.

Being able to ring Loughan House and speak with Fitzer after I was released was great. During the time of my 'slip', when I foolishly shut him out, I descended deeper into depression. But all it took was one call to him and soon the clouds began parting again, just like they did in the early days of our time spent in Mountjoy. And, true to form, Fitzer would make these calls between us all about me for the first twenty minutes or so. I was the one who had been feckin' released, yet there he would be, counselling me and making sure *I* was okay. But it was the laugh we would have on these calls that I remember best. Fitzer is the most animated storyteller you have ever met, even on the phone. He would tell a story in great detail and provide different voices and accents for each of the characters. He would build drama and tension comparable to a good James Patterson novel, and would leave you in stitches by the story's end. But there is one story in particular that I remember the most.

I'm heading home from a great day's work one day, covered from head to toe in splashes of magnolia masonry paint. Myself, Johnny, Grant and Conor (my boss Robbie's dream team) had been tackling a rather awkward pebble-dashed house, which is why I looked like someone had been flicking paint at me for fun. I say goodbye to the lads and head for my bus. As I trudge up the busy street, feeling like a walking advert for Dulux Paints, I retrieve my phone from the pocket of my overalls and punch in the number for Loughan House. After a couple of rings, I'm met with the slightly manic tones of one of the officers, Mr. Camden. I must point out that there was no emergency going on in the background to make Mr. Camden sound manic. He just always sounded that way.

'Welllll hellooo there, Loughan House Open Centre, how may I help you today?' says Mr Camden in his west of Ireland twang.

'Mr. Camden, ya headcase, it's Gary Cunningham here. How are ya sir?'

'Ahhhhh aul' Cunningham, "The Voice" eh? Good aul' *Garrr*. What the fuck do you want? You are released you know, you don't have to keep telling us where you are any more ya gobshite ya!' Mr. Camden almost shouts this at me as he begins laughing.

'Ah feck off Camden, ya head-wrecker,' I reply, 'just give the other fella a shout there for me will ya?'

'Ah yes. The other fella. Fitzer I presume. Your fuckin' shadow.' This last comment has me busting a gut with laughter. 'I'll get him now Gar, and on a serious note, I hope you're doing okay fella? I have to say, you're missed "round these parts pardner".' Camden has adopted a John Wayne tone for this comment. He places the receiver on his desk and mans the intercom: 'Would Fitzer please come to reception, that's Fitzer to reception. There is a balls rough shithead on the phone for ya.' This announcement would have been heard throughout Loughan House. Thanks for that Mr. Camden!

Soon Fitzer is on the line. 'What's the story, morning Gary ... wellllll.' He sings this opening line at me in the air of the classic Oasis tune. 'How are ya Ted?' he continues, 'everything okay with ya out there?'

'Jaysis, it should be me asking you that pal,' I reply, 'but yeah, everything is going great man. There is a whole world waiting for ya to come out to buddy. And with your attitude, you'll take to it like a duck to water,' I say.

'Ahh I can't wait,' says Fitzer, 'not long now Gar me aul' flower. Here, now, you're not to go mad yeah? But I was actually home for an overnight last week.'

'*What*?' says I, shocked, and a little hurt if I'm honest.

Fitzer starts laughing. 'Ah, don't fuckin' start, ya mad thing,' he begins, 'there was a family emergency, so they let me home for the night, as I'm now weeks away from coming home for good. I just wanted to spend every last bit of the time with Ash and Cian. I know you get that bud.'

'Of course pal. In fact, I'm delighted for ya,' comes my reply. 'Did you enjoy it man?' I then ask.

'It was perfect Gar. But here – wait 'til ya hear this…'

I always knew to prepare myself whenever Fitzer said, 'wait 'til ya hear this'.

'So,' he starts, 'I decided to ask for a lend of one of the bikes we're fixing up for the Bikes to Africa charity, so I could cycle from here (Loughan House, Blacklion, County Cavan) to Enniskillen to get me bus back to Dublin. I wanted to get the earliest bus from Enniskillen to Dublin, so the bus that brings ya from the jail here to Enniskillen was no help. I got a lend of the bike no bother, and Mr. Slater (one of the officers from Loughan House) even got me a lend of a good bike lock so I could leave the bike there overnight and cycle it back here the next day.'

All seems like a good plan so far Fitzer, me aul' flower, I think, *do continue.*

'So, I'm getting ready to go, when one of the lads comes into me room.'

'You're headin' back to Dublin Fitzer, yeah? Any chance you could post this letter and a few photos for me? It's for me missus, and ya know how long they fuckin' take in here to send your bleedin' letters,' says he.

'Of course I will,' says I, 'no bother pal. But it turned out to be quite the bother Gar,' laughs Fitzer.

'So, I gets on the bike and off I go, with this lad's love letter tucked into me back pocket, completely forgetting that the road to Enniskillen is just basically a massive bunch of fuckin' hills. More hills than Beverly, Gar, I'm tellin' ya. But I fuckin' got there, and just in the nick of time too. I lock up the bike, leg it in to grab a ticket, and next thing ya know I'm collapsed into one of the most comfy chairs I have ever had the pleasure of parking my arse on – with the love letter still in me pocket. *I'll stick it in a post box as soon as I hit Dublin, I thinks to meself Gar.* But sure, that didn't happen. I'm on the bleedin' Luas the next time I think of the jaysis letter and promise meself I'll post it as soon as I get off. But, of course, that didn't happen neither! In fact, I got off the Luas, flew into me da for a quick chat, got home to Ash and Cian, and that was that. I was in heaven, so the last thing on me mind was the jaysis letter.'

I am hanging on his every word, dying to know how this will end. He continues:

'So, next morning, I get up and spend as much time as I can with Ash and Cian, but sadly the time arrives for me to head back. I reassure the missus that it won't be long before I'm home for good and give her the biggest kiss and hug I have ever given her. I say my goodbyes and head off to catch the bus back to Enniskillen. I have to admit Gar, I was heartbroken. But I was also buoyed by the idea of life as a free man, which isn't too far away now Gar me aul' flower! Anyway, I get the bus back to Enniskillen, grab the bike, and thunder back to the prison. I gets in, get searched an' all that, and head over to me room. And just as I'm about to walk in, the "love letter" dude sticks his head out to me. "Did ya do that for me Fitzer?" says he. And ya know me Gar, I don't do bullshit. I stick my hand into my backpack, rummage around, and pull out his bleedin' love letter and hand it back to him, battered and reeking of my sweaty arse.' Fitzer and myself are in convulsions. 'Ah jaysis, God love yer man Gar, he was freaked,' laughs Fitzer, 'and all I could say back to him was, sorry man, but you know what I'm like!' Brilliant.

And almost every call I made to Fitzer during this time was filled with laughter and the same top-notch story telling. This guy saved my life in more ways than one during my incarceration, and yet if I ever inform him of this fact I'm met with, 'Would you ever fuck off ya gobshite. You're me mate, plain and simple.' And he was still playing a huge role as I began rebuilding my life on the outside. His friendship is the sole reason I am about to write the following words: *I'm kinda glad I went to prison.* How bat-shit crazy is that? But had I never gone in, I wouldn't have this man's friendship now. Of course, he still would not allow me to do anything for him while he finished his sentence ('I always look after myself Gar, then no one can let me down'), but I always did my best to make sure his family, Ash and Cian, were okay.

Every time I began missing him I would hear his voice booming inside my head: *'Snap out of it, ya balls rough gobshite. Do your whack. Gerrup outta tha' me aul' mucker. Sure I'll be home in no time.'*

Which was true. Fitzer's freedom was fast approaching.

Chapter 12

HIP, HIP BUT NO HOORAY

Life was good. I had a job, Fitzer was back in my life, my family seemed impressed with the changes in me and, most importantly of all, Antoinette and I were going from strength to strength. In Mountjoy, Antoinette became the one person I strived to impress. I would write songs for The Off#enders, or poems explaining my current thoughts and moods, and I would send them to her to get her opinion. And then it was like the old *Man from Del Monte* adverts that plagued our TV screens back when I was a lad: 'The woman from East Wall, she said *yes!*' If I got Antoinette's seal of approval, I would proceed with the song or poem. If she said, 'Eh, no Gar,' I would bin the song or poem and never speak of it again. Her opinion back then, and today, means the world to me.

Antoinette was always fascinated with my prison story, and would sit and listen intently as I meandered through tale after tale of what I achieved while I 'did me whack'. 'You should write a book about all you did Gary,' says Antoinette to me one day.

'Well...,' I start, 'it's funny you should say that. I'm about half way through that very book. I'm just not sure if people will actually be interested in what I got up to inside. Sure, my own family doesn't want to know.'

'That is only because they are getting use to the "new you" and all that comes with that,' says Antoinette, 'but I really think you should finish what you've started and see what happens.'

I loved how Antoinette could make me feel like I could take on the world without fear. Sadly, for the first time, I didn't agree with her on this one. I knew, deep down, that my story was a little different to the usual jail tale, and I was terrified of putting it out there to be dissected. So the book idea was put firmly on the back burner and I was hoping Antoinette would forget all about it. Thankfully, she didn't, and in time she would intervene.

One thing I dreaded was meeting Antoinette's family as I foolishly assumed she was harbouring feelings of embarrassment about where we met. I pictured her mam or dad asking, 'So, where did you meet this fella Gary, Annie?' and Antoinette's answering with, 'Em, well, it's like this...' But I could not have been more wrong if I tried.

The first person I met in Antoinette's family was her sister Angela with whom she shared an apartment. I remember being so nervous, and yet when Antoinette introduced me, I was met with Angela's huge smile and friendly demeanour. She engaged me in a way that made me feel like we'd been friends for years. And Angela set the tone for how the rest of Antoinette's family welcomed me. From her other sister Susan, who instantly made me feel so at ease, to her only brother David who did the very same. Even her nephews Craig and Josh, and her niece Cody, went above and beyond to welcome me into the fold. I felt so very lucky. But I still had her mam and dad to deal with, though I had no need to worry.

Unfortunately, I have a lot of guilt and regret when it comes to Antoinette's dad. We only met a couple of times, and I should have made more of an effort to get to know him. Sadly, he passed away before we got a chance to know each other properly. I have never been made to feel bad about this by Antoinette or her family, yet it remains something I feel guilty about to this day. May you rest in peace Mr. Gahan.

And then there is Antoinette's mammy, the beautiful Anne. From the second I met this lady, I loved everything about her. Such a beautiful woman, both inside and out. They say if you want to know what 'yer missus' will be like when she gets older, look at her mam. Well, I have to say, my future looks bright! And from the second I met her, she made me feel so welcome and accepted me into her family.

Even Antoinette's friends gave me an easy time when they met me first. Friends like Jackie, Janice and Mary all treated me with so much respect, and they never judged me. I am so grateful for this act of kindness from them.

Of course, Antoinette had to meet my clan too. How different my thoughts were when it came to this meeting. I was proud as a peacock as I introduced her to my brothers and my nephews and nieces, and they all instantly fell in love with her. They saw the impact she was having on my life, but it was the impact she had on my mam's life that clinched the deal.

They first met when my mam was in hospital. We went up to visit her, and I remember how nervous Antoinette was.

'God, Gary, what if she hates me?' says Antoinette.

'She won't hate ya Annie, per se,' I respond, 'maybe a slight dislike, but she won't *hate* ya.'

'Feck off, ya gobshite,' was Antoinette's reply.

But when they met, something happened that still continues to this very day. I may as well have disappeared in a poof of smoke. When they began talking, they had absolutely no interest in me. I remember asking my mam if I could get her anything in the hospital shop, asking her about six fuckin' times, only to be eventually met with, 'What Gary?

What!? Ohh, get me anything you like. Now, sorry about that Antoinette. Please continue.'

The two most important women in my life had combined to render me completely invisible, and I couldn't have been happier. Their relationship has grown and grown, and today they view each other as best friends. And Antoinette can do no wrong in me ma's eyes. I remember one night when I was living at home and Antoinette stayed the night with me. It was feckin' freezing and the duvet that covered my bed wasn't cutting it. I braved the arctic conditions and made my way to the airing cupboard just outside my bedroom door to grab one of the *many* (and I stress the word many) woollen throws that my mam has accumulated over the years. And this throw worked a treat. Instant warmth. The next day, however, long after Antoinette had left, I was summoned into the sitting room by my mother.

'Gary, don't just go taking my blankets willy-nilly. I may have wanted that one (she didn't). You didn't even fold it back properly!' My mam actually looked rather vexed as she berated me over the blanket. But I knew how to sort this out.

'Sorry ma. It's just that Antoinette was freezing last night.'

'Oh...,' she says, 'well why didn't you say?' Her frown had turned upside down at the mention of her new BFF's name. She continues, in a bright, cheerful tone. 'Take whatever throw you like for Antoinette son. Any one of them that you like. *Anything* for Antoinette.' I knew from that moment that Antoinette had taken my place in the pecking order with my mam and, like I already said, I couldn't have been happier.

One thing both these ladies had in common was a dodgy hip. My mam had had a new one put in, and so she was one of the few who knew the pain Antoinette was experiencing daily, as she had experienced something similar herself. And Antoinette was in horrific pain at this time. My admiration and respect would increase daily as I watched her try to sustain a normal life. She couldn't work in full-time employment because of how bad her hip had become. But Antoinette would never let her condition define her. She volunteered in her local youth club and was a massive hit with the kids. She regularly attended the gym and did whatever her body permitted her to do. I would find myself worrying that she was doing too much, only to be met with an attitude that inspired the life out of me. 'I can't let it beat me Gar. Some day, possibly some day soon, I won't be physically able to do any of these things. So until that day, I will keep fighting.' But unbeknownst to us both, that day was fast approaching.

I'll never forget it. Thursday evening. I had made dinner for myself and Antoinette in my mam's home. We had the place to ourselves so I told her to go in and stick on the TV while I cleaned up. Antoinette refused, and insisted on helping me tidy the cutlery away. 'Thanks hun,' I say, 'I'm just gonna run up to the jacks, then we'll cuddle up and watch some shite TV.'

'Sounds perfect Gar. I really do love you Gary,' says she.

'And I love you too baby,' came my grateful reply.

I made my way to the bathroom. Just as I flush the chain, I hear a scream that made my blood run cold. Antoinette! I bolted down the stairs and into the kitchen to see Antoinette sprawled on her back on the kitchen floor, screaming in agony. 'My leg just went from under me Gary,' she cried. I was in a blind panic. I rang for an ambulance and they got there in no time. I explained that Antoinette has Perthes disease to one of the ambulance men.

'Oh right,' says he, 'that explains a lot. It looked like a dislocation.' They began working on Antoinette, but quickly ascertained that her pain was too great. Another ambulance was summoned, one solely for the administration of morphine. That was how much pain she was in. I stood there, sobbing, feeling so very helpless. All the ambulance men were outstanding. Soon, they were taking Antoinette from my home and placing her in the back of one of the ambulances. I got into the other and we followed closely behind as they made their way, with sirens blaring, towards the hospital. But, sadly, it was in this hospital where Antoinette would be treated appallingly by some.

Quickly, x-rays were sought to give the doctors an idea of what was going on. I remember seeing one of these x-rays and I actually shuddered. My reaction was echoed by the doctor when he asked Antoinette how she actually manages to walk. The x-ray showed that Antoinette basically had no hip on her right side, it had eroded completely. Antoinette was immediately admitted to a ward. After the fantastic nurses (the only staff members to treat Antoinette well during her stay) got her settled, I took to the chair that was placed beside her bed. I was visibly upset.

'It's okay Gary. Whatever they have given me is working. The pain is subsiding. And you always tell me that things happen for a reason, so hopefully now I will get the new hip I clearly need.'

'I just want you to be okay,' I sobbed.

'I will be Gar, don't worry. Sure, you heard what the doctor said. He can't believe I can actually walk. I will have my new hip, and it will give me my life back. So be happy for me Gary.'

But we had no idea how wrong Antoinette would be with this statement. What she went through during the four weeks she had to spend in that hospital bed still turns my stomach to this very day.

But before I tell that story, I must describe the second 'divine intervention' Antoinette bestowed on me. And this one came from her hospital bed...

Chapter 13

A Divine Intervention, Part 2

Seeing Antoinette laying helpless in a hospital bed was horrid. I suppose I possess the same feelings that a lot of men do when it comes to their partner. 'I am man', 'I make fire,' and all that bullshit. Still, I honestly cannot think of a feeling worse than helplessness when it comes to the one you love. Although Antoinette was heavily medicated, the extent of the damage the Perthes had caused still meant she had moments of unbearable pain. And, shockingly, Antoinette also had to deal with the disgusting attitudes of a handful of the people supposedly taking care of her. They were actually trying to discharge her – discharge her after making comments like, 'Wow, how do you actually walk?' or 'It is very clear that you need surgery asap.' Their attitude seemed to be: We can't facilitate your operation in this hospital, so you're going to have to go home. Go home? Antoinette couldn't walk. She was on a pump that would administer an ultra-strong painkiller at the press of a button but she was still in terrible pain.

And as the days went by, I was becoming more and more irate while Antoinette handled all this negativity thrown at her with aplomb. What's even more astounding is that despite all her suffering, she still had a plan up the sleeve of her hospital gown that would change my life forever.

Antoinette has always supported me in whatever madcap ideas that came into my head. She believed in me, when nobody else did, and I constantly thanked her for that. But there was one thing that Antoinette was finding quite difficult to change my opinion on – the writing of my book. The overbearing voice that haunted my past was still too prevalent at this time: *Who would want to read your book? You are useless, ya gobshite.* Thankfully for me, Antoinette never gives up on something she believes in.

I remember one evening walking up the dimly-lit corridor towards the dull hospital ward that housed Antoinette. I could actually hear the unmistakable sound of Antoinette's laughter as I made my way towards her. A new patient had been admitted the night before and she was hilarious. This woman was dealing with a cancer that was ravaging her insides, and yet she met every day with a laugh and a joke. Even my own mother got it off her one day when she went up to visit Antoinette. This lady questioned my mam's hair, claiming it was a wig. She even asked my mam to come over to her bed so she could check for herself! But it was all done with her tongue firmly placed in her cheek, and my mam had a great laugh with her.

I made my way to Antoinette's bed, leaned in and kissed her softly on her forehead, then readied myself to listen to what particular bullshit she had to deal with that day. But Antoinette had a different idea.

'I'm sick of feeling angry about all this Gary, it's not getting me anywhere. And I can see how much it's affecting you too. Can we talk about something else please baby?

'Of course, Annie. What do you want to talk about?'

'I want to talk about how bored I am Gar,' starts Antoinette, 'but I was thinking you might be able to help. I was thinking you could maybe try to write a chapter from your book. You could then email it to me, and I could check it for mistakes, and give you my honest opinion on it.' Antoinette then said the words that she knew I couldn't say no to. 'You would be helping me out *sooo* much Gar. I love your writing, and I love the story of your stint in prison, as funny as that sounds. But you really would be helping me Gary.' Clever fecker! There was no way I would say no to this request. Although I was petrified, what my Annie wants, my Annie gets.

I headed back to my house that evening with my mind running away with itself. I had no belief in my abilities. I had begun writing this story of my shameful incarceration on sheets of A4 paper in Mountjoy, and continued the process after my move to Loughan House. There I had access to a computer and so began making a hard copy of my writing. I had been enjoying how I was trying to tell my story with as much positivity and humour as I could, but when I was released, my confidence took a hammering. Every knock back I got only fuelled my thinking: *Are ya for real Gar? You will be torn asunder if you put this story out there. People won't get it. And besides, you're fuckin' useless.* So I gave up on the idea of writing a book. But when I walked into my room that evening and fired up my computer, I had only one woman's opinion on my mind – Antoinette's. Again, just like in Mountjoy, I wanted to impress her. I wanted to help relieve her boredom, and most of all, I wanted to make her proud of me.

So on that night, with an ashtray to my right, a cup of coffee to my left, and my notes in front of me, I began writing again. The garage room in my home has a slight claustrophobic ambiance to it. With a very low ceiling and wood-chip walls, it almost reminded me of my cell back in Mountjoy, minus the wood-chip of course. When I wrote in Mountjoy, I would transcend the intimidating walls that surrounded that ancient jail and allow myself to read the words I had just written through the eyes of another. And as I began telling my story once again on that fateful night, the low ceiling of the garage seemed to rip right off as I frantically typed with the sole intention of impressing Antoinette.

And impressed she was – thanks-be-to-jaysis! In fact, she loved it. The chapter I wrote that night was entitled 'Kitchen vs Bakery' which tells the funny story of a football game I was part of between the kitchen staff and the bakery staff in Mountjoy. It has since become one of my favourite chapters, but when I sent it to Antoinette I was terrified she would hate it. I had no need to fear.

'Amazing Gary. Truly, truly amazing. Now, there are quite a few spelling mistakes, but you are telling your story perfectly. Plus you gave me something to do to help with the boredom. Thanks baby. I love ya so much. Can I expect another one in the morning?'

And with that question, Antoinette had succeeded in her 'divine intervention'. Of course I was going to write another chapter for her. I knew, deep down, that Antoinette wasn't that bored, she was in too much pain to be. But she knew how to get into my head. She knew her opinion was my kryptonite. And so, in those four weeks she had to endure in that hospital bed, I made sure to write a chapter for her every night. This process also gave Antoinette the unofficial title of my editor, and long after she came home from hospital she would still read every chapter and go through it with a fine-tooth comb.

As I recall what this woman did for me, my tears once again take over. Antoinette had saved me once more. Her belief inspired me to drive forward with no fear, and my love for her reached heights I had never experienced in my life before.

As I looked at her in that hospital bed, I longed for her to come home with her new hip. But my longing would soon be quashed. Antoinette was coming home – but without a new hip.

And there was a whole new problem for us to deal with...

Chapter 14

CRASH, BANG, WALLOP

I'll never forget that phone call from Antoinette. 'They are making me go home Gary. Yes, I'm upset and feel so let down by it all, but I'm also tired of fighting, Gar.' I was livid. At this stage, Antoinette had spent almost four weeks in a hospital bed. Four weeks of needing bed baths as she couldn't put any weight on her right leg. Four weeks of having to face the indignity of having to call for assistance in order to use the toilet. Four weeks of terrible pain.

I made my way to the hospital that evening, and as I enter the ward I see a man and a woman standing next to Antoinette's bed. They had basically been sent to explain to Antoinette that she must go home immediately. I joined the discussion just as the lady was explaining the hospital's position.

'We cannot facilitate your surgery Antoinette. The surgery must be done in Cappagh National Orthopaedic Hospital. And the fact that we can't do your op here, unfortunately, means you are taking up a bed that we need.'

I feel my blood boiling. 'So, Antoinette doesn't need this bed, no?' I ask, with an irate tone in my voice.

But it was Antoinette who answered. 'I completely understand that you need this bed. But I am honestly finding it difficult to walk. I live in a duplex on my own (Antoinette's

84

sister and flatmate Angela had met a new man, Paul, and they had moved in together), and the first thing I am met with when I open the front door is a steep staircase.'

This changes the two staff members' attitude slightly. 'Well, we can't send you home to cope on your own. We need you to try to organise someone who can assist you in getting around your home. We are really sorry, Antoinette, but it is honestly out of our control.'

I was about to jump in and possibly make things worse, when Antoinette took hold of my hand and smiled. 'It's okay Gary,' she said, before turning to the two staff members and asking, 'can you give me a couple of days and I will try to get someone to come and help me at home?'

'Of course, Antoinette,' replies the lady, 'and we can arrange a nurse to drop in on you to make sure you're okay too. We will also recommend to your surgeon that your surgery be carried out at the earliest opportunity.'

'Thank you,' replies Antoinette.

As the pair leave, I turn to look at Antoinette, just in time to see the avalanche of tears streaming down her face.

'It's not their fault Gary,' she says, 'they can't do the op here, and that's that. I'm just worried about *when* the surgery will be. And now I'm going to have to ask my mam to move in with me.'

My heart was breaking, but I had an idea that could save the day – or blow up in my face. 'Look baby,' I said, 'why don't I just move in with you? We always talked about it, so let's do it.'

I was feckin' terrified she was going to laugh in my face and tell me to get lost, but instead I was met with, 'I'd love that Gary. I'd really love that. Are you sure you don't mind?'

'Are you for real?' I say, 'I now get to say I'm living with the best thing that ever happened to me. I'm beyond happy.'

So Antoinette informed the staff that, if it was okay with them, she could be discharged on the Friday of that particular week. And although I was upset that her problem had not been fixed, in fact I honestly felt she had deteriorated somewhat, I was also elated that I would now be living with her, and I was going to do everything I could to look after her.

Then fate had her say...

On the Friday that Antoinette was being discharged, I was buzzing. It had been almost a month since we'd even hugged properly and I was looking forward to doing everything I could to look after her.

I was helping my brother Noel run a few errands that day with the promise that he would bring me to the hospital to collect Antoinette. We were sitting in his car chatting. I have always loved my relationship with Noel. He is very much like a father figure in my life. I admire him so much. The traffic in front of us was quite heavy. It looked like there was an accident ahead, and we hadn't moved in a while. Noel turns to me and says, 'I'd say you can't wait to get her home Gar. And I'm so happy you're moving in together. It's about time someone made an honest man ou' ...' *Bang!*

Noel couldn't finish his sentence. A car had just ploughed into us. I'll never forget the sound of the impact ... *Bang!* Noel's car was hit on the driver's side at the rear, just at the corner of the boot. This sent our car into a spin. The world outside the driver's window seemed to flash before me in slow motion, like the stills of a film being shown to you one at a time. As the car came to a halt, I turned to make sure Noel was okay.

'What the fuck Gary?' cried Noel. 'What just happened?'

I open my mouth to answer, but instead I let out a cry of pain. It was my hands. I had never felt anything like this before. It was like both my hands were receiving jolts of electric shocks. 'Me hands, Noely ... me fuckin' hands,' I cry.

We stagger out of the car, noting that at least neither of us was bleeding. Noel looked in a lot of pain, but his adrenaline took over.

'Were we hit by a bleedin' ghost?' says Noel in shock. There was no one there. We were in the middle of the road, with the car now sideways-on, but whoever hit us was nowhere to be seen.

Again I say to my brother, 'Noel, me hands man. Something's not right.'

Next thing we know, a young lad comes running up to us. 'I saw everything lads. Jesus. He just went straight into yas. He's just up there.' This young fella pointed up the road, and we can see the car that hit us has pulled in. The poor man who was driving was distraught. It was a complete accident, and although my heart went out to him, I was becoming more and more concerned about the pain I was experiencing.

Soon a Garda arrives on his bike. He quickly moves to ascertain what injuries myself and Noel might have. Noel complains about his back, but his adrenaline was masking the true extent of his injuries. I look at the police officer squarely and say, 'Officer, it's my hands. Something is wrong officer.'

'I'll call for an ambulance immediately lads. Do you think we can move the car to the side of the road? It's blocking the traffic.'

'Of course,' shouts Noel.

'Eh, lads,' I start,' the fuckin' bumper is hanging off. Lads? The *fuckin' bumper* is hanging off,' but nobody was listening to me. And so, as Noel began moving his car, I just picked up the wrecked bumper that was hanging on by a thread and ran along side, looking like a fuckin' eejit if I'm honest. When we got the car to a safe spot on the side of the road, I flopped down onto the ground. The officer comes over to see how I am.

'You're after going very pale Gary.'

'It's my hands officer,' I repeat. I was so afraid. I kept thinking of how the only job I could get at the moment was as a painter. I needed my hands. I kept thinking about finishing my book. I needed my hands. Or playing my guitar. Yep, I needed my fucking hands! Then Antoinette flashed to the front of my mind. Shit! I try to hold my phone in order to call her.

'Hey baby,' answers Antoinette, 'I'm sitting here waiting for ya to come get me and...'

'Antoinette,' I abruptly interrupt, 'myself and Noel have just been in a crash. I'm okay. But it's my hands Annie.' I was sobbing telling her this. But almost immediately I had to apologise and hang up as an ambulance had arrived for me. Poor Antoinette was left in a state of shock. Plus she would now have to stay another night in hospital herself.

The ambulance men were so good to me. They told me that my adrenaline had spiked and I may be hyperventilating, and that may explain why my hands felt the way they did. I wasn't convinced. Noel informed me he was okay, and that he would follow me as soon as he got the car sorted. I was brought to the A&E department of James Connolly Hospital and was being treated like someone who may have a neck injury, with my whole head in a brace. But I kept complaining about my hands.

'You're hyperventilating Gary. You're in a great deal of shock. You're hands will be fine,' said one of the nurses in attendance.

I knew I wasn't hyperventilating. How could I get these people to listen to me? Then advice from Mandy, the English teacher in Loughan House and the woman who introduced me to Yoga and meditation, came flooding into my mind. *'Follow your breath Gary. Show them you are calm.'* And so,

I closed my eyes and followed my breath, and after a couple of minutes I open my eyes to see the nurse is looking at me.

'Are you okay Gary?' she asks.

'I am completely calm, miss,' I say, 'but please listen to me. There is something wrong with my hands.' Thankfully, this worked. The nurse arranged a scan for me which confirmed I had nerve damage. I was admitted immediately.

As I was brought onto a ward, I was feeling so very low and in a lot of pain. The nurse was lovely and told me to call anytime I might need her. I began thinking about Antoinette. I can't believe on the day I was meant to collect her from hospital, I end up in fuckin' hospital myself. Between the pain in my hands and the pain in my heart, I cried myself to sleep. I was devastated.

My eyes were still closed as I began to come into the world the next morning. I let out a whimper, and as I do I feel a hand cup my arm ever so softly. I then hear the beautiful voice of Antoinette.

'Heya baby. Don't worry. I'm here.'

I must still be dreaming, I thought, but I open one eye to check, and there she was. I burst into tears. The last time I saw her, the roles were reversed, with me standing over her as she lay in a hospital bed. 'How? What? What's going on Annie?' I say confused.

'My mam came and got me yesterday Gar. Don't worry about me,' reassures Antoinette. But I was more than worried. She looked in dreadful pain, and was propped up by two crutches. But, somehow, she was there in front of me – smiling. I have never felt more loved in my entire life.

'I'm so sorry this happened, Antoinette,' I say.

'Would you stop,' Antoinette responds, 'I'm just glad you're still here.'

'It's my hands Annie,' I say, and as I do, my tears increase.

'I know, I know baby,' says Antoinette, 'but hey, *hey,* look at me.'

I open my eyes and I am met with the smile that started it all. The face that I can't get enough of. 'You're still moving in with me Gary, even if it's going to be a case of the "blind leading the blind". But you're still moving in.'

Antoinette then said the words that, somehow, calmed the anxiety that was having its fun with me: 'We'll find a way Gary. We have never had it easy from day one, but we love each other, and I really believe our love will find away. I love you, Gary Cunningham.'

And I love you too, Antoinette Gahan. And you're right. We will get through this.

Chapter 15

YET ANOTHER CURVE BALL...

I was discharged after three days. The feeling had come back into my hands except for four fingers, two on my left hand and two on my right. And these four fingers were to become a Chinese water torture of sorts for me. To try to explain what it felt like, I would say that it was as if these four fingers were trapped in a bunch of nettles and I couldn't take them out. But I had made progress, so hopefully these fingers would soon follow suit. Hopefully...

I moved in with Antoinette almost immediately after my discharge, and we instantly worked well together. I think it's fair to say that Antoinette hit the jackpot when I moved in (he says modestly). My OCD meant I cleaned – everything. I had also learned how to cook in prison, so dinner was my duty too. She landed on her feet with me all right. Of course, Antoinette may tell you different.

The pain and discomfort Antoinette was in at this time was shocking. I had taken a few days off work so I got to see her daily struggles in all their grotesque glory. Every single thing she tried to do was a massive challenge. I would do all I could to help, but I also had to be okay with the fact that Antoinette is a very independent woman. Her attitude was, and still is, 'I can't let it beat me. I can't let it drag me down.' But I was so very worried about her. Her mental health was under constant attack as she had no idea when her much needed surgery would take place. And anyone who has had to live with chronic pain will know the damage it will do to your spirit. On top of that was the fact that Antoinette couldn't work and we still had bills to pay. So, after a few days, I returned to work. I wanted to quell at least one of Antoinette's worries. But I didn't factor in the extent of my own injuries.

As the weeks went by, I began lying to Antoinette. Bare-faced lies were what I offered her daily. I hated myself for this. I hate telling lies, as I had spent way too long in my life lying to all around me. But I told myself that the lies I was telling Antoinette at this time were completely necessary – lies like that I was okay, that my fingers were not causing me that much discomfort, that I could work. But in all honesty, I was in agony daily, and work was becoming almost impossible.

But I bottled-up these feelings of pain and worry when I was around Antoinette. I knew she would go mad if she found out I was going to work in pain. But I also knew how upset she was that she couldn't work herself, and that my wages were keeping us afloat. So every morning I would get up at 4.00 am and go for a run in order to put my head in the right place for that coming day. I would then come home, make Antoinette her breakfast, smile, and kiss her goodbye as I headed off to work. But as soon as I walked out the door I would grimace in pain and cry softly to myself. Those four fuckin' fingers were the bane of my life!

I was also keeping my pain a secret from my boss Robbie. I couldn't lose this job. But I was finding holding a paintbrush excruciating. One day, I opened up to Johnny, one of the lads I worked with.

'Ah jaysis Gar,' says Johnny, a stocky lad with tight brown hair who hailed from Dublin, 'I was in a crash meself and ended up with nerve damage in me back. Jaysis pal. God love ya.'

It actually felt good to know someone had an idea of what I was experiencing.

But I was about to lose this particular battle...

One day, after finishing a particularly hard day in work, I started crying as I made my way home. I stopped and sat on a bench and just let it all out. I'm sure people were staring at the painter sitting on the bench bawling his fuckin' eyes out, but I didn't care. I needed to get it all out of me so Antoinette didn't have to see me like this. But when I started ignoring her calls as I sat on that cold, dark-green bench, I knew I couldn't keep this up anymore. Of course I hated lying to her, but I equally hated feeling like I might let her down by not being able to work. This was a tough one to deal with. But I knew what I had to do.

I arrived home and immediately began telling Antoinette the truth. I told her how most mornings when I leave for work I am in tears. I told her I'm finding work more and more difficult. And I told her all this with my head lowered in shame.

Antoinette was shocked. 'For God's sake, Gary. You can't put yourself through that every day. I love the fact that you would do that for me, for us. But Gary, I don't ever want to see you go through something like that. Take a leave of absence and concentrate on getting those fingers better.'

'But if I quit this job, how will I get another one, especially with my past? You know how hard it was to get this job Antoinette,' I say deflated.

'I believe in you Gary, but I need you to start believing in yourself now as well. You'll get another job, even if you have to take another bout of knock backs before you do. I have some savings so we'll survive – barely, but we'll survive. Please, don't put yourself through this.'

I don't know what I did to deserve this woman, but I am so glad I did it.

I had to ring my boss Robbie to tell him the news. He was gutted, but so very supportive too. I was devastated, but I knew I needed to remain positive. And watching how Antoinette dealt with her problems daily inspired the shite out of me. I now needed to test the famous saying, I had to be 'okay with not being okay'. I was never 'balls rough' in prison, so there was no way I was going to be 'balls rough' as a free man. It was time to stop feeling sorry for myself. Yes, things were hard, but many people were going through situations much worse than I was at that time. So I needed to look after my lady. And we both needed a little boost too to be honest.

Thankfully, the universe heard my call. Someone was coming home – for good.

Chapter 16

'TIE A YELLOW RIBBON 'ROUND THE OLD OAK TREE'

Picture the scene if you will...

The last of the day's sunlight illuminates the airy living room of the apartment I share with Antoinette. Cain Dingle, of *Emmerdale* fame, is looking very dodgy and is no doubt up to no good as myself and Antoinette sit in golden silence, glued to the TV that hangs on the wall in front of the 'world's most comfortable sofa' (this is open to debate). My phone suddenly bursts into life as my duelling guitars ringtone begins to play.

'Ah shite,' says I, 'pause that while I see who this is Antoinette will ya? I'm dyin' to know what that Cain fella is up to.'

'Just leave it Gar, if it's important they'll leave a message,' says Antoinette.

I pick up my phone and see the area code of the number that's calling me – 071 – County Cavan. Fitzer! Antoinette presses pause just as 'Dodgy Dingle' raises his fist to some poor unfortunate.

'Fitzer, ya aul' shite,' I start, 'how the hell are ya buddy?'

'I'm coming home, I'm coming home, tell the world that I'm coming home.' Fitzer has begun our chat by singing the P Diddy hit down the phone to me.

'*What? Really?*' I shout back to him.

'That's right Gar me aul' flower. I need ya to Tie a Yellow Ribbon 'Round the Old Oak Tree (he's singing again) for me buddy. Gerrup outta tha' Gar. I'm being released to do community service the day after next.'

You already know my next reaction to this news. This sends Fitzer into a fit of laughter.

'Would you give it over ya sap,' he says, 'did ya not realise I was gonna come home eventually, no? Give it over Gar, ya *sap.*' This unites us both in laughter.

'Ahh Fitzer, I'm delighted man. I really am. Jaysis, I can't wait to see ya.'

'Same here Gar,' replies Fitzer, 'although it'll be the day after I get home buddy. I have a wife and I'm going to show her just how much I missed her. But the following day? It's me and you pal.'

Or so he thought...

Almost immediately after his call ended, and as I was explaining to Antoinette that he was coming home, my phone rings again. This time it's Fitzer's wife, Ash.

I answer, shouting, '*Get in there Ash, he's coming home! He's coming home missus, he's coming home!*'

Ash is crying tears of unbridled joy. 'Ah Gar, I can't believe it. I've missed him so much. I just can't wait to have him home so we can begin our happy ever after together. So we can be a proper family.'

'I can't wait to see him meself Ash,' I reply, 'so you have him all day tomorrow, but the next day, he's *mine*,' I laugh.

'Gar, I was thinking you and Antoinette might come over tomorrow after he gets home as a surprise for him. I know how much he's missed you Gary.'

And this act of kindness, this longing to surprise her man, is a trait in Ash that completely blows my mind. Knowing how much this beautiful woman loves my best mate strengthens the knowledge that true love is alive and kicking today. Of course Ash was vexed at the stupid choices Fitzer had made in his past that led to his incarceration, but she loves him with every fibre of her body. And just like myself and Antoinette, true love will always find a way.

'Really Ash?' I ask surprised, 'I would have thought you'd want him all to yourself tomorrow.'

Her answer sums Ash up perfectly: 'I have forever to spend with him Gary, and I'm never letting him go again.' If you predicted that this statement made my eyes water, please 'Do pass go and collect €200'.

The next day, myself and Ash stayed in constant contact through text messages as we didn't want to let the cat out of the bag. I was buzzing, and yet I was a little nervous too for two reasons: (1) What if Fitzer thought I was a gobshite out here in the free world? And (2) I had something huge to ask Fitzer – a favour of sorts.

The favour I was after was his permission to share with the world one of the videos I had created in prison. This video coincided with the cover of 'Iron Sky' that The Off#enders had recorded for our album. Whilst we were inside, this song and video changed everything for us. We were inundated with compliments and even caught the eye of a band manger who showed interest in signing us. Fitzer's bass is haunting, but his vocals on this particular track are simply incredible. And the aul' video ain't half-bad too, if I do say so myself. So why would I need his permission to show the world? Simply because Fitzer's anonymity is paramount to him. I knew what The Off#enders achieved in prison was an incredible story – I was in the middle of writing a feckin' book about it! But although Fitzer was beyond proud of what we had achieved, he still felt a lot of shame and regret for the choices he had made. And, like me, Fitzer worried about trying to gain employment. So having his name splashed across the internet as 'The Unofficial Best Singer to Ever Emerge from an Irish Jail' might hamper his chances of gaining that coveted job. But I had a plan up my sleeve that in time would become one of my better ones.

I was like a child waiting for Santa to arrive as the hour of us standing in the world together as free men grew closer. I was so excited, as was Antoinette. We got into her car and started to make our way towards Fitzer's home when the text messages from Fitzer's wife Ash began arriving on my phone:

Ash: Oh Gar, hurry up will ya? I don't know how much longer I can keep him at bay :)

Gary: Why? What's up? Is everything okay?

Ash: He's tryin' 2get me into bleedin' bed Gar ... not that I blame him (lol).

Gary: LOL. Hang on in there missus. We're on our way.

Ash: Great. Just hurry. He's beginning to think I've gone off him (lol).

Gary: lol xxx

As I relay these messages to Antoinette, she too is in stitches. 'Oh God, Gary. He might go mad that you've cock-blocked him,' laughs Antoinette, followed with, 'by the way, what's the craic with you bringing your guitar? Sure, with your fingers the way they are, you can barely play.'

I turn and wink at Antoinette and say, 'Oh, just you wait and see.'

As we pull up to Fitzer's home, I send the last of my texts: 'Outside!'

We make our way to the white aluminium front door. I press the doorbell, and instantly I can see through the frosted glass the tall, stocky figure of my best friend as he makes his way towards the door. I lean back on the bonnet of their car, hold my guitar in my hands, and start strumming a G chord, just as Fitzer opens the door.

'*Gar*! Fuckin' deadly! Ash, it's Gary!' cries Fitzer.

I immediately begin making up a song about him on the spot. Both my hands were encased in supports that were meant to ease the pain (they didn't), but I still tried with all my might to strum my ol' six-string. As Fitzer stood there, I played and sang at the top of my voice a song that slagged the life out of him. It ended like this:

> Oh I'd say you are after getting a terrible shock?
> Well if nothing, meself and herself (Antoinette)
> are the ultimate cock-block!

What happened next will stay with me forever. I stepped into the hall of Fitzer's home and gave him the biggest 'man-hug' I have ever administered. Of course I'm crying, but this time, for once, I think Fitzer *may* have shed half a tear too.

'It's amazing to have you home pal,' I say.

'It's amazing to be home Gar me aul' mucker,' replies Fitzer.

What a journey I have had with this man.

The rest of the night was brilliant. Ash had arranged for 'Turk', a lad myself and Fitzer served time with, and his partner Lynn to be there too, along with another ex-con, 'Cronin'. The laughs, slagging, and devilment were at a very high standard. Ash also invited her sister Sharon and her hubby Ali, and Fitzer's sister Denise and her partner Dean. And before we know it, there is another knock at the door and Cunny and his partner Ciara arrive to join in the merriment. I was in my element, which was noted by Antoinette.

'You look so happy Gary. I'm delighted for you,' she says.

'We needed a boost Antoinette, and there it is, standing beside the sink slagging Cunny.' I point to Fitzer who is taking a layer of Cunny's skin off as he berates him.

I bide my time, not wanting to make the discussion all-serious-like, but soon I see my chance.

'Fitzer? Can I rob ya for a sec?' I ask.

'No bother buddy. Come on in here.' I follow Fitzer into his softly-lit and cosy sitting room. The first thing we both notice is the poem I had written about himself and Ash back in Mountjoy. Natoman, another lad we served time with, transcribed the poem in calligraphy on an A4 white board and Ash had it hanging on the wall. 'Seems like a lifetime ago pal doesn't it?' says Fitzer.

'It really does man,' I reply.

'We did a lot Gar, didn't we?' laughs Fitzer.

'We really did man, which is why I wanted to talk to ya. I would love to tell the world our story. I'm still tipping away at the book, although typing is a nightmare with my hands in this fuckin' state.' We both start laughing as I hold up both my hands in order to show off my two supports. 'But I really think people should hear your voice man. They should see what we did during the darkest time in both our lives. I will never disclose your identity or real name, no matter how many times I'm asked. I know your privacy means so much to you.'

I was terrified he would get annoyed, but instead he answered with, 'One hundred per cent, Gar. Put it out there. Yes, I would like my name and face kept out of everything, for now, but you honestly have no idea how proud I am of what I – what *we* – achieved whilst we were in "the other place". And you're writing a book man, a fuckin' *book*. How amazing is that? Now, if you start crying after what I say next, I'll fuck ya out the window, but I'm really proud of ya man. Really proud to call you my friend. And I know you'll never give my true identity to anyone. So go for it, Gar. Tell the world our story.'

My face begins to contort as I try with all my might to stop the tears that are coming. Fitzer cops this and begins laughing. 'Ah, for fuck sake. Give it bleedin' over Gar, will ya?'

So I had gotten from Fitzer the green light to proceed with confidence. In fact, not only did he allow me to tell our story, both with my book and through the video to 'Iron Sky', but together with Antoinette they instilled in me a bit more confidence. I began to wonder if anyone would actually want to hear my story – *our* story – and our songs.

But before all that could happen, myself and Annie had some life-changing news winging its way towards us.

Chapter 17

Hip, Hip (and this time) Hooray!

Watching daily the amount of pain Antoinette was in was harrowing. She really needed the surgery that would give her a new hip, and her life back. Coupled with that was the fact that my four fingers still felt like they were trapped in a nettle bush and I couldn't take them out. All of our aliments combined made for some funny situations as we tried to look after each other. For example, Antoinette would try to get up off the sofa to get a drink of water. The pain etched on her face was so apparent as she let out a small whimper. This would drive me mad.

'Annie, please stay where you are. I'll get you some water,' I would say, like her personal superhero. Reluctantly, Antoinette would agree, only to burst out laughing as she watched me struggle to even hold a fuckin' glass in my hand, never mind trying to pour the water.

'What are we like Gar?' she would laugh.

'We're happy baby,' I would say with a smile. And happy we were. We were struggling financially, struggling with our health, but we were so happy. Being out of work had left me feeling emasculated, but Antoinette would not let me wallow in feelings of self-pity.

'This is the hand we've been dealt for now Gar,' she would say, 'so we just need to get on with it. And we have each other, which personally makes me feel so very lucky.'

And, as always, Antoinette was right. But even her own positive resolve was about to be pushed to its limits.

As the pain increased for Antoinette, her independence declined. Everything was an uphill struggle for her. Even getting out of bed was an act of torture. Yet every day Antoinette would push herself as much as she could. But soon, no matter how hard she pushed, she knew she had to raise the white flag. And this was when my worry for her tripled. As the days went by she simply got worse and worse, until eventually she had to concede. She knew she was now housebound – almost bedbound. These feelings of helplessness were almost the straw that broke her back. For the first time since I had met her, Antoinette started to become introverted. Her light was dimming, and it was completely heartbreaking. I knew I had to do everything I could to help. But what could I do? Telling her 'the surgery will happen soon' wasn't cutting it. Trying to fuss after her wasn't cutting it. If only I was a surgeon!

We needed a plan...

I began thinking of what I actually *could* do. I was enjoying my new-found passion for writing, so I took a break from writing my book and turned my attention to writing to TDs in the hope they might be able to help. I wrote to Mary Lou McDonald and explained Antoinette's story. Mary Lou and her team were incredible. They contacted Cappagh Hospital to see if they could find out if Antoinette was even on a list. They also offered their ears and shoulders to us both, which we gratefully availed of. Then they gave us the advice that was to change Antoinette's life.

We were advised to write to Simon Harris, the Minister for Health, and explain in great detail how much Antoinette had deteriorated, both physically and mentally. At last I didn't feel so useless. At last I just might be able to help. I sat at the light-oak desk in the room of our apartment that Antoinette had allowed me to take over as my 'man-cave'. Roughly the size of a box bedroom, this room was my haven. Hanging on the wall was the guitar rack Fitzer had made for me in Loughan House. The room was painted purple and grey and featured positive mantras galore, my favourite being a small wooden rectangle ornament with the words *I Can and I Will* printed on its face in white.

I launch G-mail and begin typing from the heart. I informed Simon Harris, in the most articulate way that I could, of Antoinette's rapidly declining health. I explained how her pain was so great that everyday tasks were becoming impossible. I implored that Antoinette be considered for the new hip list. I begged him for help. Not once did we expect preferential treatment. We just hoped that she could at least be seen by a surgeon. The fact that Antoinette had not complained once in 38 years spoke volumes. She was willing to wait her turn. Sadly, the pain she was in made further waiting impossible.

As I hit the send button, I have to admit to not feeling very confident. The Irish health system was in tatters and Simon Harris had a lot to deal with. I feared that my plea would be lost in a million other emails.

But I had underestimated our Minister for Health. Simon Harris informed us how sorry he was to hear about Antoinette and all she was going through, and he told us he would do all he could to highlight her plight. And that is exactly what he did. Before we knew it, Antoinette had an appointment to be assessed for surgery, which was all that we wanted. We were confident that once they saw Antoinette's x-ray they would see how imperative surgery was for her. Simon Harris had saved the day, and myself and Antoinette are eternally grateful to him and Mary Lou McDonald. Not all politicians are bad.

I'll never forget that appointment. The surgeon Antoinette was seeing was the highly-skilled Mr. Cashman, who actually completed a fellowship in the 'Young Adult Hip'. We were seen by one of his team, and as we waited for him to familiarise himself with Antoinette's case, we smiled at each other as we noted the expression on his face as he viewed Antoinette's x-rays.

'My word Antoinette. How do you actually walk?' he asks shocked.

'You're not the first doctor to ask me that,' replies Antoinette.

'Well,' says the doctor, 'I plan on being the last.' And he was!

After a few more appointments and a successful pre-op, the day of Antoinette's surgery had arrived. I hadn't seen Antoinette this happy in so long. I had the biggest lump in my throat, but knew I needed to keep it together for her. We arrived onto the ward and we were met by a wonderful nurse. Antoinette got changed into her hospital gown, and was then met with the news that I knew was going to drive her mad.

'It'll be around lunchtime when you go down Antoinette,' said the young nurse.

Antoinette is the most impatient person I have ever met. 'Ah jaysis Gary. That's fuckin' ages away,' she moaned, but with a smile.

'You've waited thirty years Annie,' I say, 'I'm sure you can hang on for a bleedin' hour or two.' We both have a little giggle at Antoinette's expense. She was glowing in that hospital bed. I was so happy for her. And when the time arrived, I was allowed to accompany her right to the door of the theatre.

'I love you Gary,' says Antoinette, 'I'll see ya later – with my new hip.'

I watch the swinging doors close behind her, and then I just stand in the middle of the hospital corridor, sobbing. What else did you think I would do? I'm Gary Cunningham. I cry – a lot.

After what seemed like a lifetime had passed, and with still no word on Antoinette's progress, I rang the hospital to see how she was.

'Oh yes, Antoinette has just been brought from surgery into us here in the high-dependency unit,' said the friendly nurse. 'I'd maybe leave coming up until tomorrow,' she added.

High-dependency unit!? I'm not sure if I even thanked that nurse. I just remember bounding to the hospital in order to see if Antoinette was okay. I was shaking. *Why is she in the high-dependency unit? Jesus. Did something go wrong? Please let her be okay,* were the thoughts that ran through my head.

I sprint up a narrow corridor that twists and turns and eventually leads to the doors of this high-dependency unit. I stop myself. I take a deep breath and wipe away any remnants of sweat that may be on my face. I sheepishly enter the ward, fearing the absolute worse, only to be met with the unmistakable, and very infectious, laughter of Antoinette. I make my way towards this laughter, and soon I see my girlfriend sitting up proud, laughing and joking with a nurse – laughing and joking!

'Ah, heya baby,' says Antoinette.

'Are you okay Antoinette?' I almost roar at her, which makes her laugh.

'See? I told ya he'd be up the walls.' Antoinette says this to the nurse that is assisting in the fluffing of her pillows. 'I'm great Gar, just great.' And as she uttered those words to me, and I lean in and give her a cautious hug, we both find we are bawling. But they were tears of complete joy.

Hip, Hip (and this time) Hooray!

Antoinette had her new hip. Of course, there would be a long period of recovery, but I knew this wouldn't bother her. For the first time in a long time the light reappeared in Antoinette's eyes. Her whole aura glowed and seemed to be on show for the world to see. I was beyond happy for her. And as bad as it had been, she kept her moaning to a minimum and never gave up. She was truly my hero, and her strength is a constant source of inspiration for me. And now, thanks to some help from a couple of TDs and Mr. Cashman's unparalleled skills, Antoinette could begin dreaming of a pain-free life – of a normal life.

But she was in a relationship with yours truly, so a normal life may be asking for a bit much!

Chapter 18

TAKE A CHANCE ON ME

It was great having Antoinette and her shiny new hip home, although I have to admit I had two big concerns. Firstly, with Antoinette being so independent, I worried that I might annoy her by trying to look after her, by maybe doing too much. But thankfully, I had no need for concern. In fact, I'm pretty sure 'the missus' was quite happy being waited on hand and hip! And I loved nothing more than looking after her, so it was a wonderfully mutual agreement.

My second worry was echoed by Antoinette's surgeon. She longed for her life back to such a magnitude that we fretted she would literally try to run before she could walk. Getting back to the gym and to living her life were paramount to Antoinette, and I feared her drive (and lack of patience) would push her too far. But I had no need to worry. Antoinette followed all the instructions she was given by her doctors, nurses and physiotherapist with zealous dedication. And although I knew she was feeling post-surgery pain and discomfort, never once, not *once*, did I hear her complain. In fact, I don't think I ever saw her so happy, except, of course, the day we became a couple (he says hopefully).

I remember looking at Antoinette one day and feeling inspired to the gills. I watched as she performed the exercises that were required to assist in her recovery. I could see she was finding them difficult and painful. But it seemed the more it hurt, the more it spurred Antoinette on. To be honest, it made me take a long and hard look at myself.

Yes, my feckin' fingers' still felt trapped in a feckin' nettle bush, but watching Antoinette push herself through her recovery made my mind up – I needed to get back out there and get a job. I needed to ease at least one of Antoinette's worries, as I knew her savings were becoming depleted and soon we would be struggling to make ends meet. So it was my time to step up. It was time for me to dig deep and find the resolve I needed to work through my pain, just like Antoinette was doing on a daily basis. Antoinette was not in full agreement that I should return to work.

'Please don't put yourself through that baby. We'll manage,' she would say.

But I didn't get into a relationship with Antoinette so she could 'manage'. I have always strived, and still do to this day, to give Antoinette the life I feel she truly deserves.

And getting a job would assist me in this quest. Of course, my stint in Mountjoy would be a massive thorn in my side as I again began to look for employment. Though this time around, I changed tack.

I now had a greater reason to bag myself a job, so I knew I needed to take the knock backs and rejections in my stride. I needed to learn from them and adapt. But my God, it was tough.

'Sorry, no Mr. Cunningham' or 'I'm afraid you haven't been successful this time Mr. Cunningham.' It seemed that the vocabulary of every establishment I applied to only consisted of those two sentences. I began finding it funny as I'd watch some interviewers go from:

'Hmmm. We have a good one here Mary. Ticks all the boxes. Friendly, and he seems like a hard worker. Jackpot, Mary, jackpot!'

To:

'Sweet mother of mercy, no! What a filthy scumbag. We have a bad one here, Mary. He ticks the one box that overrules all the others. He was, wait for it Mary, in prison!'

Maybe I shouldn't laugh, but I found the changes in potential employers once they found out I was in prison almost amusing. I remember one interview I went for I decided to open with, 'Good Morning, and thank you so much for this opportunity. Before we go on, I'd just like to inform you that I'm an ex-prisoner.'

'Thank you for coming Mr. Cunningham, you can see yourself out,' came the reply. I laughed that day I can tell you.

As I'd walk away from these interviews, instead of feeling down I decided I would focus on how I had impressed them right up until my criminal past reared its ugly head. I looked for the positives in these negative situations, just like I had done in the most negative of environments – prison. Behind bars, I coined the phrase, 'It's not the time you do, it's what you do with your time,' so I needed to focus on what I was going to do to improve this particular time in my life. And one of the most positive things to come from these rejections was the fact they spurred me on to finish writing my book in the hope that I might change at least one person's perception of a reformed ex-prisoner.

But I still needed that job...

I'll never forget the job advert: *Maintenance Painter Required Immediately For Busy Hotel.*

I'll have a bit of that, I thought to myself. And so I began my ritual of sending off my CV with a cover letter attached that basically declared that I was the world's greatest painter and decorator – ever! I then sat and prayed for a reply, which came that very day. I was offered the chance to sit an interview. I was thrilled.

On the morning of the interview, my nerves were running away with themselves. My OCD ensured I knew the exact directions to this hotel, which was actually outside of Dublin. Yes it meant an hour's bus drive, followed by a 15 minute walk, but logistics should never come into play when seeking employment. Antoinette filled me with confidence as I kissed her goodbye. 'Good luck Gar. You've got this. And remember, they would be so lucky to have you work for them. Go knock their socks off baby.'

I used the hour bus ride to refresh my memory about everything I had learned about this hotel. I arrived, way too early of course, but this time my earliness stood to me. As I sat in the magnificent reception of this picturesque hotel, I marvelled at how welcoming it was. I began dreaming of becoming a cog in the wheel of this establishment, a cog that would ensure it kept its decoration to the highest of standards. I was dragged from this daydream by the calling of my name.

'Gary? Howya, my name is Ken, and I'm the duty manager here. It's great that you came early as I'm up to me feckin' eyes today. Come on in here and we can get this started.' Ken is a very welcoming man, with a polished bald head, a stocky frame, and a huge smile. He instantly put me at ease, as I was beginning to feel the tie I was wearing tighten around my neck. I followed Ken into the hotel's bright and airy bar and we took a seat at one of its tables. 'Can I get you anything Gary?' asked Ken.

'No thank you sir,' came my nervous reply.

'It's Ken, Gary,' smiled Ken. 'Okay,' he continued, 'it looks like you have all the experience we require, so tell me a little about yourself.'

I could feel the sweat on my palms as I tried to paint a good picture of myself. I was polite and articulate as I spoke of the years I worked for my late father's company. I tried with all my might to ensure that Ken liked me, in the hope that he might see past the question I assumed was coming. *'Ever been in prison Gar me aul' flower?'*

But, the question never came...

Instead, Ken asked me if I had any questions (which I did – I inquired what paint was being used on the woodwork, as acrylic-based paints are the way forward, which impressed the shite out of Ken). And his next words sent my emotions into overdrive.

'Can you start tomorrow Gary?'

What?!? I had to pinch myself. I stutter the words, 'Eh, absolutely Ken, a million percent I can.'

'Great,' says Ken, 'can you start at 8.00 am, maybe 8.30 am? I know you have a bit of a commute.'

I'll book a fuckin' room here Ken, and start at 5.00 am if you want were the words running through my mind, but I answer with, 'I'll be here for 8.00 am Ken. And thank you. Thank you so very much. You won't regret this.'

'I don't think I will Gary. Just once you know you are now part of the staff here and so you may be required to do duties outside of painting,' says Ken.

'There is nothing I won't do Ken. Thank you so very much,' I reply, my gratitude going through the roof of the hotel's beautiful bar. I left, took out my phone out to tell Antoinette, when suddenly I stopped. I realised Ken hadn't asked the question I feared so much. I knew I wasn't obliged to disclose my shameful past, but suddenly I felt a wave of guilt come over me. Ken, and this hotel, were offering me the one thing I longed for the most. Maybe I should go back in and be honest? Maybe I should also have told Ken about my fingers, although they would never prevent me from working. I would never let them. Still, I was torn. After spending the majority of my life telling despicable lies, I hated the feeling I was now lying to these people. I needed advice, and luckily I had the greatest of advisors waiting at the end of my phone.

I called Antoinette and roared, 'I got the job baby, I got the bleedin' job.'

'Oh Gary, I'm so proud of you. You never gave up. Wow. I love you so much,' says Antoinette.

'Thanks baby,' I start, 'though I do have a concern.'

I tell Antoinette of my worry, only to be met with, 'No! They didn't ask you Gary, and the legal route is, if they don't ask, you're not obliged to tell.' She was right. I decided not to say anything and I headed out of the hotel's expansive gates feeling very proud. I was so excited for the next day.

I arrived to my new job the next morning fresh as a daisy. I was introduced to Jonas, the maintenance man, and instantly we hit it off. A tall man, Jonas is very friendly and highly skilled with his hands. I'm introduced to some other staff members and find all of them very welcoming. From the girls tasked with cleaning the guests' rooms to Amanda, the young girl who works in the bar, everyone made me feel an instant welcome. I was taken to meet the hotel's manager Brian, and the head of HR, Denise, and again I am flattened by the welcome I received. I was given my first guest room to paint, and I knew this was basically a test to see if I actually knew what I was doing. Everything was going perfectly.

Right up until...

My first day was drawing to a close. I had finished the room to a very high standard and made sure to hoover, clean and dust the furniture, make the feckin' bed – I made sure to do everything. I was on my knees in the en suite sweeping up some dirt when Brian the manager entered the room.

'Gary. Can we have a little chat please?' said Brian as he closed the room's door tight behind him.

The blood ran from my face. I stood up, looked in the mirror, and I remember thinking, *So close Gar. You were so close.* I come out of the toilet with my head bowed like a scorned child.

'Now Gary,' starts Brian, a tall man, who is always immaculately presented, 'before I start, I must say to you that I am a massive Kerry fan.' This catches me off guard. I knew he was referring to the (mighty) Kerry Gaelic football team, but why was he telling me? And, of course, my love for the Dublin Gaelic football team came flying out of me in an almost knee-jerk type reaction.

'Oh yeah? We'll I'm a massive Dubs fan,' I say with pride. So what if he is my boss – *Up the Dubs!*

'I know you are Gary,' laughed Brian, 'I heard the song and saw the video you did for them on YouTube.' He was referring to the song I penned about the Dublin team before the All-Ireland final that year. 'In fact,' continued Brian, 'I've seen everything about you Gary.'

I had been feeling a slight dread all day, as I feared they would Google my name and see that I had spent time inside. And I was right. But what Brian said next, is something I will never forget.

'We know you've spent time inside Gary, but already you have impressed us, and so we want to give you a chance.' I again find I am crying as I type this. You have no idea how much those words meant to me. I began crying in front of my fuckin' manager for God's sake! 'Keep up the good work Gary. You have an amazing opportunity here so don't mess it up,' says Brian.

'Thank you so much. Honestly, thank you. I am so sorry I didn't say anything in my interview,' I say.

'Not at all Gary,' replied Brian, 'we never asked you. Just don't let us down.'

And I didn't. In fact, I became one of the hardest workers this hotel ever had. And no, I'm not being big-headed saying that. I just went above and beyond to repay them for their trust in me. I remember one day being told that someone had written on the comment cards that are placed in each guest's room, '*Wonderful stay. The painter was so very helpful and very friendly.*' Wow. But I always made an effort to be bright and cheerful and very positive if I ever encountered a guest. I would put down my paint brush and assist them with their cases and so on. Yes, my fingers were fucking killing me, but knowing I was earning a living again, knowing I was easing Antoinette's worries as she tore through her recovery, made any pain I was experiencing so very worth it.

I said in an earlier chapter that if an employer was to give an ex-prisoner who has learned their lesson a shot, they would never regret it. And every day, I made sure these wonderful people never regretted giving this ex-prisoner a chance.

For the first time in a very long time, I felt very proud of myself. I never gave up, despite the constant rejections. I believed in the light at the end of my tunnel. I believed in myself. And now, thanks to this hotel, I began believing in the existence of the beautiful side of human nature.

Chapter 19

I'VE STARTED, SO I'LL FINISH

It amazes me how easily you can make your day better with just a simple choice. Choose positivity over negativity, and instantly your day will begin to improve. Sadly for some, this simple choice can be the most difficult one they ever have to make. But I firmly believe if you can make a conscious effort to remain positive, you will reap the rewards. I was so very negative prior to my incarceration. I was 'balls rough'. When I think back to those dark days, I realise I had so much support around me. I was just too caught up in my own shite to see it – to see the people who would have done anything to help me. Yes, I struggled when I was first released. Yes, I slipped and became a drunk again. But isn't that what humans do? Isn't that what makes us human in the first place, the ability to make mistakes?

I knew I needed to feel at ease reaching out for help to those who loved me. And, again, I can't stress enough the true power of talking about how you feel. If you're in a negative downward spiral, simply talking to someone can begin the healing process. And as you heal, you will find that making the choice to remain positive becomes much easier. No, I don't think a positive mental attitude can cure everything. You can't cure an illness solely with positive thoughts. But if you combine positivity with the appropriate medicine, or apply positivity to your treatment, recovery will be so much easier. I am a shining example of this. I was a horrible human before my time in prison, but today I embrace life with positivity, love and, most importantly of all, gratitude.

Antoinette never let me forget about finishing my book. My fingers were improving – slowly, but improving none the less. My new job had given me back some confidence so I felt I was ready to do something I never dreamed I'd be able to do. I was ready to give it my all, as I brought my first ever book to a close. Every evening after work, I would come home and cook for myself and Antoinette, ensure she had everything she needed, and then I would disappear into my man-cave and wouldn't re-emerge until I had two chapters done. I would email them off to 'me gaffer', Antoinette, in order for her to check for spelling errors and, more importantly, give me her opinion on them. It was a great system, even when, the very odd time, her opinion wouldn't be favourable!

My mam was equally as important at this time. I would tease her by reading out a random chapter, only to be met with tears. 'Where do you get the words Gary? You make me so proud.' Hearing these words from my mam only motivated me more to make sure this book was as good as I could make it.

I loved meandering down memory lane as I recalled the men I served my time with, and how each and every one of them made a massive impact in my life. I wanted to show that the Irish Prison Service can come in for some unfair and harsh criticism. Of course it's not perfect, but what organisation is? I met some officers who were really good men, and who displayed a certain amount of empathy. I met teachers who, to this day, I feel were sent down from above as they gave us prisoners everything they had in the hope that we would better ourselves. And, of course, there was the story of meeting Fitzer, starting The Off#enders, writing a musical called *Journeyman,* meeting Antoinette. Yep – I had a story to tell all right. So I decided to tell this story with as much positivity and humour as I could, which scared the bejaysis out of me. Prison stories should be dark and bleak, right? Well not this one.

Antoinette, still in recovery mode, filled her day trawling the World Wide Web looking for potential publishers. She would compile lists of links to publishing houses, bios about these publishers, and the information that each required with a submission. This would vary, but most wanted a synopsis, proposal and the manuscript's first three chapters.

I need to confess that I have a bloody cheek making reference to Antoinette's lack of patience. Although I am, for the most part, quite patient, this all changes when I send an email, or even a text message. I expect a reply, instantly. Stupid, I know, but at least it made Antoinette laugh.

I would go through Antoinette's detailed list and fire off my submissions, and amazingly I didn't have to wait long for my first rejection. Yes, it was an email of rejection, but the woman who sent it complimented me on the writing of the first three chapters but my story was not a fit for their publishing house. Still, I felt good about that rejection, though the next feckin' hundred rejections began to annoy me.

Shockingly, I was being told that my story seemed – are you ready for this? – a bit 'too positive'. I shit you not. I was actually told by one that the story needed tales of beatings, drugs, intimidation etc., all of which goes on inside every prison the world over. I just chose not to focus on that negativity. Sadly, these rejections and being told my book was too positive began messing with my state of mind. The voice of belittlement from my past started whispering in my ear once more: *Ya gobshite. Write a positive book? Are you kidding me? You'll never amount to anything. A fuckin' book. Who would read your story ya gobshite?* And people who suffer with confidence issues will know how overbearing this voice can become. But only if you let it. This time, I chose to stand up to this voice: *You're the gobshite. I have never been useless, and I will never give up on myself again. So fuck off, and fuck you!* Antoinette knew I was struggling at this time. One night, after I made sure she was okay, I entered my man-cave to submit my tale to more publishers. I see a hand-written note sitting on the silver keyboard attached to my computer. It was from Antoinette and it simply said the following:

> Gar, One of your favourites, Mr. Stephen King, had the classic *Carrie* rejected 30 times before it was published. And 'yer wan' (lol) who wrote Harry Potter (harry-feckin'-potter Gar), Mrs J.K. Rowling, had Harry's tale rejected 12 times and told to 'not give up the day job'. So, if some publishers could have passed up on these classics, then some are going to pass up on your classic. Keep the faith baby.
>
> I'm so proud of you,
>
> I love you.
>
> Annie xx

Wow...

And as much as these words went straight to my soul, it was the actual location of the note that brought the uncontrollable sobbing. The note was on my desk, in my man-cave, which is up two flights of stairs. Antoinette had climbed the stairs in considerable pain in order to leave me this note. I run downstairs, and it was as if she knew exactly what state I was going to be in because, as I enter out living room, she was in the very same state – sobbing.

'You made it up the stairs baby. Up the fuckin' stairs,' I cry, 'that is amazing Annie.'

'I wanted to surprise you baby,' says Antoinette through tears, 'I know you're struggling, but look at how good your life is when you don't let the negativity in. So I wanted to help, and remind you how amazing I think you are. You wrote a *book*, Gary. Never forget that. It's an amazing achievement.'

'I adore you Annie,' I say as I hold her tight.

How many times is this woman going to save the day for me? Will I ever stop being surprised by her drive and determination? Can I actually love her any more than I already do? Well, the answers to these questions are as follows: Antoinette will always save the day. She is my constant. I will never stop being surprised by this woman's strength. And as seconds turn into minutes, my love for her continues to grow, and grow, and grow.

Thanks to Antoinette, I learned from these rejections. I adapted. And I had a really good idea, one that might help both the publishing of my book and my buddy Fitzer.

But what happened next, none of us saw coming. The true power of positivity was about to burst into my life. And I was ready and willing to gratefully accept it.

Chapter 20

HEY JOE...

The digital age has truly taken over, hasn't it? We wake up and immediately check our phones. We Google 'how to make an omelette' so we can make breakfast. We have apps for everything from counting how many steps we take to ones that make us sound and look like film stars. We commute throughout the city with our heads buried in our hand-held devices – and personally, I love it. Don't get me wrong, too much of anything is bad for you, and I do feel we should sporadically leave our phones or tablets at home. At least then we could take in what is going on around us. A perfect example of this is people at a gig. The excitement is building. People are readying themselves for the arrival of their favourite band or artist. Suddenly, the house lights dim, the guitarist strums a chord, and the crowd go wild ... *after* they take out their phones in order to record this moment. And then they watch their heroes through the screen on their phone. Silly really – though I am guilty of doing this myself. Ah yes, ya gotta love progress.

There is one app in particular that I have always loved. JOE.ie is a news website and app aimed primarily at young Irish men and women. I find that JOE has mastered the perfect balance of delivering the world's most important news stories along with viral videos and funny content. From 'all-things-Trump' to a family in Kerry losing their minds as a bat flies around their kitchen, they tick all my boxes. So when I got the green light off Fitzer to put our story and our cover of 'Iron Sky' out there to be dissected by society, I knew JOE. ie was the best outlet to facilitate this. And boy, was I right.

The first thing I did was construct an email that contained the story of how we formed The Off#enders inside Mountjoy. I started this by saying that I hoped my story wouldn't offend, as I have a very different view on prison life. I explained in detail the journey Fitzer and I embarked on after the band's creation. I also spoke of the book I had just finished that told all this and more in quite a positive manner, and how I was trying to get it published. I attached the video for 'Iron Sky', an image of my book's front cover that I had designed in Photoshop, and a random chapter. Someone also recommended that I start a blog in order for potential publishers to get a better feel for my writing, so I included the link to www.garcunningham.wordpress.com. I described how I had been a disgusting person before my incarceration and that prison had saved my life.

I gave Fitzer a ring and read out this email to him. 'Jaysis Gar wha? You're some man. That's brilliant pal. I've always said it buddy. Andy Dufresne hasn't a bleedin' patch on ya!' Fitzer is in knots of laughter as he again compares me to Stephen King's famous character.

'So, I can go ahead Fitzer yeah?' I ask.

'Proceed with confidence ol' boy. Hold fast and remain calm. Jolly good show what, what?' For reasons only known to Fitzer, he has decided to say all of this in a Winston Churchill-like accent.

I laugh, thank him, and 'bid him a good day' in a similar tone.

I next asked Antoinette for her opinion and thankfully she loved it. What she also did was calm my nerves somewhat, as it had dawned on me that I was about to tell anyone who cared to listen that I am an ex-prisoner. I was about to explain in great detail what an absolute gobshite I was prior to prison. I was petrified. But I really believed in The Off#enders. I really believed in my tale. And, most importantly of all, I really wanted to try to highlight that people can come out of prison changed and reformed – and remain that way.

So as the sun set on a Saturday evening, and with the backing and blessing of my two best friends, I sent my email to editorial@JOE.ie. And, of course, because they didn't reply instantly, I assumed they thought the whole story was basically just a bag of shite.

How wrong I was...

The very next morning, as myself and Antoinette cuddled under the covers and decided that this was the best way to spend this particular Sunday, my phone beeped for my attention. As I pick it up, I saw that I have a new email from JOE.ie. I leap from the bed, which scares Antoinette half to death, and began reading:

> Hi Gary, Tony here from JOE.ie. Far from finding your story offensive, I find it inspiring. Often we get great stories like this sent into us but the music isn't up to scratch – that is absolutely NOT the case here. The cover version (*of Iron Sky*) is fantastic and it will really resonate with a JOE audience, thanks so much for telling us your story. Let me just ask you one thing – are you okay with us sharing all of the details you gave us, including your name? If there's anything you'd like me to leave out in the writing of the story then please let me know. I'll be working until 5pm on Sunday evening, then back in the office on Wednesday. I won't write anything until I hear back from you.

I looked at Antoinette in complete disbelief. I couldn't believe how much this guy, Tony, loved not only 'Iron Sky' but also my story. I was impressed with the respect he showed me, as he was willing for me to remain anonymous. But I honestly hoped my story would put a human face on what some parts of society deemed a monster, so anonymity was never an option for me. As I begin reading all of this out to Antoinette, I realised Tony had wrote some more, and this completely and utterly blew me away:

> On a personal note, and I hope you don't mind me asking, but I think I may have met you before years and years ago in Cappagh Hospital. Does that ring a bell? I just remember a lad with a guitar called Gary Cunningham and he was an absolute gentleman. It may not have been you but I said I'd ask anyway. Hope to hear back from you soon re: publishing the details of your story.
> All the best, Tony.

I look at Antoinette, stunned.

'Were you in Cappagh Hospital years ago Gar?' asks Antoinette. I open my mouth, but nothing comes out. I just collapse onto the bed as the tears begin to flow. Antoinette places her arms around me and says, 'It's okay baby, be proud. This is amazing Gary.'

I pull myself together enough to say, 'Believe it or not, I'm not crying because they want to run my story, although I can't believe that they actually want to. It's Cappagh, Antoinette. I haven't thought about my time in Cappagh Hospital in years. I was only a kid. I had osgood-schlatter disease when I was 12 or 13, which was a condition that affected my left knee. I had to stay in Cappagh for about a month, maybe more, as a result. There was a young lad from Mayo beside me...'

I find I have to stop talking. This young lad's name was Robbie, and he meant the world to me. Robbie's whole body was being ravaged by cancer. When I met him first, he wouldn't speak to anyone, but I wouldn't give up on him. I handed him a pen and paper one day, and asked him to write down why he wouldn't talk. He wrote that he hated losing his hair. God love him, the poor lad was embarrassed. But I knew how to fix this. I got my brother Noel to bring up some hair clippers and I shaved my head. 'Now, neither of us has hair Robbie,' I laughed. And, amazingly, Robbie laughed too.

He soon started talking to everyone, and he was simply one of God's better people – even at his young age. I loved looking after him and I always tried to entertain him and the others in the beds around us. I got my guitar brought in and daily I would play Guns 'n' Roses and Green Day songs (badly) in the hope it would keep everyone on the ward entertained enough to forget why they were there. I don't really remember the other kids on that ward, but I'll never forget Robbie. I became close with his wonderful parents, and when he was moved to Crumlin Children's Hospital, I remember Robbie's dad taking me to see him. But unfortunately, Robbie lost his courageous battle with that horrible disease and it ripped me apart. I was young myself and I just remember feeling an anger like I had never experienced before. Robbie was such a beautiful, bright young boy and his passing was heartbreaking. And although I have never forgotten him, I have to admit I hadn't thought about him in a long time.

I sent an email to Tony, firstly thanking him a thousand times for his reply, and confirming that, yes, I was in Cappagh all those years ago.

Tony instantly replied, saying, 'I never forgot your name. I was only on that ward with you for a couple of days, but I never forgot how you used to play your guitar for everyone. Even as a kid, you were so kind and giving.'

How incredible is that? The story of my shameful past, of my band, my book and everything in between, lands on the desk of a man I was in hospital with all those years ago. I admitted I didn't remember Tony, but he didn't care. He remembered me. I impressed him enough for him to never forget my name. And now, he was impressed with my story and was willing to run it on my favourite site and app. Although it's widely known that I cry at the drop of a fuckin' hat, I'm sure you'll agree the tears I shed because of Tony and his incredible memory were completely justified.

Tony kept in touch with me over the next few days and he treated my story with so much care. He even sent it to me before it went public to make sure I was happy with it. I loved it. There was a picture of me at the top of the page, with the headline, 'Prison Saved My Life'. Tony had incorporated every single thing I had sent to him into his fantastically written article and the feckin' thing went viral. The views for 'Iron Sky' just kept increasing and increasing. The interest in my story was unbelievable, and I think the main reason for this was my brutal honesty. Having lied my way through a bleak, drunken life before prison, I now stood tall, telling my story with utter honesty. It scared the shite out of me, yes, but I was proud. And all of this was thanks to Tony and JOE.ie. But Tony wasn't finished yet.

As is standard practice these days, Tony and I found each other on Facebook and have remained good friends ever since. He is funny and articulate, and just so happens to love Liverpool FC as much as I do! After my story went live, Tony shared it on his personal Facebook page. But he didn't feel the need to tag me in this post. I stumbled across it, and I was so touched by what he wrote. He described the above story from Cappagh Hospital in his own words, pointing out that it was 25 years ago. He explained how shocked he was when fate put my story on his table. And he referred to me as a 'charismatic, talented, and very kind man'. I was stunned.

This was a huge moment in my life, the moment I really began to believe in myself. This is when I knew I could proceed with confidence. People loved 'Iron Sky' and they wanted to know more about my story. And Tony and JOE.ie were the ones who started all this off for me. I shall remain eternally grateful.

And soon, thanks to this article, I was offered a chance to chat with a personal hero of mine.

Jaysis, 'me nerves'.

Chapter 21

A FAN OF FANNING...

The reaction to Tony's article was unbelievable. Of course, I faced some negative feedback, with some leaving comments like, '*once a criminal, always a criminal,*' or, '*are we meant to be impressed with this scumbag?*' But with the new-found sense of belief I had, I took on board these negative comments and completely understood where they were coming from. If anything, these nasty comments spurred me on, as I wanted more than anything to show these people that they were wrong. Take the guy who sent the 'scumbag' comment. He decided to leave this comment on my Facebook page, which I have as a public page so people can interact with me if they choose to. At first, I was beyond irate. But the old Gary would have reacted by spitting bile, by using vile and threatening language in my reply in order to exert my 'manliness', which when you think about it is ridiculous. Antoinette was telling me to forget about it, that I was going to have to get used to people saying such things. But this guy was being quite rude and had decided to leave this comment on a platform where my family and friends could see it. So I composed myself and sent him a private Facebook mail. I asked him why he felt the need to attack me and why he felt it was okay to call me a scumbag when he didn't actually know me. His reply was just as vile as his comment. He continued to call me names and used foul language. He said that *no one* can come out of prison reformed. He actually called me pathetic! *Pathetic*? Now I was fuckin' fuming! But instead of fighting fire with fire, I again composed myself enough to send the following reply:

> Does it make you feel better calling me names? Let me give you my opinion. I really think you should have a long, hard look at yourself in the mirror. It seems that it would make you feel more comfortable if I had of come out of prison and immediately broke the law once more. It seems that you would feel a lot happier, and totally justified, if I had of gone back to the arsehole I was prior to my incarceration, putting pints of Guinness before everyone and everything. It seems that you almost expect me to go back to being a drugs mule, so that you can turn to whoever will listen to you and say, 'See? I told you so. Once a scumbag, always a scumbag.' Well, let me tell you something. Yes, I *was* a scumbag, a complete waste of space actually. Yes I *did* break the law and I deserved every day that was handed down to me by the judge. But I did everything I could to change every single thing about me in order to show the world how sorry I was. I achieved so much whilst I was locked-up. And now that I am released, I am striving to show how much I've changed, how much I am filled with remorse for my past, and how I'm not the only ex-prisoner that has these feelings. But all of this makes you feel uncomfortable. You would rather I fucked up again. So I ask you, what does that say about you?

His reply came in about five minutes and only consisted of a mobile number. I rang this number, ready for a fight, but instead I was met with an instant apology. 'Fuck,' he starts, 'you got me there man. I am really sorry for calling you a scumbag. Everything you said was so right and true.'

I really appreciated this man's bravery. None of us like to admit we are wrong, so I really admired him for allowing a conversation to take place between us. I thanked him and told him not to worry. 'I have very thick skin sir,' I said, 'sure, ya have to in prison – it's full of *scumbags*.' I pause enough for this man to sense my sarcasm.

'I deserve that Gary,' he laughs.

'Look man,' I start, 'don't get me wrong, of course there are some really "bad eggs" in prison. But I honestly believe you would be shocked at how many are exactly like me. Mortified because of the choices we made that landed us in jail in the first place. Longing to make it up to our loved ones, and terrified what society is going to think of us when we are released. Can I ask you, were you the victim of a crime yourself?'

He informed me he was. His home was broken into and he was assaulted during this raid. The men were caught and sentenced to, what he deemed, was a very light sentence. And as I listened to this man, it felt like a cluster of clouds began to part in my mind. Of course there are victims of crime, and these crimes may be of such a magnitude that forgiveness may seem utterly impossible. To this day, I will always be grateful that this man allowed me to explain my side of the story, as by doing so, and by understanding why he called me a scumbag in the first place, I learned a valuable lesson. I became more mindful of all the victims of crime, and as a result, I would now proceed with more caution and respect as I tried to tell my story of reform and redemption. Who would have thought being called a scumbag would have such positive results?

There was also an avalanche of love and support from people that read the JOE.ie article, and a lot of interest in my story. I was being asked onto radio talk shows for a chat, but one lady beat them all to it. I received a private Facebook message form a woman called Grace, who is a researcher on Ryan Tubridy's Radio 1 show. She informed me that she saw Tony's article, loved the cover of 'Iron Sky' and, best of all, said, 'I thoroughly enjoyed reading the chapter from your book – in fact, I'm dying to know what happens next.' Wow. Grace asked if I would be interested in coming onto Ryan Tubridy's show in order to tell my story. She left a contact number which I instantly dialled. Grace answered and was so polite and upbeat, and today I am proud to call her my friend.

We had a great laugh over the phone that day, and I found that my slightly manic ways didn't put Grace off one bit. 'So,' starts Grace, 'would you be interested in coming into us for a chat?'

'Too feckin' right I would,' I replied gratefully. I then proceeded to tell Grace the story of how, one day in Mountjoy, Fitzer predicted I'd meet Ryan Tubridy. He was really impressed with a song I had just penned for The Off#enders.

'I'm tellin' ya wha', Gar me aul' mucker, you keep this up and you'll be on the fuckin' *Late Late Show*.' He then picked up a bottle of shower-gel, sat on his bed in his cell, and recreated the fantastic scene from the movie *The Commitments*, where Jimmy Rabbit sits in the bath and acts out his appearance on *The Late Late Show*. Fitzer's impression of Ryan Tubridy was eerily accurate. There is not an impression this man can't pull off.

Grace is laughing at this tale, but then informs me that, unfortunately, Ryan would be on holiday and it would actually be Dave Fanning that would be conducting the interview.

'Really?' I almost shout, 'even better so.'

'I'm sorry?' asks a confused Grace.

Shit. I didn't mean it like that. 'God, I'm so sorry Grace,' I say sheepishly, 'I've just always been a "fan of Fanning", so to speak. I think aul' "Tubs" is a legend if I'm honest.' I sound like I'm backtracking, and thankfully Grace decides not to prolong my torture any further.

'Ah, you're grand Gary. And Dave Fanning *is* a bit of a legend all right.'

'He sure is,' I say.

'So, next Wednesday okay with you to come in Gary?' asks Grace.

'I shall be there with bells on,' comes my predictable reply.

The morning of the interview, I was rattling with my nerves. 'What am I doing Antoinette?' I asked my guidance councillor.

'You are telling your story Gar, and I personally know what an inspiring story it is. So just be yourself and you'll be fine,' comes her reply.

Antoinette and I made our way to the RTÉ studios, and as soon as we enter the gate I can feel that morning's breakfast making its way from my gut to my mouth. I was so nervous. We enter the building that houses the Radio 1 studio, and as soon as we get to the door we are met by a smiling Grace, her glasses sitting perfectly on her nose, her blonde hair draped over her shoulders. 'Hi Gary. This must be Antoinette? I have to ask. Did you really meet in prison?'

Antoinette and I both laugh and reply almost in unison, 'Yep, we sure did.'

'Aww wow,' gushes Grace, 'that's amazing. Now, are you okay Gary?'

The caveman in me wanted to reply, *Of course I am. Why wouldn't I be? I'm a bloody man I'll have you know.* Thankfully, my better-half piped up. 'He's shitting, Grace,' says Antoinette.

'Ah don't be Gary. Look, think of it like this. It will just be you and him in a room chatting, with massive headphones on your heads and large microphones shoved in front of your faces. Easy-peasy right?' This makes me laugh and I start to feel a bit calmer. Truly my 'Saving Grace'.

We walk through the corridors of this famous studio, its walls dotted with the faces of past guests. I remember thinking to myself, *One day Gar. One day your photo will be on that wall.* Nothing wrong with dreaming now is there? We arrive outside the studio, and Grace offers us everything from a glass of water to a feckin' four-course meal. The butterflies in my stomach are still flapping their wings and I'm worried about what I was going on to talk about. Grace informs me I'll be heading in in two minutes – just enough time for me to run to the toilet. I head to the sink and splash water on my face. *Be open and honest Gary. Own your shortcomings and the mistakes you made. Be confident and speak with openness of the heart and clarity of the mind.* I say all this to my reflection in mirror. I gather my thoughts, and head out to meet a hero of mine. *Oh shite*, I start thinking. *I hope I don't 'fan-girl' him.*

The show is on an ad break as Grace leads me into the studio. Antoinette is sitting on a sofa outside and will be able to hear every word. As Grace pushes open the first door, I see we are in a control room with the controls being manned by some more really friendly people who all greet me with a smile and a wish of good luck. Grace then pushes open another heavy door and suddenly I am face to face with Dave Fanning. I know he's not everyone's cup of tea, but I personally think the man is a fuckin' legend. Every Christmas, I would purchase *Fanning's Fab 50* as I found his taste in music was very similar to mine. I loved watching him on *The Movie Show* on RTÉ as he reviewed the latest movies. And now, here he was in front of me, greeting me with a huge smile and a hearty handshake.

'Good man Gary. How are ya?' asks Dave.

'Absolutely shitting, I'm a big fan,' I stutter.

'Would you go away out of that,' he laughs, followed by 'grab a seat, get comfy, and don't worry, I'll sail you through this. Now, before we go live I have to say your band's cover of Paulo's "Iron Sky" is fantastic. Is that you singing?'

'Jaysis no,' I reply. I explain to him all I can about Fitzer.

'Right, right. And you guys recorded it in prison, yeah? Wow. Very impressive Gary.'

Hang on. Did Dave Fanning just say my band impressed him? Stick a fork in me, I'm done!

'What music influences you Gary?' asks Dave.

'Oh quite a lot,' I reply, 'but The Doors would be at the top of my list.'

This makes Dave Fanning laugh, and as the show comes back from the ads he begins slagging me, live on air. He makes reference to the fact that I was too young to have been around when The Doors were at their peak. I had to counter, of course, but what I didn't realise was that this ribbing was to ease my nerves, and it worked a treat. Dave Fanning handled myself and the interview with such care and consideration. He did ask me all the questions that made me feel so embarrassed, like what was I arrested for, how was I involved in the drug culture that is such a burden on our nation, how it felt to know I had let down everyone in my life and so on. I answered all his questions slowly, clearly and with complete honesty. I referred to myself as a vile human prior to my incarceration, and I offered nothing in the way of excuses as to why I ended up in prison. 'I ended up inside because I was a selfish, self-centered bastard Dave,' was the answer I gave.

Dave Fanning also allowed me to talk about the positive sides to my story. He played a clip of 'Iron Sky', and I was proud as punch to hear my buddy sing. He mentioned the name of my book, and how I am trying to get it published. He even gave out the link to my blog. All in all, the way he and the staff treated me and Antoinette was incredible. They say you should never meet an idol as they may let you down. Well, Dave Fanning quashed that myth for me.

The reaction to this interview was nothing short of incredible. Before I gained the confidence to speak out and tell my story, I had about 20 friends on Facebook. Two hours after the interview that number had tripled and continued to grow. My mam and my family all said how proud of me they were. Fitzer text me the following: 'Fuckin' incredible Gary. You don't hear honesty like that these days. You completely owned your mistakes. You're an inspiration buddy. Now, *fuck off!*' (Fitzer's usual ending to his texts). But walking out of the studio – after taking a ton of selfies with Dave Fanning – and seeing Antoinette standing there with her arms open, well, I'm sure you can guess what that did to me.

'Jesus, Gary, you were amazing baby. I don't have the words ... I'm ... I'm just ... fuck Gary, I'm beyond proud of you.' We share a hug that shuts out the rest of the world, which was not a nice thing to do as Grace was standing there waiting to escort us out.

'Aww that's so sweet you guys,' says Grace as her beautiful smile lights up her face.

I thank Grace for reaching out to me in the first place, and wish her nothing but success for her future.

'Oh, we'll keep in touch Gary. I have a funny feeling that people are going to love your story, and I have a feeling that book of yours may see the light of day sooner than you think.'

And what happened almost immediately after myself and Antoinette got into her car in the RTÉ carpark would have people wondering if Grace was a feckin' clairvoyant!

Chapter 22

TWO MEN,
TWO LIFE-CHANGING OFFERS...

The sun was enhancing every flower in the RTÉ carpark as myself and Antoinette got into her Ford Focus. We were both enjoying an adrenaline rush after my very first radio interview. 'You came across fantastic Gary. I'm so proud of you. My phone hasn't stopped. It seems like everyone was listening,' Antoinette laughs. As she navigates her way out of the carpark, I too take out my phone.

'Do you really think I came across okay, Annie?' I ask worryingly. I never feel good enough. I always feel like I've made a hash of things. I know I am conditioned to think this way, but it still always gets me down. Plus, I hate sounding like I'm feeling sorry for myself, or fishing for compliments.

'Of course you did baby,' starts Antoinette, 'you were brutally honest and hid behind no excuses. I'll tell you what Gary, I promise I'm going to make you realise just how special you are. Even if it kills me, which it just might.' Antoinette starts laughing and I find myself joining in. I know I'm very hard on myself, but I feel I have legitimate reasons, ones I don't feel the need to divulge. And I suppose I was even more worried having just told my story live on-air.

But then *this* happened...

As Antoinette exited through the massive gates of RTÉ, she decided to turn left. 'So what,' you might say, but I was perplexed. Okay. I am quite the neanderthal when it comes to being a passenger in Antoinette's car. *'Put your lights on Annie.' 'Why would you even think about going this way Annie?' 'Will I drive Annie?'* Shite like that. I convince myself that I am an encyclopedia of directions that would give Google Maps a run for its money, when in all honesty I just come across like a complete arsehole.

'Gary! Don't you mind what way I'm going, okay? Jesus,' says Antoinette angrily.

'It's just that if you had of turned...' I stop talking as my phone comes to life in my hand. Notification after notification came flooding in which was amazing. But the reason I stopped 'mansplaining' to Antoinette my personal reasons for turning right instead of left was the arrival of two emails.

The first is from a man named Brian Langan. I read the email's content and then scream at the top of my voice to Antoinette, 'It's an email from a publisher Antoinette. An email, from a jaysis publisher!' Unfortunately, the way I decided to scream this news about my future almost ended both our futures there and then. Antoinette got such a fright we were almost involved in a serious car crash. In fact, only for Antoinette's adept driving skills that would have been our end. I have some neck making comments about this woman's driving abilities, especially when she is a far better driver than I am.

'Gary! For jaysis sake! You scared the shite outta me there,' shouts Antoinette. I could tell she was annoyed with me, but I knew how to fix this.

'Listen to this, Annie, listen to this,' I say with vigour. I then read the following email from Brian:

Dear Gary,

Many thanks for your submission to Transworld Ireland earlier this month, and apologies for the delay in responding to you. I read your sample chapters last week and found them hugely entertaining. There's a raw edginess about your writing, and you have a great (and very funny) way of telling stories. And there's something uplifting and redemptive about the story of The Off#enders, so I'm keen to read more. It could make for a great movie along the lines of *Sing Street*.

I had been about to email you to ask you to send on the full manuscript when, coincidentally, my father heard you on Dave Fanning this morning, and rang to let me know about the interview. I'll have to listen back when it's available online! But do please send me on the manuscript. I will be on holiday for two weeks from this Friday, but will try to get to read the manuscript as soon as possible after my return, so do bear with me. I will also pass it on to our publisher, Eoin, as I had already spoken to him about the book's potential.

Kind regards,

Brian Langan

Myself and Annie were stunned, and my God did it feel good. 'That's amazing Gary. And his dad heard you this morning? How crazy is that?' says Antoinette, but I'm gone. I'm sitting beside her in body, but my mind is gone as I immediately begin my reply to Brian. I thank him and explain that I was a passenger in my partner's car when I received his mail, and that my reaction almost caused us to crash. I tell him I'm almost home, and that as soon as I get in I will send him the full manuscript.

Brian's reply comes straight in, and he expresses his gratitude that I wasn't driving the feckin' car as he, quote, 'wouldn't want an accident on my conscience'. He also emphasised that this is only the very first step. He wrote, 'There are many hurdles to get over – so no guarantees – but it's a good start.'

I was floored, not only by his interest, but by his compliments. *'A raw edginess about your writing, and you have a great (and very funny) way of telling stories...'* Fucking hell! From that day, myself and Brian developed a really good relationship, albeit solely through email. I'll come back to Brian and his intervention later, but now let me tell you about the other email that was sitting in my inbox.

This one came from a man named Ronan, and his email address informed me that he worked for RTÉ. His email was very minimalistic: 'Hi Gary, Ronan here from *The Late Late Show*. Could you give me a shout when you get a chance? Here's my number... Cheers, Ronan.'

Now, if you thought my reaction to Brian Langan's email was hysterical, you really should have seen my reaction to Ronan's. The pitch of my voice went to new levels. I'm pretty sure I could see cracks begin to appear on the windows of Antoinette's car.

'The jaysis *Late Late Show* Antoinette. *The Late Late Show!*' I roared.

'Jesus, Gary! A bit of warning if you're gonna go all Beatles Fan on me please,' says Antoinette, slightly annoyed but very excited at the same time.

We pull up to our apartment, and as soon as I'm in the door I am punching Ronan's number into my phone. I don't know if being an all-round lovely human is part of the criteria when applying for a job in RTÉ, but, like Grace, Ronan was such a nice person to talk to from the second we started chatting. He told me he had read the JOE.ie article, and that he had heard my interview with Dave Fanning. He said he was both impressed and very intrigued by my story. He then asked would I be interested in coming on *The Late Late Show* to tell my tale? I was completely stunned into silence – which can make phone calls quite difficult.

I think I said something along the lines of, 'eh, emm, yes, yes, I would love to Ronan,' or something like that. Ronan found my reaction quite funny.

'That's great Gary. Now, this might sound crazy, but it won't be until maybe January or even later than that' (it was July). Ronan said there would need to be an embargo of sorts to not tell my story in public until then. I told him if he needed me to change my gender I'd give it a go, and I thanked him – about a hundred times. Ronan said he'd keep in touch, and as he hung up, I raise my head and meet Antoinette's gaze.

'They want me to go on *The Late Late Show* Annie,' I start, before bursting into tears.

Antoinette followed suit, and as we embraced on our staircase I could feel a wave of pride come over me. 'They want you because of *you* Gary. Your book isn't even published, yet they still want you. That is just amazing baby.'

I couldn't answer her. My mind had gone into overdrive. Here I was, a guy who was a complete waste of space before my incarceration, a guy who had broken the law and ended up in prison. But I was also a guy who had changed and who wanted to show the world that it's possible to right your wrongs. And now I had been invited on to a show that has been a staple of Irish culture for many years. I was going to be on the fuckin' telly! Wait until I tell 'me ma'.

'God, Gar,' starts Antoinette, 'imagine if your book got published before your *Late Late* appearance? That would be something else.'

It sure would be, Annie, it sure would. But only time would tell...

Chapter 23

MY MAGNIFICENT THREE

'*I sentence you to three and a half years Mr. Cunningham.*'
When the judge peered at me and uttered those words, I felt my whole world collapse. But I deserved it. I deserved every day that I was to be incarcerated for what I had done. Hearing my mam sob as I was led away from the court is a sound that is forever etched into my memory. As I was taken away, I doubted I would make it through prison. I felt so sorry for myself. Ironic, right? I broke the law. I was the arsehole who decided to ignore everyone and everything around me so as I could tend to my selfish needs. And yet I was feeling sorry for myself! But that was so typical of me back then. So being sent to Mountjoy prison, a place I assumed would be the epicentre of negativity, was certain to be the straw that would break this camel's back. But yet again, I was wrong.

For inside that ancient jail, I was to forge friendships that I know will last a lifetime. I was to achieve more inside her tall, grey walls, than I ever had in my entire life on the outside. Incredibly, it was in Mountjoy where positivity began its battle with negativity in my mind, and positivity kicked negativity's arse. You have already met Fitzer through the pages of this book, and I'm sure you have gathered what a positive entity he is. Well, I met him in Mountjoy. You have walked with me as I try with every stroke of my pen to highlight Antoinette's allure. Yep, that's right, I met her in The Joy too! I am not for one minute suggesting you should try a stint in jail. In fact, I pray you never have to see the inside of a cell. I just can't believe it was in the very place I thought my own personal negativity would grow, that it was almost banished forever from my life and was replaced with the immense powers of a positive mind. The glass was always half-empty for me before prison, but today it overflows with joy.

There are three individuals I met in prison who I refer to as 'My Magnificent Three'. The first of this trio you have already met, Antoinette. So now I would like to introduce the other two. I would like to show you how they have helped shape me into the man I am today. How their support and words of encouragement, both in prison and once I was released, takes my breath away.

So let me introduce you to Magnificent Lady No. 2: Maggie Byrne.

Maggie came thundering into my life after I had been locked up for about six or seven months. I had written a musical, *Journeyman*, inside my cell on C Wing, which impressed Paul Byrne, the music teacher in Mountjoy, so much that he insisted myself and Fitzer record rough versions of the songs so he could give them to a colleague of his.

'Her name is Maggie lads,' Paul said to us one day, 'and she is the drama teacher in the Medical Unit' (another section of the vast Mountjoy campus).

Myself and Fitzer recorded the songs for this musical on a dictaphone. Paul then gave the recordings to Maggie and after a couple of days we were introduced to her. Instantly we hit it off. There is a radiance that greets you when you first encounter Maggie, her golden hair always gleaming, her soft English accent adding to her mystery. She loved my musical, and decided to dedicate her free time every Wednesday evening to facilitate drama workshops for anyone interested in partaking in the construction of this play. I had gathered quite a few men who wanted to be part of this, and these men came from all walks of life. Yet Maggie handled each and every one of us with such care and ease. Wednesday became the one day of the week that we all lived for. Maggie had ways of allowing us to cast-off our inhibitions and step completely out of our comfort zones. Each and every man who attended these workshops loved her, but none more so than I did.

At the end of every session, Maggie would ask myself and Fitzer to stay back as she would walk us through her vision for putting my musical on the stage. And it was during these special moments that I began seeing how thoughtful this woman truly was. She would pull me to one side and ask was I okay. She had many questions and concerns as to where I gained my inspiration for *Journeyman*, which I quickly answered whilst doing all I could to ease her concerns.

'It's about no one in particular and more an amalgamation of everyone, if you get what I mean Maggie,' I explained to her, and of course she got it.

After walking away from Maggie every Wednesday, I truly felt like I could take on the world. I wasn't used to receiving praise, and yet Maggie showered me with it whenever she could. She believed in me, and she helped me believe in myself. Sadly, I was then plucked from Mountjoy and moved to Loughan House. Although I was grateful, I was quite sad too. I was leaving Maggie and all her hard work behind. We almost got to stage *Journeyman* too. Alas, it wasn't meant to be.

Maggie promised to write to me once I got settled in Loughan House. Shamefully, I must admit that I thought she was just saying that to make me feel good. I suppose I didn't expect her to write. Why would she? And yet, amazingly, she did write to me ... twice! I know this sounds silly, but I knew then that this woman would remain in my life forever. And that's exactly what happened.

And as for *Journeyman*? I can't believe I'm writing this, but we are currently gung-ho trying to stage it out here – outside the walls of where it was created.

Now ladies and gentlemen, please take to your seats and allow me to introduce to you 'Magnificent Lady No. 3': Deborah Blacoe.

Deborah Blacoe. Even writing her name invokes heavenly thoughts, and yet I know how much she will squirm after reading that line. Deborah's late brother was the remarkable Phil Chevron, one of the most talented men this island of ours has ever produced. From being the frontman in his band, The Radiators from Space, to being the lead guitarist in The Pogues, Phil had done it all. But sadly, it was his passing, and his guitars, that were to bring myself and Deborah together.

In his will, Phil had asked that three of his favourite guitars be donated to the school in Mountjoy. What an incredible thing to do. The presentation of these guitars happened at a ceremony in the school of Mountjoy, and was attended by various strands of the Irish media. Even Billy Bragg was there that day, as he spoke about his memories of Phil and how himself and Phil wanted to get Billy's scheme Guitars Behind Bars brought into Ireland, which I certainly hope will happen. Although I would say that now, wouldn't I?

The Off#enders were asked to play a few songs at this ceremony which we jumped at. But before we got onto the stage, we sat and listened to all the various people speak so lovingly about Phil Chevron. It was such an emotional day, with Billy Bragg reaching for one of Phil's guitars at the end of his speech, and performing a beautiful, haunting version of Bob Marley's 'Redemption Song'. But it was Deborah who blew my mind.

I hung on her every word as she allowed us a glimpse of her life with her brother, rather than the star Phil had rightly become. She stood at the podium and spoke with such clarity.

There was a softness to her voice that made you almost transfixed to her. She displayed confidence in abundance, and yet nothing could be further from the truth. I had the honour of speaking to Deborah after the ceremony had ended, and she told me she was petrified as she stood there and spoke.

'You would never have guessed it,' came my shocked reply.

We spoke that day for what felt like hours, and then Deborah said something to me that has never left my heart since. I was weeks away from being released at this stage and, if I'm honest, I wasn't ready. I was terrified of what was going to happen to me on the outside. I told Deborah this, and she took both of my hands in hers and said words that will remain private between us but went straight to my heart.

And then Deborah was pulled away to do an interview with Tom Dunne for Newstalk. Fitzer was standing beside me as I spoke to Deborah, and had heard almost every word.

'Jaysis man. That was lovely. Fair play to her Gar,' he starts, 'I'll be fuckin' bawlin' now meself in a minute.'

'I'm just so glad I got to meet someone as special as her Fitzer,' I reply, 'even if it was only for a few minutes.' Oh, how wrong I was, again! It's lucky I have no problems being wrong isn't it? It seems to happen a lot.

Skip forward to my interview with Dave Fanning on RTÉ Radio 1. Deborah happens to be sitting in her kitchen enjoying a cup of java with her radio tuned to that very station. *Gary Cunningham? That's the Gary I met in Mountjoy,* thinks Deborah. She instantly logs onto her Facebook, finds yours truly, and the rest is the most perfect of fairytales.

Deborah has done more for me in the short time I've known her than the so called friends I had spent my life with before my incarceration. She actually saved Christmas for me, but I know the type of lady she is, and I know I would embarrass her if I was to disclose that information. But she did it, and I am confident she knows how much it meant to me. She is one of the most beautiful and descriptive writers I have ever come across, and I long for the day that I am holding a copy of her book in my hands. So I constantly push her to write more and more. Even some of her Facebook posts are passages of unbridled beauty. I love this woman with all my heart, and every day I give thanks that I am lucky enough to share this life with her. Such a beautiful lady, The Magnificent Deborah.

So there you have it, three amazing women whom I met in the most negative place on earth. But it was in that very prison that I realised that Mountjoy, or anywhere in life, is only as negative as you allow it to be. I hope that each and every one of you reading this story will find your own Magnificent Three, or Thirty-Three, or One Hundred and Three. I would love for the power of positivity to wash over you the way it did me, and for you to enjoy the benefits of it.

Chapter 24

WE'RE JAMMIN'...

'Here Gar me aul' mucker, let's hire a rehearsal room and get the aul' band back together, wha?' These were the words that came down the receiver on my phone from Fitzer one day. And they were the words I had been longing to hear. Life was going pretty good at this time. I was enjoying working in the hotel, with my main goal being to secure employee of the month. Myself and Antoinette were falling more and more in love with each other. Even Brian Langan was keeping my spirits up with sporadic emails as he decided if my book was a good fit for his company to publish. Yep, things were good. So, when Fitzer suggested we reunite The Off#enders and jam as free men, I was beyond excited. I thought fondly back on the hard work and long hours we put in as we recorded our very own album, indeed, learning how to record a feckin' album as we went along. We were a true band of misfits. I was the only musician who was playing longer than a few months at the start of our 'career'. Fitzer was learning the bass off Paul Byrne in the school in Mountjoy. Sweeny-Todd was enhancing his rhythm guitar skills in the same school, and as for Cunny? Well, he taught himself how to play the drums, which was astonishing. And of course, there is Fitzer's voice – but then I *may* have mentioned that already!

We became a distraction for some as we performed in various jails. I remember after playing a thunderous gig in Castlerea prison, myself and Fitzer actually received fan mail in the post to Loughan House. One of these letters made Fitzer feel a little uneasy, though, which in turn delighted the rest of us. The chap that sent this particular letter seemed to have a bit of a soft spot for aul' Fitzer. He spoke of how he 'loved the way the sun came through the window and illuminated your face as you played your bass, and sang so beautifully'. He even wrote Fitzer a little poem.

'Ah me arse! Give it bleedin' over will ya?' was Fitzer's response, which just made us take the mickey out of him all the more. 'Still. I don't see you shitebags gettin' poems sent to yas now do I?' laughed Fitzer. 'At least we now know who the top dog in The Off#enders is, wha'?'

Even back in Mountjoy, we had gained somewhat of a rock star persona. Lads would encourage us in ways only prisoners can: 'Here! Are ya listenin'? You's are bleedin' *rappa* lads, yeah? Like, I'm not even messin,' yiz are fuckin' deadly boys. *Hon The Off#enders!*'

Yes, fine praise indeed. Of course, we also had men who would bring our egos back down to earth with a thump. Men like The Little Fella or Budgie. 'Fuckin' rock stars me arse. Yiz are shite!' would be their particular choice of words. But deep down we knew they loved us. So, with Fitzer's suggestion lingering in my earlobe, I Googled available rehearsal rooms and found one that I felt would be perfect.

Let's do this!

In the days leading up to the reuniting of one of the most famous bands in the history of the Irish Prison Service, I practiced my guitar until my fingers actually bled. I began imagining us standing on a stage in front of our loved ones, and playing the songs we had created in prison for them. I turned to Antoinette and said, 'I can't believe we're actually going to stand in a room and jam together without the knowledge that an officer will have to come in and end our session.'

'It's full circle Gary,' replied Antoinette. You're right Annie – full circle.

The day of the rehearsal was upon us. Even in work that day, I found myself playing air-guitar as I ran through the set-list I had constructed in my mind. I got home, packed up my guitar, gave Antoinette a massive kiss, and bounced out the door. When we jammed in Mountjoy or in Loughan House, we had a connection that nobody could break. Finding the groove of a song, and playing it on a stage with your closest friends is a far better high than any drug will ever offer you. On my way to the rehearsal room, which was right in the middle of Dublin city centre, I actually bumped into two lads I had served time with. Sadly, life wasn't good for these two upon their release. They seemed caught in the stranglehold of addiction, and all the horrible shite that brings with it. But they recognised me, and on seeing the guitar on my back, one of the lads says to me, 'Ah Gar, 'member The Off#enders? Jaysis, you's were alrigh' pal ya know that?'

'Cheers man,' I reply, 'sure, that's were I'm goin' now lads, to jam with The Off#enders.'

'Ahh no way pal, yeah? Fuckin' nice one. When yiz are giggin' I'll go in and see yas, yeah?' comes this lad's reply.

'Sounds like a plan,' I say. I wished the lads all the best, and I have never meant those words more in my life. I hope they are both doing okay.

I arrive at the rehearsal room at the same time as Sweeny-Todd and Fitzer. We can see Cunny's large smile beaming at us from the building's reception. I find that I am becoming emotional, and although I have 'previous' when it comes to public displays of bawling, I think we all felt very emotional to be honest. We entered the room assigned to us, which felt very small, with a low ceiling painted in black, and the four walls a blood red colour. Cunny sits behind the drum kit provided, and it hits us all hard. No longer will he have to play on the kit that was so kindly donated to us by an officer from Loughan House, Mrs. Mulligan. It was her teenage son's old kit. It was bashed and battered, and it had fuckin' 'Dora the Explorer' stickers adorning its kick-drum! But, back then, all of our band's equipment was donated to us and in a terrible state of disrepair. But we were in prison, so what did we expect? Life gave us lemons, and we made some sweet lemonade. 'Look at yer one behind a drum-kit that's not in bleedin' bits,' laughs Sweeny-Todd, which in turn makes us all giggle. You could feel that anticipation in the air.

The time had come. *Come on The Off#enders...*

From the first striking of a G-chord on my guitar, we were completely and utterly *shite*! I cannot stress this enough. We were like a bunch of people who had never met before and had no idea how to play musical instruments. It was like we had just been forced together in order to create music. Well, it was far from fuckin' music we created that night! At one stage I looked at Fitzer, and we both just fell around laughing.

'Jaysis, were we this bad in jail lads?' laughs Cunny. Honestly, we were shite! Talk about delusions of grandeur.

So why have I told you this little tale?

Because this isn't a movie, this is real life. If I told you we walked into that room and played like Pink Floyd, you might have raised an eyebrow. We were useless. But, just like in prison, we improved more and more with time. And being able to stand in a room with these three friends and play songs which we either wrote ourselves or which inspired us throughout out sentences will forever be an unforgettable moment for me.

An early photo of Gary and Antoinette

Ash and Fitzer

Gerry Adams, another fan

Gary's mam Lily buying her first
copy of *Joys of Joy*

Cunny and Dee Keogh, who has been a huge support for him

Gary and Eilish O'Carroll from *Mrs Brown's Boys*

Niall Boylan and his producer Helena

Gary and Siena at the launch of *Joys of Joy*

Gary, Fitzer, Cunny and Sweeny-Todd
(The Off#enders) at the book launch

Gary with Ronan from
The Late Late Show

An emotional moment on *The Late Late Show*

Antoinette and Imelda May

'It's Kevin Kilbane, Antoinette!'

Gary signing his book for Imelda May,
while she signs her album for him

Kathi from Delaware arriving in Dublin

Gary, Lily, Ryan Tubridy and Antoinette

Gary, Baz Ashmawy, Simone and Michael

Joys of Joy on the road in America

Fitzer's birthday gift to Gary, sitting on the guitar rack Fitzer made for him in prison

Gary with the Dundalk YouthReach group

Antoinette and her mam Anne

Fitzer and Annie working hard in BIMM College

A prisoner no more

So we kept working hard. We had a dream to play a gig, even just the one. We wanted our journey that began in Mountjoy to end with the coming together of our family and friends so they could see just how good we actually are.

A gig eh? Hmmm. I wonder...

Chapter 25

SPAM-A-LOT...

My commute to work every morning was a bit of a hike. It consisted of having to leave the apartment at 6.30 am and walk 25 minutes in order to catch the 7.00 am bus. The bus then took a little under an hour, and when I reached my stop I had a further 10 minute walk up a feckin' hill. I would make it in just shortly after 8.00 am, and I was really proud of that. I would have commuted to England daily if it meant I could secure employment, so I never complained about this hike. Instead, I used the time to focus my thoughts and get my head in the right place. I was still dreaming about my book being published, but I have to admit I was beginning to worry. It had been quite a while since I had heard from Brian Langan. I had sent him my full manuscript, so I thought it would be respectful to cease sending my submissions to other publishing houses. But a lot of time had passed with no correspondence. I knew how incredibly busy this man's day could be, but it didn't stop me from worrying.

I was reading the famous book *The Secret* around this time, and I have to say I was really buying into it. Some might say this book is all mumbo-jumbo bullshit, and perhaps they are right, but I like to think of it as a placebo of sorts. The basic premise of this book is simple: If you think negative thoughts, you will be surrounded by negativity. If you think positive thoughts, you'll be surrounded by positivity. Easy, right? Well, for me it actually was that easy. Throughout my life, I was famous for making statements like, *Ahh sure why would I do that, that won't work for me, nothing ever goes my way.* And then I'd waddle my fat arse off to a pub and drink myself stupid. All this book wanted me to do was stop putting myself down, to stop thinking good things won't happen to me because I'm a 'bad person'. *Well, that's bleedin' handy,* I thought to myself. But when things started happening in my life – positive changes and more good news than bad – I realised that buying into this book's idea was working out for me. Some might say that my luck just changed and that the book did nothing at all. Maybe my thinking that this book was helping me was nothing more than the placebo effect. I'll let you decide.

Sitting on the bus to work one morning, I had as usual been meditating for the first 20 minutes or so. I found it the perfect way to start my day and still do. Now I didn't sit with my legs folded in the aisle of the bus, eyes rolled, repeating mantras over and over again. God no. All I did was close my eyes, smile, and begin my day being thankful for all I had. I would then focus on something, in this case hearing back from Brian Langan, and instead of thinking, *Ahh he's never getting back to me,* I thought, *He's a busy man. He will get back to me. And, remember, he may not like my story. Either way, I'm prepared.* Unfortunately, after about a week of shifting my focus, the familiar ping of my phone goes off and there was Brian's email – and it wasn't the one I wanted.

In it, Brian apologised profusely, explaining that his hectic workload and a family holiday had prevented him from mailing me sooner. But he also disclosed that his company wouldn't be moving forward with my book. I was crushed. But I refused to lay down. In all the emails between myself and Brian, I always remained polite, gracious and extremely grateful. So if this was to be my last email to this man, I would keep to that formula. I thanked him from the bottom of my heart for taking the time to read the manuscript in the first place. I explained that he was the first to ask for the full story, and even though it was a no, I would now get back on the horse and keep trying. Even typing those words in that email to Brian had the desired effect on me. Before, I would have given up. An example of this was how I reacted after one of the rejections I received before Brian's. I turned to Antoinette and said, 'Who was I fooling? Who the fuck would want to read my story. I'm deleting the whole stupid thing off my computer.' Bit of an overreaction, but I was my own worst enemy back then and I was still living in Negativity City.

After receiving Brian's email, I fired off a very grateful reply, and I wished him nothing but happiness and success for the future. He replied almost instantly with the most cryptic of responses:

> Thank you for taking it in such good spirits Gary. Those emails are probably the most difficult (and least enjoyable) parts of my job. But leave it with me. It may take a couple of weeks, but I'll get back to you. Brian.

And that's just what he did. But this email was one I really didn't expect. In it, Brian gave me his critique of my book, explaining that these were his views and his views alone. But he also had spent his time compiling a list for me. A list of publishers, agents, hints and tips for good submissions, the works. It was honestly one of the kindest gestures anyone had ever done for me. I had never met this man, yet here he was sharing his wealth of knowledge with me. He urged me to never give up. I was stunned and beyond grateful, which I made sure Brian knew in my reply to him.

At the very top of his list of publishers, Brian wrote the following: 'The Liffey Press – David Givens: David is a gentleman. I worked with him for ten years, so when you submit, definitely use my name with him.' *Well*, I thought to myself, *seems like a good place to start*. So I sent off my submission to David and put my faith in the hands of the universe. But after a week? Nothing. So, I went back to Brian's list, found the next publisher he suggested, and started again. And then the universe started paying more attention to me.

I was on the bus to work one morning, doing my meditation, and I'll never forget that particular morning for two reasons. The first, and most important, I'll come to in a minute, but I'll also remember that morning for the embarrassment I felt thanks to an old jail buddy of mine, KG. I had just finished that morning's meditation and was bringing myself back into the world. I picked up my phone to write that day's positive thought into my 'positive thoughts list' (how original), when I see KG has sent me a Facebook mail. I open it and see that it is a video with the caption, 'Does anyone know why my motorbike sounds like this?' I was intrigued. I hit play, and listened as the guy explains his concerns over the sound his bike is making. But just as he turns the key to give us all a listen, the audio morphs into a woman having the loudest orgasm you have ever heard. I was absolutely mortified! The bus I got each morning usually had the same passengers, and they were mostly women. I tried with all my might to lower the volume on my phone, which was at its highest, but the damage was done. The looks I got. Thanks KG!

After my embarrassment began to subside, I read a few pages from *The Secret*, and one of the things they wanted me to do was close my eyes and picture myself holding what I truly wanted in my hands. That was easy. I closed my eyes and pictured the cover I had designed for my book. I pictured this design encasing my book as I held it, with both my mam and Antoinette on either side of me at the book's launch. Feck it, if you're gonna dream, dream big. I continued that thought throughout the day until I arrived home. After dinner, I headed up to my computer in order to begin sending submissions off to more publishers. I have no idea why I did what I did next, but I checked to see if I had any spam. I never check to see if I have spam. Who does? Spam is the product of the devil right? I click the drop-down arrow and am met with this horrifying message: *SPAM 1*. You have got to be kidding me. It was from, wait, *what*?

'Annie. Antoinette. *Annie!*' I roar down the stairs.

'Jesus Gary, what?' comes her joyful reply.

'I have an email here from The Liffey Press!' I am still shouting. I open the mail and see that not only did this man, David Givens, like my first three chapters, but his wife actually acted out the scene from Chapter Three, 'On the Bus'. He asked me if I would send on the full manuscript. Then my blood ran cold. I looked at when David had sent the mail. Almost a fuckin' week ago! I frantically reply, gushing with apologies and explaining the whole spam situation. But I had no need for concern. I knew instantly from David's early emails that he is one of this world's better people. I fired off the full manuscript and, three days later, David informed me that he would love to publish my book. I couldn't believe it. I ran to Antoinette, where she was waiting with open arms, smiling her head off. I rang my mam and there wasn't a dry eye between us. The same reaction happened with my brothers, nephews and nieces. So you see? I'm not the only Cunningham who cries a lot.

Myself and David got on from the get-go. A taller man than myself, sporting a beard and a very distinctive American accent, he quickly became much more than my publisher. He was fascinated by parts of my story. He spoke of its creative arc, but he also slagged the shite out of me. 'My *God,* Gary,

I get it. Fitzer is amazing! You only tell us, like, a thousand times in the first few chapters,' he boomed through his thick American tone. 'Don't get me wrong Gary,' he continued, 'it needs a lot of work to tidy it up. But the story is fantastic – even "amazing" in parts.' I knew this was a dig at me, but I didn't care. He could slag me all he wanted to. He was about to make my dreams come true.

Over the next few weeks we would meet in the reception of a beautiful hotel right in the heart of Dublin. We would make our way to a table, order coffee, and go through everything we needed to do to get this book out there. I signed my contract and everything about this man, his company, and the way he carried himself put me so much at ease and gave me an abundance of confidence.

I will never be able to fully thank both Brian Langan and David Givens for having faith in me. I just hope the book does okay now. Shit. I hadn't thought about that...

Chapter 26

I Must Be Frank with You...

My meetings with David were becoming the highlight of my week. I could also see, at this time, how proud Antoinette was and this made my heart sing. The same went for my mam and the rest of my family. For the first time, each and every one of them could see the wholesale changes in me. They could see I had found my voice, both from the writing of my first book, to becoming almost a regular on *The Niall Boylan Show* on Classic Hits 4FM, and to a lesser degree on 98FM's *Dublin Talks*.

I had given my story to two ladies whose opinions meant the world to me, Deborah and Maggie, and I asked them to be brutally honest and tell me what they thought. Antoinette had already read the book a few times and had given me her seal of approval. Deborah got back to me first. 'I couldn't put it down Gary, in fact, I read it in one sitting.' Wow. She loved it.

Maggie loved it too. She asked if we could meet for a coffee. I said I could meet her in the same hotel where I was meeting David later that day. I actually needed to meet her first if I'm honest, as I was actually dreading this particular meeting with David. He had sent an email explaining that his brother-in-law, Frank, had read the draft and had some thoughts on it. Frank is a published author, playwright and journalist and

David holds his opinion in the highest of esteem. But then David wrote something that made me stop and worry.

'Gary, Frank feels there are a few missed opportunities with this story. I would like him to come to our meeting so we can flesh them out.'

Ah no, not again! All I read from that mail was that this guy Frank was going to tell me the story was a bit too positive, that there needs to be more violence and so on. I was pissed. I had had my belly full of people saying my book was too positive. How the hell can something be *too* positive? I get that it's a story about prison life, but I really wanted to try something different with this tale. And the way I chose to do this was to avoid talking about the countless horrors I faced and witnessed, daily, during my incarceration. People already know the horror stories that can come from prisons, so I wanted to try to write a story filled with more than a hint of positivity. I explained to Antoinette that I will 'fuckin' pull this bleedin' book, it'll never see the light of day, I'm tellin' ya!'

Luckily, Antoinette had become quite the Jedi knight when it came to my completely over-the-top reactions. She just smiled, nodded and said, 'Okay Gar. You do whatever you have to.' It was almost like she was saying 'there, there' to a toddler. And I suppose, in many ways, she was.

So on the morning I was to meet the dreaded Frank, I arranged to meet Maggie first. She gushed about my book, telling me she loved it. She also pointed out, in a very 'matter of fact' way, that I had gotten some tiny details wrong about the games we had played in her drama workshops back in Mountjoy. That's why I love her – straight as an arrow. I tell Maggie about the pending arrival of 'Count Frank' and all his wicked ways.

'No Gary!' comes Maggie's firm reply. 'You have found your voice. Don't you dare let anyone change that, okay?'

As I let Maggie's words linger, I turned to see David has walked in with Frank! The two lads grab a seat, and as I say my goodbyes to Maggie she again reminds me, 'This is your voice. Don't lose it.'

Too fuckin' right I won't Maggie me aul' mucker were the thoughts that popped into my mind. I was ready. Ready to do battle. *A few missed opportunities is it, Frank? Well, we'll see about that.*

If at this point you are thinking to yourself, *I bet ya he's bleedin' wrong about this Frank fella*, then please come up and collect your prize. I could not have been more wrong about an individual if I tried. Frank was an absolute gentleman. He praised my book and I felt like such an idiot. The advice he gave me was, I suppose, 'emotional' advice. Let me give an example.

In a chapter from *Joys of Joy*, myself and another prisoner get sent from Loughan House to Dublin in order to sit a music exam in a school, which is quite a funny story. Frank simply asked how it felt when one of the schoolgirls who had noticed my tattoos and Mohawk haircut (don't ask) asked the teacher if she could move to a different seat. 'Ah, I felt like...' I pause, smile, and look at Frank. 'I felt like shit Frank,' I say as the penny drops.

'And there you go Gary,' says Frank, 'put that in the story. Just that line, "I felt like shit." That, to me, is just a missed opportunity.' Brilliant.

Frank had four small points in total, and I respected his advice so much that the four changes he suggested went into the book. He is an absolute gentleman, one who has become a very close friend. I did tell him that I initially thought he was Beelzebub, and we always have a laugh about that to this day. But, yet again, I found myself floored by the kindness of an individual towards me.

One thing Frank did say about my book – and he wasn't the first – was that it would make a great movie. A feckin' movie? Give it over now, Franky Boy. I just hope the book sells even one copy.

A feckin' movie? 'Would ya go 'way outta tha'.'

Chapter 27

WHAT A PAIN IN THE ARSE...

(Please note: this chapter has the word 'arse' in it quite a lot. A necessary evil in telling the story I'm afraid.)

Life, what a ride. In fact, Ronan Keating, the most unlikely of sources, sums it up perfectly: 'Life is a rollercoaster, you just gotta ride it.' Wise words indeed. Well, the rollercoaster I was on was about to go around the dreaded loop-the-loop once more. Everything was about to get turned upside down on me. And this time, it was literally a 'pain in the arse' for me to deal with.

My diet and the manner in which I lived my life pre-prison were deplorable. My food intake consisted of fast food and 'rubbish' aplenty. As a result, I never really felt healthy. So when one day in my late teens I found I had bled after a bowel movement, I immediately put it down to the fact I had consumed a ridiculous amount of pints and shorts the night before. I ignored it.

Skip forward to me being incarcerated in Loughan House. I am drink-free and in the best shape of my life. The gym and eating well had become my new addiction. So when one day after going to the toilet and seeing almost the entire toilet bowl covered in blood, I panicked. The staff in Loughan were great, and I ended up in Sligo General Hospital for three days as tests were carried out. It was discovered I had infectious colitis, along with one other ailment that, for the duration of this chapter (and probably my life) my embarrassment levels insist I keep to myself. I feel it would be a case of, what is it the kids say today? TMI (Too Much Information). Let's just say, to this day, it is a massive 'pain in my arse'.

These bouts of crippling cramps and blood in my stool would sporadically come in and out of my life after my release. I would have a couple of bad days, and then I'd bounce back. But just as my life had begun to find some stability and structure, just as I was about to publish my first book, these bouts became a lot more intense and a lot more frequent. Yet again, I find I am lying to Antoinette. She was making incredible progress with her new hip, but it's a long road and one that can't be rushed. So once again, I would find myself heading out the door to work, disguising the pain I was in. I'd make that hike to the hotel, but as soon as I got there I would be crippled with pain. Of course, I would then hide that from the staff in the hotel, and I would try to get on with my work. But the pain was excruciating. I was bleeding more regularly, and just getting through the day became very difficult. I couldn't lose this job – not another one. I had already had two jobs, which was two more than a lot of ex-prisoners I know could secure, but I was fading fast.

One morning, as I began lying again to Antoinette, I forgot to factor in how tuned in this woman is. Nothing gets past her, and I really mean nothing. In fact, it is one of the many traits she possesses that I am incredibly attracted to. 'Eh, what's wrong with you Gary?' came her worried question.

'Me? Nothing. I'm bleedin' grand, ya mad thing,' I offer as a reply.

'Funny that,' starts Antoinette, 'I don't remember falling in love with a bloke that looks like he has something stuck up his arse as he talks to me. Tell me what's wrong baby.'

As she said these last words to me, she grabbed hold of my two hands and looked deep into my soul. I broke. In fact, I shattered into a million pieces. I opened my mouth and everything came out. Antoinette was shocked, and very pissed off with me.

'Why Gary? Why feel like you need to be the hero? And for a second time too. Do you think I'm happy with you going into work in that much pain? How could I be? Gar, I am beyond grateful that you would do that for us. But baby, we'll survive. We'll find a way.'

I explained I was also terrified of losing another job, as my criminal record would forever hamper my chances of gaining employment.

'Are you nuts?' asks Antoinette. 'If anyone is going to get another job, it's you Gary. What I've always admired about you is your drive. If you want something, you go get it. And you won't stop until you do. Besides, you don't know if you are going to lose your job yet. I just can't have you trying to support us when you're finding it hard to support yourself.'

I rest my head on Antoinette's shoulders and let out a sigh. She rings the hotel and explains that I will be out for the foreseeable future. They were so understanding and to this day I really appreciate each and every one of them for that. But I knew whatever was wrong with me was getting worse, and I was a bit scared if I'm honest. But the team of professionals I was to encounter soon eased my fears a little.

First up was my GP, Dr. Mary Chambers. What a woman. She has always treated any illness I might have with aplomb. She even tackled the dreaded man-flu with me once, although that particular illness was a bridge too far for her. But then, it's man-flu, so what do you expect? When I told her I had lost another job as a result of the 'pain in me arse' she immediately got on the case.

Dr Chambers arranged for me to attend hospital, and soon I became a patient of the next bunch of professionals to assist me, headed by Mr. Mulsow. This team of doctors were tasked with 'getting my arse into gear', literally. They quickly ruled out the major worries, and ascertained in no time what my problem was. And they were so very sympathetic to my situation. When I say they explored every avenue to try to ease my discomfort, I'm not exaggerating. I found each member of Mr. Mulsow's team to be friendly and supportive, including the receptionist, Aine, who myself and Antoinette hounded on occasion yet she never gave the impression that we had annoyed her. We felt we had to hound her, simply because I had now become a cog in the wheel of the disgraceful healthcare system we have in this country. But that's a topic for a whole different book.

The pain and discomfort I was experiencing was dreadful. After going to the toilet, I would feel drained, like I had just done twelve rounds with Mike Tyson. I was finding it hard to get a resolution. In fact, I was finding it hard to get a bloody follow-up appointment. So I started taking pictures of my blood-stained toilet bowl. I then sat down at my computer and poured my heart out in an email to Mr. Mulsow about how I felt my mental health was also taking a bashing as I tried to deal with what was wrong with me. Once again, just like with my fingers, I found myself in chronic pain. So I begged him to try to help me. He replied almost instantly. An appointment was made, and soon I was being told that I was to have surgery, and that hopefully the 'pain in me arse' would be no more. Result! Or was it? You didn't think it would be that easy now, did you? Silly you! There is one more health issue that will throw a bag of spanners into the works. I'll get to that in a later chapter. You're on this journey with me now, so you may as well stay on until the end!

This illness has emasculated me. I'm out of work … again. I'm not providing … again. I feel like shit … a-fucking-gain! In my head I'd think, *Antoinette deserves so much more than this.* Antoinette's answer to this? 'I deserve you Gary, so shut up being a gobshite.'

Then one day, out of nowhere, Antoinette turns to me and says, 'I have been trying to get my old job back for the last while, and today they said yes. So don't worry baby. You supported us when I was out of action, now it's my turn.'

And that is just what she did. Was it a bit early in her recovery to be heading back to work? Personally, I think it was. Did Antoinette care? Not one bit. When she needed to stand up and be counted, she did just that. Instantly she eased our money worries with her selfless act. I felt like shite about the whole thing, but that is just the neanderthal in me rising to the surface again.

I must admit, though, that I am proud of that neanderthal in me. In an age where equality is to the forefront in almost every discussion, and about time too, I am still proud that I have a longing in me to support my partner. It's fuck all to do with her being a woman, and more to do with a protective side of me. I want to help give Antoinette the greatest life I can. So with me being out of work, I did feel emasculated, and I'm not one bit ashamed of that. I am not for a second saying, *She should be at home, while I work,* fuck that. Those days are thankfully long gone. But I should be able to say I want to support my partner without feeling like I'm going to be attacked by certain people who might (incredibly) deem that sexist. I adore women. In fact, I'd be nothing today without all the strong women I have encountered in my life. And I live my life treating all around me as equals. I am currently in a minority myself, being an ex-prisoner, so I know what judgement feels like. Okay, rant over (sorry about that).

So my 'pain in the arse' has become a massive 'pain in the arse' to deal with. But old Gary would have hit the bottle to cope with this problem. Old Gary would have wallowed in self-pity. But not now. I would now have to dig a little deeper and find the positives in what was a very negative situation. I began reciting the mantra I had constructed in Mountjoy Prison:

'It's not the time you do, it's what you do with your time.'

Chapter 28

THANK YOU FOR BEING
A FRIEND...

*T*he *Niall Boylan Show* on Classic Hits, 4Fm opens the airwaves to the public to discuss the burning topics of the day. These topics can range from harrowing stories of struggle to funny situations. Niall has a wonderful ability to first rub you up the wrong way and then in the next breath be an incredible source of support. I love this show. I had become something of a regular on it, with the show's producer and researcher, the wonderful Helena and Garrett respectively, always knowing that they could reach out to me, especially if the topic was all-things-prison. But it was my honesty once I was on-air that seemed to pique Niall's interest in me, and what happened next I never saw coming.

Niall had added me as a friend to his private Facebook page. I was feckin' chuffed. I'm sure what I was feeling was comparable to a Donny Osmond fan receiving personal letters from aul' Donny himself. One day, Niall displayed what I would deem incredible strength and courage as he put up a post about bullying. Bullying is simply unacceptable, and yet it happens all around us on a daily basis. Even in prison, bullies are dealt with swiftly. Of course, we worry about our kids being bullied, and we must all remain forever vigilant, especially in this digital age we live in. But Niall's post reminded us that adults too can very much be the victims of bullying. In this particular post, Niall informed the reader of the bullying he faced as a child, and the affect it had on him. He then shared a story of how as a grown man he had to deal with a bully again. I admired this post so much. Niall never named and shamed anyone, he didn't even point a finger. He just used his fame to highlight an area of our lives that is happening daily and needs to be discussed. His honesty resonated with me so I sent him a private mail telling him just that. As I hit send I almost instantly regretted it. *Ah shite!* I think to myself, *He's gonna think I'm a bleedin' weirdo now! Well done Gary ya sap!* But instead Niall's reply appeared on my screen and he was thanking me. He asked for my mobile number, which I sent back to him, and almost immediately he rang. I felt like a bumbling fool. It's crazy what meeting a 'celeb' (although Niall would never consider himself one) can do to you. All of a sudden I had lost the ability to fuckin' speak:

Niall: Hello there Gary. How are ya man? Thank you so much for your mail. It meant a lot ... eh ... hello? Gary?? Are you there??

Gary: (Silence).

Yep, like a gobshite I froze. How embarrassing. I eventually blurt out something like, 'ahh yeah man. No bother, in-all-an-anyways'... or something ridiculous like that. I can hear Niall's laughter, and realise I am being a tool. 'Sorry Niall. I'm just a bit of a fan if I'm honest.'

'Funny you should say that Gary,' replies Niall, 'because I admire you so much myself. I think your honesty about the mistakes you have made is quite refreshing. And I get great craic out of you on the show.' I was flabbergasted, but not as much as I was after what happened next. 'Gary? Do you mind if I talk to you about something?' asked Niall.

'Of course not,' I replied.

The next conversation and the many we had after that are of a personal nature to Niall and it is not my place to disclose what we talked about. But I still can't believe that a man I admired so much was actually reaching out to me, looking for someone to talk to. I realised that there were two Nialls: 'the radio show host' and 'the loving father and gentle guy who has his own insecurities'. And it was meeting the latter that made my admiration for this man soar.

Over the next few weeks, we would chat on the phone and I would listen as he unloaded. I'd offer any advice I could, but mostly I would just listen. We became good friends. Yes he can 'wreck yer head' with the views he shares on his show, but I've had the honour of seeing him without the microphone in front of him, and he is hands down one of the kindest, funniest, most caring people you could ever meet. Niall never once judged me for being an ex-prisoner. He would listen to my own worries about trying to find my way as a free man. It always amazed me that we would chat on the phone about how he was feeling, and then twenty minutes later I would tune into his show and listen as the professional in him took over. Not one person would know he was dealing with anything in his life, and this inspired the shite out of me.

I started to look at myself and how I handle my own problems. I learned so much from Niall in the early days of our friendship and I'll be forever thankful to him for that. He also gave me the chance to do something that I actually love to do – be there for others. I know how dark life can get. I have tried to kill myself. I have found myself in situations that have almost pushed me over the edge. And even if I was the creator of most of these situations by being a dickhead, still, I've been there. And when you are down in that hole the worst possible feeling is that you have nobody to turn to. So once I got on top of my own demons, I set about offering my ear to anyone who might need it. From posts on Facebook to being there when Niall or others needed me, I will always make myself available to anyone who might be struggling. It costs nothing in this life to care or to help. I've been on that shitty road, so I know what it feels like.

My friendship with Niall continued to grow, and when I informed him I had a book coming out, I could sense the pride in him. 'You're a good man Gary, never forget that,' he would say to me regularly, quickly followed by, 'and if I ever catch you with a pint of beer in your hands, I'll clip the ears off ya!' Niall's friendship meant more to me than he knows. The ex-prisoner who faced an abundance of knock backs befriended by one of our nation's most successful talk show hosts? That's the stuff dreams are made of. So what I decided to do next seemed like the most obvious thing to do.

'Here, Niall me aul' flower? Are ya free April 6th by any chance? I'd be honoured if you'd MC my book launch?' I nervously asked.

Niall, being the no ego bloke that he is, of course said yes. I was bleedin' made up! Then it hit me. I am going to have a book launch. Oh sweet mother of Jaysis...

Chapter 29

GETTING READY FOR THE LAUNCH, PART 1

The weeks leading up to the launch of my book were filled with so much excitement and anticipation, coinciding with feelings of utter dread and worry. The reason for the excitement was obvious – I was launching my feckin' book! But the worry stemmed from the fact I was petrified nobody would turn up, excluding Antoinette and my family, and they had to go.

My publisher David and I would meet in the same hotel in town and talk about things I never dreamed I would discuss with someone. At this stage, David had edited my tale. It was my first excursion into the world of writing, so poor David had quite a bit of editing to do. But when he handed me a copy of the finished article, printed on sheets of A4 paper, I was stunned at the level of work he had put into it.

'Gary,' says my American publisher/editor/friend, 'when I started editing I thought, *gosh, there is a bit of work in this all right,* but once I got into it I found it so enjoyable. I love this story Gary.' As soon as I picked my jaw up off the floor, I thanked him. 'I'm going to be honest with you Gary. You should reserve some of that thanks for my wife, Darina. When I first received your manuscript, I wasn't sure. But Darina loved it. She turned to me and said, "you have got to take a chance on this guy," and luckily for you Gary, I always listen to my wife.'

'Wow, please pass on my utmost gratitude to your good wife,' I say.

'Sure, you can thank her yourself Gary. She will be at the launch along with my mother-in-law, my son Luke, and your new buddy Frank. They always help me out with a book launch.' My first thought was, *Brilliant. That's three people who will definitely be at the launch*, but I was also loving the fact that David involved his family at his launches. I thought there was something really special about that.

One bright Wednesday afternoon, as we sat in that hotel, sipping coffee and enjoying the late March sun as it illuminated the hotel's bar, David broached the subject of a venue for our launch.

'How many would you guess will go Gary?' he asked.

'I've invited fuckin' everyone and their grannies David,' came my honest answer. So we decided to go for quite a large venue. I decided to stop focusing on people not going, and instead pictured a room filled with my friends and family. We were running through different venues when the most unlikely of buildings came up, the Freemasons Hall on Dublin's Molesworth Street.

'I worked there as a painter over many, many years David. Well, at least my brothers did. I mostly just annoyed them, but I know the place very well. The porter, ahh, what was his name now? Paddy, yeah, Paddy. He's a character David. He loved me and my brothers. Will I try to reach out to them? I could mention my late dad's name. They all loved my dad in there.'

'Sounds like a plan Gary,' replied David, followed by, 'I have a place we can use if all else fails, but it is a bit small. We want a big room Gary.'

'If you want a big room David,' I reply, 'then a big room you shall get.'

Before we left that day, David turned to me, and knowing full well he was taking the piss out of me, he said, 'Oh, and if you want, but only if you want, maybe you could drop by my office tomorrow. The first copies of your book will be there.'

I almost passed out. 'I'll sleep on the doorstop of your office tonight, so I can be there when you open up,' came my cheeky reply. Honestly, though, I was beyond excited. But first, I had to secure this room for the launch. Time to fire up my computer.

The email I sent was like a trip down memory lane, as I fondly remembered serving my time as an apprentice painter and working in this magnificent building. I don't fully understand the Freemason Way, but I do know their building is simply stunning. Sitting proudly on Molesworth Street near Dáil Éireann, its large steps and massive columns which lead to its entrance allow this building to stand out on its own. I fired off an email and got an instant reply offering us the chance to come view the room they had on offer. And the use of my late father's name helped a lot too. Thanks dad. We arranged our meeting for a day later that week, and when I informed David, he seemed really impressed.

'That's fantastic Gary. Well done. I'll see you in my office in the morning. I have a book I think you might be interested in.' *Too bleedin' right Davey ya fuckin' legend* was what went through my mind, but instead I just thanked him.

The next morning, I was picked up by my brother Noel and we drove to collect the very first copy of my book. I was an emotional wreck in the car, so I was more than happy to have my brother with me. He has always been there for me, through good times and bad, so it meant a lot that he was there to witness this huge moment in my life. We arrive at

David's office, and climb the stairs to the very top, where David is standing, waiting and smiling.

'Welcome lads,' he starts but quickly follows it with, 'are you okay Gary? You look in quite a lot of pain.'

'It's just me arse Davey, nothing to worry about,' I joke back. 'Now, where is this book of mine?'

When David handed it to me, I did what I am doing now. I bawled my eyes out. It looked so impressive. David had tweaked my original cover and I loved his version. I held it in my hands, and I was overcome with a barrage of emotions. I thought back to my life before Mountjoy and how bleak it was. I thought about the times I *don't* talk about in the book I was now holding, times in prison were I struggled or felt fear. I opened the book at a random page, and I held it close to my face so as I could drown in the fragrance of fresh print. I love that smell. It reminds me of happier times when my mam would bring me into Easons and allow me to buy another *Famous Five* book. I really wanted people to enjoy that feeling of getting stuck into a new book. I cried. Noel cried. David? Not so much. But then, this wasn't his first book.

Later that day, once Antoinette got home from work, the two of us went to each of my brothers' homes so we could share this moment with them, their wives and their kids. But, of course, I saved the best 'til last. I will never forget walking into my mam's kitchen, and seeing the look on her face. She was so overcome with emotion, and all she kept repeating to me, over and over, were the words, 'I'm so proud of you Gary. I'm just so proud.' It was one of the most special moments in my life.

The next day, myself and David met outside the Masonic Hall. As we entered through the massive double doors, I was instantly brought back to my youth. I remembered bringing in endless scaffolding bars and buckets of paint through this wondrous hall. I turned to tell David of my nostalgic thoughts, but I am interrupted by the calling of my name. 'Gary Cunningham. Well, would you look at you. All grown up, and what a sexy man you have become.' Paddy the Porter! I couldn't believe he was still working here after all these years. Paddy is a very proud gay man, and he loves to have a little flirt. A small man, with tight greying hair, he carries himself off with such style. He instantly started making remarks about my build, my clothes, everything. I was in stitches, but I think my laughter was coming more from the fact that David didn't know where to look.

'You're some man Paddy,' I start followed by, 'it's great to see you man.' We hug, he grabs my arse, and we all fall about laughing. Paddy the Porter. Legend.

We were brought down into the room they were offering and I was suitably impressed. While David and the guy in charge fleshed out a deal, I allowed my mind to wander. I saw a podium and realised I would have to speak at this event. Luckily, I am partial to a bit of talking. I was dragged from my daydream by David calling out to me.

'I think we're good Gary. It's a big room. Do you think we'll fill it?'

I took one last gaze at the room that was to hold the launching of my book and replied, 'I fuckin' hope so David...'

Chapter 30

GETTING READY FOR THE
LAUNCH, PART 2

And so the day had arrived. My stomach felt like it belonged to someone else. I must have looked like I was sponsored by John Player Blue as I don't remember not having a cigarette in my hand, even in the shower. Niall Boylan had agreed to act as MC, and incredibly I had secured Mr Brian Murphy, who was then Governor of Mountjoy prison to launch it. I had met Mr. Murphy whilst I served my time. He held a very different role in the Irish Prison Service back then, but he was always very friendly and approachable. He told me he remembered me and all I had achieved during my incarceration, and agreed instantly to launch my book on the night. I mentioned to him that I would be honoured for any staff members from the Irish Prison Service to attend too, especially Mrs. Gavin and Mrs. Carrick, the Governor and Chief respectfully of Loughan House when I was housed there. I speak highly of these two remarkable ladies in *Joys of Joy*, so I mentioned that it would mean the world to me if they could come. Mr. Murphy promised to mention it to them. Fingers crossed. I also reached out to the teachers from Loughan House, especially Conn, the I.T. teacher, and Mary, the cooking teacher, as they were always so supportive of me and my writing. Unfortunately, they both lived in Fermanagh so I didn't expect them to come.

That morning, I went to my usual barber in order for him to work his magic. His name is Christian, and he is not only a fantastic barber, but he is also one of the coolest blokes I know. With a style unique to himself, which I suppose is 1950s-inspired, he is always wearing a stylish hat and sports an impressive handlebar moustache. He also happens to be extremely funny. I loved getting my hair chopped by this fella. We soon realised we both had a love for the great Laurel and Hardy, and we would share with each other our favourite scenes. So it was with huge pleasure that I got to invite this man, and his stunning partner Sorcha, to the launch. As Christian sculpted my hair, he gratefully accepted my offer. Great. That's two more.

I arrived home and could hear Antoinette singing. I love when she sings. I quickly jump into the shower and then into my suit. *God Gar*, I think to myself, *the last time you donned a suit, you got three and a half years*. I smile an uneasy smile as I remember receiving my sentence in Court 5 that day. You've come a long way, baby. I enter our bedroom and am floored by Antoinette's beauty. Her black hair seemed to glisten, her smile washing the entire room in its light.

'We did it baby,' I say.

'You did it Gar,' comes Antoinette's reply. We hug, and I will never forget that hug.

Antoinette and I arrive at the Masonic Hall way too early. My OCD can be a fuckin' pain sometimes. I suggest to Antoinette that we head to the bar across the road to kill a half hour. I'm felling quite dapper in my suit as I enter the bar, and I feel nothing but pride when I order a Budweiser for Antoinette and an orange for myself. How times have changed – for the better. As I'm waiting for the drinks, I turned and let out a gasp. Sitting at a table eating dinner were Conn and

Mary from Loughan House. I couldn't believe it. I run to their table and there isn't a dry eye between us. They made that two and a half hour journey for me. Jesus. Conn looked great, with his gray hair and matching beard trimmed to perfection. Mary looked beautiful too, although she always does.

I introduced Antoinette, and as I do, I turn to see my nephew Mark and his partner Christine walk in.

'What are you doing here,' laughs Mark, followed by, 'everyone is behind me.' And true enough, my entire family walked into the bar. I look up to the sky, and in my mind I say, *Thank you universe ... thank you.* I introduced Conn and Mary to my family, but especially to my mam who looked stunning that night. And all she did for the whole night was smile. This wonderful moment was shattered by a text to my phone from David: 'ETA 2 min ... could do with a hand to get the books in.' I grab Antoinette and Noel, and we run. As I look back, I see my mam, Conn and Mary deep in conversation. I feel complete.

As we entered the Masonic Hall, I am greeted by Niall Boylan. I was really taken aback, as this was my first time to meet him in the flesh. He looked very dapper in his suit, but what impressed me most was he rolled up his sleeves as soon as David arrived and helped bring in the copies of my book. He also helped my brother Noel arrange the seats, while cracking jokes and making us all laugh which, personally, really helped me. I was starting to get very jittery altogether. When my mam came over and saw Niall, I thought she was going to pass out. She has a bit of a thing for good ol' Boylan, and the way he handled my mam was fantastic. (I found out later that Niall had just had one of the worse days in his life, but he never showed it. He told me he would never have let me down. What a good man.)

All of a sudden people started to appear. I was starting to contemplate 'leggin' it', doing a runner ... *leaving*! But when

I turn and see Fitzer and his gorgeous wife Ash, followed by Sweeny-Todd, Cunny, Smithwhicks, Redmond, Kellyer and a few others I 'did my whack' with, I feel a massive lump form in my throat. Fitzer cops this.

'Ahh here we bleedin' go. We haven't even started yet and all ready "yer wan" (yours truly) is bleedin' off. Give it over will ya?' We both laugh and hug it out, and as we do he whispers into my ear, 'I'm so fuckin' proud of you man, and I'm so proud to call you my friend.'

I break from the hug and run into the toilet. I'm not having him slag me again. But to know that the man who meant so much to me inside was standing here tonight with his wife, well, it doesn't get much better than that.

I come out of the toilet and the number of people seems to have doubled. Oh God. I see Brain Murphy chatting to Niall Boylan. I make my way towards them, and Brian smiles as I arrive.

'Ah good man Gary,' he says, 'I brought a few with me. This is Michael Donnellan.'

But Mr. Donnellan needed no introduction. He was the Director General of the Irish Prison Service. I couldn't believe he was there. 'Congratulations, Gary, on a remarkable achievement,' he says.

I am about to answer when my publisher's wife, Darina, interjects and says to Mr. Donnellan, 'You guys should really employ this man.' I was slightly embarrassed, but I equally loved her so much for saying that.

Mr. Donnellan is saved from giving an answer by Mr. Murphy. 'And these two ladies are here two Gary.' I turned to see both Governor Gavin and Chief Carrick standing there. He had brought everyone I had asked for. I just couldn't believe it. As I embraced both ladies, words failed me. But they both understood. These women saved my life by believing in me. They gave me the tools and encouragement to turn my entire life around. I mention that they play a massive part in the book about to be launched, and although they were both slightly embarrassed they were equally very proud.

The room was almost full. I couldn't believe it.

David reminds me, 'just make sure you mingle.'

Right, I'll do that now I think, but as I was about to, a lady I know called Tanya walks up to me and says, 'I want to be the first one to get the book signed.' I was feckin' delighted! I grab a pen and go down on one knee in order to sign it for her.

David cops this. He grabs me and says, 'No Gary. It's better if you sit down to do that. Here.'

He pulled a seat out for me, and I never moved off that seat for the rest of the night. It was so overwhelming. The only time I got off that chair was to give my speech, a speech which was filled to the gills with thanks and praise and foul language. When I looked out, I could see a room filled with all the people I loved. Filled with ex-prisoners and current prison officials. It was beautiful. I marvelled at how professional Niall Boylan was as he MC'd the evening. I was left sobbing after Brian Murphy got up and spoke about me. And as beautiful as those moments were, what was really special was sitting in that chair signing copies of my book. The queue went the whole way around this large room. I knew I was under time constraints, but I made sure to write something personal on each copy. Then my barber Christian and his beautiful wife arrived. They both looked incredible, decked out in their best glad rags. Christian handed me a large gift beautifully wrapped. 'Wait 'til your home to open that. Proud of ya buddy.' What a lovely thing to do. Then I looked down the queue and spotted someone, and time stood still.

A lady by the name of Siena Guidera had reached out to me on Facebook. She was a regular listener to Niall's radio show and loves when I'm on. We got to know each other on Facebook so of course I invited her to the launch. But sadly she informed me she probably wouldn't make it as she was suffering from a quite horrid strand of cancer. I told her not to worry, and that I would bring a signed copy to her. But when I saw one lady I didn't recognise who needed to move her seat each time the queue moved, I knew it must be Siena. I couldn't help what I did next. I apologised to those who were ahead of Siena and brought her to the top of the queue. I then told David and the others in the queue that this would take a minute or two which everyone completely understood. And for the next couple of minutes, I just sat and held this woman's hands.

'You always cheer me up when I'm down Gary, so I got you this, but please don't open it until you get home.' I was speechless. A moment in time I will never forget.

As was the rest of the launch. Every time I looked up, I was shocked to see who was standing in front of me. From Deborah and her son David to Maggie who had brought teachers from Mountjoy with her. Family, friends, my head was spinning. It was just perfect.

When it was all over, I had a panic attack, which poor Antoinette bore the brunt of.

'I never fuckin' mingled Annie,' I ranted.

She was great. 'You couldn't Gar. You sat on that seat and everyone came to you. It was amazing baby, you're amazing.'

As we left the Masonic Hall that evening, I was delighted when Fitzer and Ash said they would come back to our place. I love that about Fitzer. A few were heading off for drinks, but he decided to stay with me. 'You're not drinking, so I'm not drinking,' he said. Myself, Antoinette, Fitzer and Ash all jumped into a taxi.

'Gerrr*up* outta tha' Gar,' roared Fitzer from the taxi's back seat. 'That was some night pal. You're a bleedin' legend.'

'Always remember buddy,' I reply, 'there would be no book without you. I love ya man.'

'Give it over now Gar,' laughs Fitzer.

We get back and all have a great laugh in my kitchen. Fitzer then says to me, 'So what are the presents ya got? I'm bleedin' dyin' to know.'

I open Christian the Barber's first and it is a boxset of Laurel and Hardy, all enclosed in a box that looks like a miniature suitcase. I burst into tears, while everyone else laughs at the fact I'm fuckin' crying, again! But what a thoughtful gift.

I then open Siena's, and this time the whole room, even Fitzer, sheds a tear. It was an ornament of a heart, with the words, 'Friendship isn't a big thing, it's a million little things' printed on it. Today, it hangs on the guitar rack Fitzer made for me in Loughan House, in the very room where I am sitting now, typing this book. What a beautiful and thoughtful gift to receive.

What a day. What a night. What a launch.

But I had no time to linger on these feelings. I had a date with Ryan Tubridy the very next evening.

'Ma. I'm gonna be on the telly.'

Chapter 31

THE LATE LATE SHOW

About a week before my impending appearance on what is most certainly one of Ireland's most famous television shows, I met up with Ronan, the man who had approached me about appearing in the first place. We met outside a small café on South William Street, in the heart of Dublin. I was feeling petrified about the whole 'going on live TV' situation, although there was no way I was going to show it. But after a few minutes of talking to Ronan, my fears began to slowly evaporate. He almost jumped out of his chair in order to greet me, and he insisted on buying the coffees. A little shorter than me and sporting a well sculpted beard, Ronan embodies what it is to be a perfect gentleman. I assumed that all who appeared on *The Late Late Show* would first have to meet this man, and I could now see what a vital role Ronan plays in calming their nerves.

We got the pleasantries out of the way and then Ronan got down to business. 'Gary, I have to congratulate you on your book. I read it in a couple of days, and I loved it,' he said through a beaming smile.

'Wow Ronan, eh, *wow*! Em, thank you so much,' I stuttered as a reply. What I really enjoyed about meeting Ronan was that once we had finished talking about what would happen on the evening of my appearance, we sat there and just talked about everything. From football to his love for his daughter, we covered it all. I thanked him for making me feel so welcome and calm. We said our goodbyes, and I walked away with my head in the clouds. I was going to be on the 'bleedin' telly'!

It's the morning after my book launch and I'm up at 'stupid' o'clock. In truth, I didn't get much sleep. I was still hyped and emotional by the evening's events. I was still trying to come to terms with how many people had turned up, but I had no time for reflection. I made breakfast for myself and Antoinette, and then I headed to my mam's. If I was going to be on *The Late Late Show*, then my mam was going to be by my side, and she was buzzing. I get to the front door of her home, and there she is, standing in the doorway waiting for me. I allow myself a moment and feel waves of love and pride wash over me. I can feel the tear ducts in my eyes begin to open, and so I snap myself out of it. *No tears today Gar me aul' flower,* I think to myself. Yeah, right. Who am I kidding?

I had a great laugh with my mam as we headed back to mine. To hear her speak about how proud she felt as I stood on the podium at last night's launch made every star in my solar system align. My mam kept saying to Antoinette, 'Jesus, Mary and Joseph. Can you believe it Antoinette? My son. On *The Late Late Show.*'

Antoinette simply replied, 'Of course I can believe it Lily. He deserves it.'

And so, with the three of us wearing our Sunday best (on a Friday), we all pile into the taxi Ronan had sent to pick us up. The driver, a man in his late forties with a receding hairline and a large gut, was great craic. A real Dubliner.

Driver: 'So, which one of yiz are on the show with aul' Tubbs tonight then?'

Nervous Gary: 'Eh ... that would be me.'

Driver: 'And what the fuck is so special about you?' followed by a large booming laugh.

Nervous Gary: 'Emm ... I wrote a book about being in prison, and I'm heading on to talk about my experiences.'

Driver: 'Did ya now? I better keep me an eye on me aul' wallet, wha'?' followed by an even larger, more booming laugh.

That last line did the trick. We are all united in laughter as the taxi made its way to the RTÉ studios in Donnybrook. The driver actually did more for me than he realised. With the amount of questions he had for me before I left his car, I felt like I had already done a feckin' interview. But I'll never forget his parting words. 'That's some story Gary. If you tell it tonight, the same way you just told me, then you have nothing to worry about. And I'll be buying your book tomorrow. Best of luck to ya.'

Standing at the door of the studio is Ronan. He welcomes us and takes the time to have a chat with my mam and Antoinette. He escorts us down the famous narrow corridor that leads to the show's green room, and once we arrive we see a table has been kept for us. Ronan tells Antoinette and my mam to make themselves comfortable, and then whisks me off to make-up. 'So, how are you feeling Gary?' asks Ronan.

'I'm actually okay sir,' I reply. And I really was. The taxi driver was right. All I had to do was tell my story. My only fear was people hating me, or them thinking I wanted anyone to feel sorry for me. I could handle the hate. Prison makes your skin very thick. But I had Antoinette, my mam, and my family to think about, and I didn't want them to get upset. Yet again, Ronan put my fears to bed as he reassured me everything was going to be okay.

When I get back to the green room, I become a bit of a sap if I'm honest. The other guests from that night's show are all standing around chatting, while my mam and Antoinette, who both looked stunning by the way, are sitting at our table with massive smiles on their faces. I see Kathryn Thomas, whom I had actually met before when I was a contestant on the first airing of the Irish version of *The Voice*. She looked as beautiful this evening as she did back then. She was going to be joined on the show by ex-Ireland international soccer player Kevin Kilbane. Seeing Kevin made me become even more of a sap. In my eyes he is a legend, plain and simple.

My morphing into a sap continued when my eyes found the one and only Colm Meaney, an Irish actor who needs no introduction. 'Get up and introduce yourself Gary,' suggests my mam.

'I will in me arse,' I reply, followed by, 'besides, I'm on soon. I need to keep my head in check.'

The 'keeping my head in check' idea soon got launched out of the window with the arrival of the last person to make my transition to an absolute sap complete – the beautiful Imelda May. She was running late, and had burst into the green room like a freight train. My mam and Antoinette love this woman, as do I. But our love for her reached new heights that evening. Imelda came over to us, and started talking to my mam and Antoinette like she had known them for years. My mam informed her I was about to go on to tell my story.

Imelda looked at me and said the words I will never forget: 'You're not the only one to have gone to prison Gary, so put that worry out of you head. Tell your story with confidence. I can't wait to hear it. I'll be watching as I get my make-up done, which I better fly and get done now.' I cheekily ask could I take a photo of her with my mam and then with Antoinette, and of course she was only too happy to oblige. Such a beautiful woman.

Next, in comes Ryan Tubridy, and I watch with admiration as he goes from table to table greeting all of his guests and their family and friends. He was so good to me, and told me not to worry. 'It's just me and you having a chat Gary.'

And so, my time had come.

After I embraced the two most important women in my life, Ronan tells them that he will be back to bring them to their seats. He leads me backstage where I am mic'd up, and then he brings me to the side of the stage and leaves me in the hands of a really cool lady, who I assume runs the backstage area.

'Good luck Gary. You're going to do great,' says Ronan.

I take a little peak out from behind the curtain and I shiver. The audience is full. Ryan Tubridy is yapping away to them as the show was on a commercial break. The lady left in charge of me, who was sporting massive headphones which had a mic attached, turns to me and says, 'Can I give you a bit of advice Gary?'

'Any advice you have would be greatly appreciated,' I reply.

'Okay. When you walk out from here, pause, and wave.'

What? Is she off her head? 'Ah you must be kidding me,' I start, 'I can't wave and be like, *Hi everyone. It's me, Gary, your friendly ex-prisoner*. I'd be bleedin' mortified.'

The backstage lady laughs, but then shows me an example. 'Here, watch this.' She pulls back the curtain and, with her head down, makes her way towards Ryan. She then comes back and makes the same trip again, only this time she pauses, smiles and waves. I could immediately see her point, and I thank her for such good advice. Then, all of a sudden, Ryan Tubridy is giving my introduction.

Here we go...

I appear from behind the curtain and am met with applause, thanks-be-to-jaysis. I pause, smile and wave, and although I feel like a fool, I'm glad I did it. I make my way to Ryan, but suddenly my blood runs cold. The ongoing problem

I was having with 'me arse' decides, *Hey, he is about to appear on national television. Let's run amuck.* Just as I go to place my bottom on the soft, brown leather chair, I feel a pain rush through me. *You have got to be kidding me*, I think to myself, but there was no way my health issue was going to hamper this interview. So I gritted my teeth and got on with it.

And it was one of the most amazing moments in my life. Ryan Tubridy's handling of my story was fantastic. He wasn't afraid to call me out on the actions of my past, but he also allowed me to tell my story, my way. And my way consisted of not hiding behind any excuses. I wanted anyone who was watching to see that I had been nothing short of a disgusting scumbag, who was also the most selfish bastard you could ever meet before I went to prison. And I wanted people to see how far I had come. I was as honest and as open as I could be. I spoke highly of the Irish Prison Service, and how I believed that they had helped to save my life. I spoke about Fitzer and how much his friendship meant to me. I told funny stories that actually made the audience laugh. And then Ryan moved on to my mam and Antoinette, and true to form, yours truly began fucking sobbing, on *live national television*! I later found out that Fitzer had started a WhatsApp group with some of the other lads we served time with betting on how long it would take me to cry. Arseholes! Although I did find this funny.

When Ryan began speaking about these beautiful ladies, I broke down. And do you know what? I am proud that I did. We lose way too many young men in this country to suicide, and I know a lot of men find it hard to show their emotions for fear they will be viewed as 'less of a man' or some stupid bullshit like that. The number of men who reached out to me after my *Late Late* appearance and thanked me for showing that it's okay not to be okay took my breath away. For once, I was proud of the fact I am such a whinger.

The interview seemed to fly by, and soon I am looking at Ryan Tubridy as he holds a copy of my book to the camera and plugs the shite out of it. I am, quite literally, blown away. The cameraman informs Ryan that the show has gone to a commercial break, and he turns to me, grabs both of my hands, and with huge concern asks if I am okay. 'You went white just as you sat down Gary,' he says.

Me feckin' arse was bleedin' killin' me Tubbs me aul' *mucker* was what I wanted to say, but instead I found a much more appropriate way of saying it. Ryan then tells me he felt the interview went really well, and says that he would see me after the show. I make my way backstage and standing there, with his arms open, is Ronan.

'Wow Gary. You did amazingly well. You're such a natural.'

'Jaysis. Thank you so much Ronan,' I offer as a reply. As we make our way through the backstage area, I look up and see Colm Meaney is being mic'd up. He comes over to me, grabs my shoulders and says, 'That was fuckin' brilliant. You don't hear honesty like that on the TV these days. Be proud of yourself.'

I almost pass out, but not before I tell him that my favourite thing I have ever seen him in is *The Birth of the Dubs*, an excellent documentary he narrated about the Dublin GAA team of yesteryear. I actually said to him, 'Forget all that Hollywood shite and make another Dubs documentary,' which made him laugh.

As he walks off to go out and do his interview, he bumps into Antoinette and my mam. He takes my mam by the shoulders and says, 'Your son is a feckin' legend,' and then just walks off. Me ma was chuffed.

We enter the green room and everyone congratulates me which sends my head spinning. I remember Antoinette taking a picture of me with Kevin Kilbane, and I kept repeating, over and over again, 'Annie, it's Kevin Kilbane.' Yep, I am a sap all right. But all the while I'm thinking, *Why can't everyone treat the ex-prisoner side of me this way?* It was as plain as the nose on your face why I was on the show. I was talking about life in prison. It's not like I could have said, 'Ah no. I was pulling your leg this whole time – in fact, I have actually lived a teetotal lifestyle, and I am currently studying to be a priest.' Everyone knew why I was there, and yet everyone treated me so well, even passing compliments on me. If only potential employers could show the same trust in me. I never once felt judged by any of these people, from the stars of today to the people who work behind the scenes in both television and radio. And I am so grateful to all of them for that.

I got to speak to Imelda May again, and I also got to meet her beautiful sister Edel, who to this day I am honoured to call my friend. Imelda informed me she was signing copies of her new album in town the next day and suggested I come into her with a copy of my book, which I did. And it was fantastic. We only spoke for a second that day as she was so busy, but I signed my book for her and she signed her (brilliant) album for me. Wow.

Ryan Tubridy entered the green room and made a beeline for my mam, and they just sat and spoke. He really took his time with my mam and she really appreciated it. I can honestly tell you that Ryan Tubridy is a total gentleman. He told Ronan to make sure my mam received the *there's one for everyone in the audience* package that was given out that evening. He took his time with all of us, and made us feel so very special, as did Ronan.

The drinks were flowing, which began to get to me a little, and so I asked my mam and Antoinette did they mind if we left. My mam looks at Antoinette and says, 'We don't mind in the slightest if he goes home Antoinette, do we? I think we'll be okay here, with all our new friends.'

'Yeah, Lily, you're right,' says Antoinette, 'you toddle on home there Gary. Myself and Lily are hitting the town with Imelda. We still love ya though.'

The two of them are falling around laughing as they take the piss out of me. I actually begged them to stay. I didn't want the fact that I was keeping alcohol at bay to ruin their night, but they were having none of it.

'We're only winding you up Gar,' says Antoinette.

'Of course we are Gary,' says my mam, 'besides, we'd probably feckin' need you with us to get us into these fancy places.'

Again, that mischievous laugh comes flowing from my mam. I love seeing her happy like this. Free from the drama and strife that unfortunately has always been a factor in her life. She could take the piss out of me for eternity if it made her happy. A taxi is arranged to bring us home, and before we all pile into it, I embrace Ronan one last time and thank him for everything.

'We'll stay in touch Gary,' he says, and I believed him.

When we get back to our apartment, Antoinette loads up the recording of my interview and the three of us watched it in tears. I felt proud, empowered. I also felt that I was most probably going to face a massive backlash. I was ready for that. But at that moment, nothing was going to alter the levels of pride I was experiencing.

In the days that followed, I received the following email from Ronan:

> Hi Gary, Just to let you know we got huge viewing figures on Friday night and 50% of people watching telly in Ireland were watching your interview (nearly 550,000), which is massive. So well done and thanks a million.
> Ronan.

As my mam would say, 'Jesus, Mary and Joseph'. How amazing is that? It truly is sublime what having some self-belief can do for you. Did I feel proud? More than I can even begin to articulate.

Oh, and Ronan kept his word and sent my mam her gift to her home. What a gentleman. What an experience!

What next?

Chapter 32

THE TRAVELS OF JOY

After my appearance on *The Late Late Show* the sales of *Joys of Joy* went through the roof. I was stunned. My friends' list on Facebook was increasing daily too, which made me feel so grateful and blessed. And it was a combination of these new friends, and some of the friends I already had, that saw the creation of a trend that did two things to me: (1) It made my heart skip a beat – countless times. (2) It made me really, really jealous.

My story seemed to resonate with a lot of people, and people were taking to social media in order to tell me so. From posts thanking me on writing the feckin' thing in the first place to full on reviews and recommendations. I never saw this coming. In fact, I had told my publisher that it might sell at least five copies, and then I would be dragged onto O'Connell Street in the heart of Dublin's fair city and tied to the Spire for a public flogging! Dramatic indeed, and probably not the best thing to say to a publisher who had just taken a massive risk with me. But that's the thing. Here I was, still trying to find my way as a free man. A guy who always had very low self-esteem, who carried the weight of the bad choices he had made like a chain around his neck. Yes, I wanted to try something different with how I told my prison story, but I honestly thought it would flop. I should have had more faith in myself. At the end of the day, if you don't believe in yourself, how do you expect others to believe in you? And if my publisher hadn't shown a belief in me? Well, I wouldn't be sitting here now, writing this sentence.

So I was moved and touched by people's kind words – daily.

My jealously came from a global trip that my book embarked on. It was so surreal. It started with photos from sun loungers. These photos were like the obligatory ones we receive from our family or friends when they are on their holidays. You know the ones, two tanned legs (either hairy as hell or smooth as silk) at the forefront, while the background consists of a beautiful swimming pool in a scene of pure tranquillity. But in the photos I was receiving there was a copy of my book resting on the thighs of the sender. And, remarkably, I had never met the people who sent me these snaps. Photos from Spain, Italy, South Africa, Germany – even feckin' Russia, although there were no tanned legs in that one. My book has seen more of Central Europe than I fuckin' have. I was quite jealous. Then, one day, Mrs. Kathi Twohig Hamelin came bursting into my world like a big ray of sunshine, and she did both of the above. She made my heart skip a beat, and made me really jealous.

I had met Kathi on Facebook, and our introduction came from another reason my book made me grateful. It got me back in touch with a guy I went to college with before my incarceration, Pol Ó Muireadhaigh. I was such a prick to this man back then, which shouldn't come as a surprise as I was basically just a prick to all. But Pol stood by me, never turning his back on me. He and his partner Lisa have been a constant stream of support, and I am very thankful for that. Pol is a patriotic Irish man and not afraid to speak his mind. He had set up a page on Facebook relating to the 100 year anniversary of Ireland gaining its independence, and one of the followers on this page was Kathi. They got on like a house on fire, and with Pol acting as my unofficial PR agent at this time, it wasn't long before he pointed Kathi in the direction of my book. Obtaining a copy would prove a waiting game for Kathi, as she lives in feckin' Delaware in the USA. But she ordered a copy through The Liffey Press website, and next thing I know she has sent me a friend request, which I happily accepted. Kathi then proceeded to give me daily updates as she digested my tale, and she really seemed to be enjoying it. I loved her quirky sense of humour, and she in turn loved my book. In fact, she loved it so much she did something amazing.

My publisher David rang me one day with a question: 'Hey Gary. Do you have family in Delaware?' I didn't, but I happened to mention Kathi's name to him. 'Yep, that's her. She has ordered, like, twenty copies of your book.'

I was stunned, but not as much as I was when I realised what she was doing. She loved my story so much that she wanted it to reach as wide an audience as it could. She would hand my book to friends and strangers and implore them to get in touch with me after they had finished it, which almost all of them did. She then took to the road. My book was about to embark on a real life road trip across the United States. And I was really jealous. Kathi would send me photos from famous landmarks, from the Grand Canyon to Salt Lake City to the streets of New York to the grave of an Irish Freedom Fighter in Philadelphia, my book was seeing it all. I was completely gobsmacked. Each photo would come with a wonderful story. Each person Kathi would meet on these *Travels of Joy* (as she christened it), would walk away from her knowing more about Mountjoy Prison than a lot of Irish folk do. I have never seen a blade of grass up close in America, and my newly acquired criminal record meant gaining access to the Land of the Brave would now be quite difficult. Yet here was my book doing fucking laps of this vast country. I was so jealous, yet extremely proud.

My friendship with Kathi has continued to grow. Her concern for my health is ever present, and her kind words help me when I'm struggling. I even received a gift in the post from her one day. It consisted of two hand-knitted pouches with the wool being woven by Kathi herself. Inside each one was a Mary Magdalene medal, and each medal had been blessed – twice! One of these medals was for me, and one was for Antoinette. We were both quite moved by such a thoughtful gesture so we decided to video call her via Facebook, and she got some shock. Her face when she saw us pulling funny faces as she connected to our call was priceless. I love this woman and her family with all my heart. So, the last thing she did for me really made me feel special.

Kathi wanted to surprise me, so through Pol she arranged for herself and her husband Raymond to come to Dublin. The initial reason for her coming was to surprise me at something The Off#enders were going to be a part of. More about that later. But for now, just know that she made that trip to meet me, and of course Pol too. I couldn't believe it. We sat in Café Nero beside St. Stephens Green Shopping Centre, and became one with the moment. Pol had his children with him, and soon we were joined by his partner Lisa. It was such a wonderful and special day. I had introduced Kathi to the sport of GAA football (hurling was a little too much for her American senses), and of course she was now an honorary Dub. So I gave her my Dublin jersey, which was a huge thing for me to do – I wouldn't give that jersey to Antoinette for God's sake! But knowing it would be worn on match day in Delaware was enough to win me over. Of course, Kathi was not to be out done. She yet again hand-knitted me something, this time a Dublin scarf. It has a wonderfully retro tone to it, with the majority of the scarf being sky-blue, with navy stripes. I love it and I love this special lady so much too. And to think it all started with Kathi reading all about how I served my prison sentence. How amazing is that?

I am still very jealous of how much of this beautiful world my book is seeing though. *Travels of Joy* you say? Jammy fecker of a book I counter!

Chapter 33

(Strong) Women Rule the World

Thankfully, Antoinette is not the jealous type. I say this because there have been a lot of women from all walks of life who have reached out to me after reading *Joys of Joy*. There have been plenty of men too, and I am the polar opposite of sexist, so I would be equally proud if it was a man or a woman who shared their opinion of my book. But no matter who gets in touch with me, I always reply to them. I want them to know how good they have made me feel by taking time out from their day to talk to me.

One day, I came across an advert looking for writers for a film production company. It was being set up by a young lady by the name of Shireen Langan. I don't know what came over me, but I gathered the confidence from somewhere and applied. I suppose my thinking was pretty simple. I needed money as I was still sidelined with 'me arse' and all the problems it was giving me, and I suppose I felt I could easily sit and write for a living. I couldn't believe I was about to apply for a position completely outside my comfort zone and qualifications.

I ran it by Antoinette, and she said to me, 'Why not Gar? I personally love your writing, as do all the people who have read your book. Go for it.'

So, with Antoinette's backing, I sent an email to Shireen that was comparable in length to this book you are now holding. She replied almost instantly asking if I would like to meet up. I asked if the same Café Nero from a previous chapter would be okay, and it suited Shireen perfectly. We arranged a time, but as I made my way in to meet her, I began my usual fretting. *What are you doing man? You write one bleedin' book and now you think you're Wordsworth?* I thought to myself. I even stopped halfway and contemplated turning back. But I am many things, and thankfully rude is not one of them. And once I met Shireen, I had no reason for concern.

She was sitting outside Café Nero as I approached, sporting very cool shades as her long, dark hair shone in the day's sunlight. I ambled over and burst out with, 'Howya. Gary. Pleased to meet ya. Can I get you anything? And by the way, thank you so much for agreeing to meet me.'

'Eh ... okay. Take a breath there, Gary,' laughs Shireen, followed by, 'I'm good for coffee thanks.'

I laugh and join her at the table, and we hit it off almost instantly. This young lady is a tour de force of talent. Sitting proudly at the age of 23, she has done more with her life than I could even dream of doing with mine. She had worked as an intern in radio and television, and was currently studying both disciplines in college. She informed me that she was also currently the manager of a band as well. I was waiting for her to tell me she had just discovered the cure for cancer over her breakfast that morning. I was very impressed with this young lady's drive and ambition. Shireen had asked me to bring samples of my work, but of course, I only really had one sample. And so I handed her a copy of my book.

'Oh, wow, that is really impressive Gary,' says Shireen, followed by, 'so, please – tell me everything.'

Jesus Shireen, you may have talents coming out of your ears, but you still have a lot to learn about me. Asking me to tell you everything is a risk you take at your own expense.

I finished telling my story, non-stop, after about twenty minutes or so. I gave her the edited version! But Shireen was really impressed. Yet again, I find being open and honest about my story really stood to me. Shireen tells me of her idea of starting up this film production company, and I am really impressed. She was doing all of this by herself. She had secured cameramen and sound engineers, and she felt my writing would be the perfect compliment. I was stunned. I realised this wasn't a 'job' in the conventional sense, but I felt I had just found someone who would encourage my own creative thoughts. And that is just what happened.

Shireen has interviewed me about my time spent in Mountjoy for her college work, and we also came up with the idea of interviewing people from all walks of life, thus proving that every single one of us has a story to tell. We decided to call this project *The Secret Voice Inside My Head,* and after considering the kind of people we would love to interview, I almost jumped out of my seat as I say, 'I've got the most perfect lady, who I am pretty confident would allow us to film her telling her story.' Shireen seemed intrigued, so I began telling her of the second strong woman from this chapter – Jenny.

Jenny must have been *Joys of Joy's* biggest fan, after my mam of course. But the way in which we got chatting ... well, our friendship almost never happened at all. Jenny read my tale and sent me a private mail on Facebook asking, 'Here Gary? Did you do a poem for "such and such" (she mentioned a name here) while you were in Mountjoy?' What Jenny was referring to was the fact that I would write poems whilst housed in Mountjoy for the lads to give to their loved ones. I would make it look like they sent it, and would charge a half ounce of tobacco for my services (I had to live). I would never disclose the identity of these men as, firstly, it was not my place to name anyone who has spent time behind bars, and secondly, I would never break the trust these lads put in me.

Jenny's mail continued: 'A friend of mine, her fella was in there and he gave her a poem, and I fuckin' doubt this fella created it for her. In fact, I doubt this fucker can write.'

As much as Jenny's mail made me laugh, I moved quickly to nip this in the bud. My reply was simple: '*I will never* give away the identity of any man I served my time with.' I thought that Jenny would most probably never get in touch with me again after that, but she replied instantly and told me how much she admired me for saying what I did. I didn't expect that, if I'm honest, nor did I expect the friendship that has grown between the two of us since.

Jenny is one of the more special humans that inhabit this planet of ours. And trust me when I tell you that this incredibly strong woman does not have it easy. A single and very proud mother to three beautiful children, Jenny's role as a mam is pushed to its limits daily. Her youngest son is on the autistic spectrum, as is Jenny herself, albeit only slightly in her case. She faces challenges that most of us would run a mile from and she embraces them with a gusto that is quite remarkable. She never moans or plays the 'poor me' card. She is so very inspiring. She is also an incredible writer, but sadly, like a lot of us, she has not one drop of self-belief. But when she decided to put up a post on Facebook, which was basically a review of *Joys of Joy*, she showed the world just what she can do. The feckin' post went viral. It is honestly hilarious, but also hard hitting and heartfelt. I even showed it to my publisher David, who agreed with me that it was excellent. And so, to this day, I try with all my might to encourage Jenny to write. I feel she has a masterpiece inside her that is just waiting to be unleashed. I got her to start a blog, and I got excited every time she put up a new entry. Jenny has a way of telling what should be a heart wrenching story, such as how autism controls the smallest of things in her family's lives, in the funniest, most positive way possible. So when I told Jenny about myself and Shireen's project, she of course said she would allow us to film her telling her story. And although life has prevented that from happening so far, I know it will happen, and then all will get to see just how special this lady is.

And that goes for Shireen as well. She has way too many talents to remain anonymous, and I can't wait for the day when she finally lands her big break.

My book was bringing all these wonderful and special people into my life. I was quite moved by it all. And they just kept coming...

Chapter 34

DEE(LICOUS) AND EILISH(OUS)

Jenny was telling everyone she met that they had to read my book. In fact, she was giving away copies and replacing them almost daily. Jesus! But Jenny had one last trick up her sleeve for me, and that was to facilitate a meeting for me with Dee Keogh.

Jenny and Dee have known each other for years, but with Dee moving to Kerry it had been a long time since they had seen each other. But the universe did what it had to do, and one day Jenny spots Dee – in feckin' Dublin! She runs over, and without saying hello, she instead rants, 'You have to meet the fella who wrote this book.' Jenny, acting like my very own PA, then hands Dee a copy of *Joys of Joy*. 'This book is like American Express to me, I never leave home without it,' starts Jenny, followed by, 'he is the male version of you Dee.' And that, right there, is the best compliment I have ever received. Although being compared to Dee Keogh is an honour I'm not convinced I am worthy of.

Phone calls are made, and soon Dee was arranging to come up from Kerry to meet me. She had read my book in one sitting and informed me that she was, quote, 'fuckin' dyin' to meet me. And from the second we were in each other's company, nothing has been the same in my world ever since. Dee is the most beautiful person, both inside and out, and it's her positivity and outlook on life that sets her apart. She trains people in a programme known as STEPS, which gives all who attend the tools and abilities to realise their fullest potential. Dee works for an organisation in Kerry known as NEWKD, and on the morning of our first meeting she informs me, in no uncertain terms, that she wants me to be a keynote speaker at an event they had coming up entitled 'Powering the Community, Plugging into Potential'. Basically, she empowers all who are lucky to be in her company. All she wants is for you to know what a special person you truly are.

Dee and I became very close. She loved Antoinette solely from reading about her in my book, so the day they finally met was a beautiful moment in my life. I knew there was one other person who would greatly benefit from a good 'dose of Dee' – my mam. And that particular meeting was also very special.

I had arranged to hook up with Dee in Dublin's city centre. She had told me there was someone I needed to meet and she would bring this person along with her. I asked would it be okay if my mam joined us, and this made Dee very happy. She was dying to meet my mam, but she seemed even more excited that it was going to be this day that she would get to meet her. Mam and I met in town that morning, but my heart grew heavy as I listened to her insecurities come flowing out of her. 'I won't go with you to meet this lady Gary. I'll only be in the way,' she said. This side to my mam has always broken my heart. She never feels good enough. But I knew what just five minutes with Dee would do for her, and so I insisted she came with me.

'If you're not going, then neither am I Lily,' I said to her.

'Okay Gary, but if I'm in the way, I'll just leave.' Little did we know that this particular day was going to be all about Lily Cunningham.

We arrive at my favourite Café Nero, and inside sits Dee, holding the biggest bunch of flowers for my mam that I had ever seen. I had already told Dee everything about my mam, and she had also met her through the pages of *Joys of Joy*, and had seen her face on the night I appeared on *The Late Late Show*. So when they meet, Dee embraces my mam and tells her over and over again how much she loves her. A massive smile formed on my mam's face, and it was about to become even bigger. Dee kept winking at me and saying, 'Wait 'til ya see who is coming in. Both of you are going to love her.'

Next thing we know, a well-dressed, very attractive lady is giving Dee a hug. She says hello to myself and my mam and then quickly heads to the counter in order to buy everyone a coffee. My mam has turned into a bit of a 'Beatles Fan' whereas I am sitting there, completely oblivious. Dee says to me, 'Do you not recognise her Gary?'

'Should I?' I say, half sounding like a bit of a smart arse.

'*Mrs. Browns Boys*,' starts Dee, before the penny came thundering down in my head.

'*Fuck off!* Is that 'Winnie' from *Mrs. Browns Boys*? Is that Eilish O'Carroll?' I am almost attacking Dee with these questions.

'The one and only,' replies Dee. 'Oh, I *knew* it,' says my mam. And that was what made this so very special. My mam is one of the biggest fans of *Mrs. Browns Boys*, and her favourite character from the show was at the counter buying her a coffee. When Eilish returned, she received the hero's welcome (and a barrage of 'sorrys' from yours truly) that she duly deserved. We spent hours together that day, with Eilish and my mam hitting it off like a house on fire. In fact, at one stage, my mam was correcting Eilish on her lines from *Mrs. Browns Boys*. Like I said, my mam is a super-fan. Eilish has a heart so big she could give love to the entire human race and still have some left over when she was finished. What she and Dee did for my mam that day is still ever-present in her. They empowered her and reminded her of her true worth. Dee, Eilish and Lily are still very close today. Three ladies. Three friends. Three nutters!

We then all took a little road trip down to Tralee together. Eilish and I were keynote speakers at the aforementioned event that Dee was running. And what a day that was. The day was filled with inspirational speakers who stood in a room filled with over 200 people and told their stories. Each one would make the hairs on the back of your neck stand to attention. In fact, I actually questioned if I could take to the stage after hearing these people share their own hero's journey in all their glory.

I went to the toilet and began splashing water on my face. The toilet seemed empty so I began talking to myself in the mirror. 'Believe in yourself Gary. You can do this. Look at all the wonderful people you have met today who really want to hear you speak. Snap out of it now Gary. Cop on and get out there.' As I finish my mantra, I hear a toilet flush in one of the stalls behind me. I felt a little embarrassed, but decided to face it like a man, right up until the door of the stall opened and there stood a very elegant lady. I nearly fuckin' died! I thought to myself, *Well, that's you off to Mountjoy again Gar*. As I apologised profusely and grabbed hold of the door to make my exit, I see from the sign that it was actually not me that was in the wrong toilet. This lady and I share a brief laugh before I cancel the prolonging of her embarrassment and make my way out of the toilet. Very strange indeed.

My talk went really well. Every single person in attendance took the time to congratulate me, and again I was so touched by their total lack of judgement towards me. But there was one very special moment towards the end that hit me hard. While I was serving time in Loughan House, I entered the Writing in Prison competition, which was part of Listowel

Writers Week, and I won it – twice. And as I gave my talk that day in Tralee, I noticed a man sitting in the very front row. It turns out that this man, Séan, had graded my first entry in the Writing in Prison competition, and it was his decision to award me first place. It was such a wonderful moment in my life, as I gave a hug to the very first person who encouraged me as a writer.

Eilish's talk that day was fantastic too. She finished with a song she wrote herself, and we were all only too happy to join in and sing with her.

Dee had one more thing she wanted to do for me, and this included my mam. After my talk, I was presented with a beautiful ornament of a slate. The artist and creator of the piece, Liz Brown, had drawn the cover of my book on its face. Below it was the phrase I coined in prison, 'It's not the time you do, it's what you do with your time.' I was blown away. Dee then grabs the mic and says, 'Could we have Lily Conway (my mam's maiden name) up to the stage for a second please?'

My poor mam could be overheard saying, 'Oh, please don't ask me to talk.' But Dee just wanted to give her a gift of her own. And that gift was a slate similar to mine, only this one had beautiful flowers hand-drawn on its front, with the lyrics to the song I wrote about her in Mountjoy sitting proudly beside them. I called this song 'She' and it tells the story of my love for my mam through music. I will always be proud that this quite uplifting song was created in a very dark and negative place.

On the back of mam's slate were these words: 'Thank you, Lily, for sharing your inspirational son with us.' I burst. In fact, I actually couldn't see my mam's reaction through the tears in my eyes. The entire room was moved. Dee then hands me a guitar, and asks me to sing that very song. Was she fuckin' insane? I could barley speak. But Dee whispered in my ear that she believed in me. And so, somehow, I managed to sit on a stool, and sing my song for my mam straight to her in a room full of strangers. It was pure magic, as was the whole day. And this day happened because of Dee Keogh and NEWKD.

So having Dee and Eilish around has actually been life-changing for me, Antoinette, my mam and my entire family. Antoinette and I have been to the home of Eilish and her beautiful and very funny partner, Marian. The two ladies cooked for us, and it was a perfect evening. Eilish and Marian went even further when they brought Antoinette, my mam and Antoinette's mam backstage at a live performance of *Mrs. Browns Boys* in Dublin's 3 Arena. My health prevented me from going, and when I heard from Antoinette and the two 'mammies' how well they were treated, I have to admit to feeling a little jealous. What a lovely thing for Eilish and Marian to do. The two ladies also joined Dee one Saturday afternoon, as I brought them to my brother Gerry's home. Dee got to meet Cunny that day, and she was delighted. She has a bit of a thing for aul' Cunny. But she also sensed a sadness in him, and she wants to help him. And that is exactly what she is doing today.

The future for Gary, Dee and Eilish looks quite exciting too. Whatever could we be up to?

All will be revealed ... in time.

Chapter 35

Heading Back Inside and Reaching Out to YouthReach

The reaction to *Joys of Joy* in the prisons dotted around this island seemed quite positive. This made me happy, as I had made a conscious effort not to attack the Irish Prison Service when telling my tale. My thinking was, *why would I speak badly of a service that assisted in saving my life?* So when I was asked to go back inside in order to speak to some of the lads, I was really honoured. I received invites to three prisons, Wheatfield, Portlaoise and The Midlands. Here's how they went...

Wheatfield

I had been asked by an officer connected with the school in Wheatfield if I would come in and talk to a small group of men who were attending classes there. I happily agreed, and on the morning of my talk was filled with nervous excitement. I got two buses over to this intimidating structure, and as I made my way up the long driveway that leads to the prison's entrance, I found I was beginning to feel nervous. It wasn't meeting the prisoners that brought on these nerves. Why would I be nervous meeting them? It wasn't long ago that I was in their very position. It was the prison officers I was nervous to meet. I was worried that they might be of the impression that I thought I was something I'm not. And nothing could be further from the truth.

The first officer I met at the jail's entrance seemed a little off with me. I explained who I was, handed him my passport as a form of ID, and he just mumbles something under his breath and walks off. Great start! Soon the same officer returns and escorts me to an area with lockers in order for me to leave my phone and other belongings in a safe place.

'So, you wrote a book, yeah?' he asks.

'I did officer,' I reply.

'Good man yourself. Now, grab a locker there, put your stuff in, and head back to the entrance. They'll look after you there. I am fuckin' wrecked. Long aul' shift. Best of luck in everything you do Gary.' I felt like a fool. He wasn't off with me, just tired. I can be such an idiot sometimes.

Soon, the officer who invited me appears and escorts me through the corridors of this vast prison. I almost instantly get that 'Mountjoy' feeling inside me. The similarities were a little too close for comfort. I stop at every locked gate and wait as the officer opens it, which transports me back to the dank D Wing of The Joy. The officer was great craic, though, and she kept my mind off these thoughts.

We arrived at the school, and I see one tall stool, surrounded by a few of the famous grey plastic chairs that I spent two years and nice months plonking my arse on. The school in Wheatfield prison seemed a lot bigger than the one in Mountjoy. It basically consisted of a long, wide corridor with doors on both sides leading into the various classrooms. Soon the lads started to arrive, and I am amazed to see that a lot of them are holding copies of my book. I had never done anything like this before, yet I was feeling very confident. But as soon as the lads take to the plastic chairs, and I ease myself onto the stool ('me arse' was still torturing me), one of the men feels he must pull me up on something.

'Howya. Listen Gary, I have a bit of a problem with one part of your book. You refer to a prisoner as a 'tablet-guzzling zombie'. I don't think it's right to make fun of his addiction, especially with you being an addict yourself.'

I was frozen to the spot. Everything I wanted to say to these men went out the window. The lad who pulled me up on this was referring to a prisoner from *Joys of Joy* who had actually given me a punch! In the chapter, I do call him that, but in my head I was creating a caricature of him. I never thought my description of this fella would upset anyone, and that was never my intention. I was ashamed.

I could see that this lad held quite a lot of pull with the other prisoners who were there that morning. I also got the impression that he would have no bother going toe to toe with me – either physically or through the spoken word. But I had no argument with him. I just had one point to make.

'He gave me a fuckin' dig,' I start, 'if someone hit you a dig now, you wouldn't be like *ahh, what a lovely, lovely person*. You would most probably call him every name under the sun.'

'I'd fuckin' knock him out,' replied this man, who for now I will refer to as 'A'. This brings laughter to all.

'Great answer,' I reply, 'but what I am trying to say is, of course I was going to slag him off in the book but, believe it or not, I meant the slag to be more of a joke. I never looked at it in the way that you just explained it. And I feel a lot of regret now if I'm honest. I feel like I dropped the ball on that one.'

This honest answer seemed to be okay with 'A' and he actually informed me he really enjoyed the book.

I tried my best to give my talk, which was tough, as I was a little distracted and nervous. But when I began talking about The Off#enders, the mood in the room lifted. I was asked a barrage of questions ranging from how we would write songs to my personal favourite, 'How the fuck did you record a bleedin' album?' One of the lads even stood up and did a rap, and he was excellent. At the end of the talk, I showed the lads The Off#enders video for 'Iron Sky', which really impressed them. And as the video played on the large projector, 'A' approached me and thanked me for how I handled his critique.

'We were all convinced you were gonna be a prick about it, and we were ready for that,' he said.

'Not at all man,' I reply, 'in fact, thanks so much. You really opened my eyes. I just hope you now understand my thinking.'

'I do pal,' says 'A,' followed by, 'I'll look ya up when I get out, yeah?'

'Make sure you do,' I say, 'and stay safe man.'

That evening I took to my blog and wrote about the day I had just had with these lads. I then sent the blog's link to the officer who had invited me, and I asked if she could print out a copy and give it to 'A'.

I really hope she did.

Portlaoise

This time I was invited by one of this famous jail's psychologists. I arrived at the daunting gates where she was standing waiting for me. 'Thank you so much for coming Gary,' she says with a smile.

I have to admit my confidence took quite a hammering after Wheatfield. The last group of people I wanted to let down were prisoners. So I shifted my focus. I began constructing a talk in my head that would hopefully instil in these men the knowledge that, with the right amount of hard work and self-belief, a life outside these prison walls is achievable. I was ready to rock. Alas, my bum wasn't. I was in crippling pain that morning. But in the email I had received from this lady, she told me how much these lads were looking forward to me coming in. So there was no way I was going to let them down.

Walking into Portlaoise prison is quite unnerving. This is Ireland's maximum security prison so it has gun towers manned with armed Irish soldiers. As you make your way towards the entrance, you can't help but feel there is a gun trailing you. 'I make this short walk every morning, and it still makes me feel uneasy,' says the psychologist. We then met the officers at the jail's entrance, and their mood was starkly different.

'Ahh, it's yer man who wrote that book,' laughs one of them.

'It was shite, keep him in,' offers another.

This goes a long way to calming my nerves. I also met an officer who asked me if I would sign a copy of my book for him. It was a huge honour for me. Unfortunately, he hadn't got it with him, and although we arranged to meet when I was heading back out of the jail later that day, it slipped both of our minds. I was raging to be honest, as I would have loved to have signed that particular copy.

We made our way to the school, which again seemed so much bigger than the one in Mountjoy. I entered the large, airy classroom and was shocked to see how many lads had turned up. There is a notable ceasing of conversation between the prisoners as I enter, which unnerves me a little. I look around the magnolia-painted classroom and note that every one of the lads in attendance is staring at me. Suddenly, the room begins to feel less airy and bright. I am introduced by the head of the Irish Red Cross (prison division). This man had already met me before, during my own incarceration, when I was the leader of the Red Cross faction in Loughan House. I thank him for his kind words in his introduction, and note a slight quiver in my voice. I was feeling really nervous. I knew I needed an icebreaker.

'Howya lads, my name is Gary Cunningham. Lads, look, me arse is like a bag of fuckin' lego here, so don't mind the faces I pull or the fact I can't sit down. Right, let's get this show on the road.' The room unites in laughter. Phew! That talk was incredible. I was asked a ton of questions, and I tried to answer them all as best as I could. Some of the lads took to the floor to highlight their own personal struggles, and I felt very privileged as I listened to their tales being told in such an open and honest fashion. I tried with all my might to give the lads a bit of self-worth. I urged them not to write themselves off, as there was already a world out there willing to do that for them. I recommended that they didn't go down the road of feeling sorry for themselves once they were released, and I begged them not to give up at the first knock back they received, as there was going to be a few of them to deal with. I actually got a standing ovation, but this may have come from the fact I played a guitar and sang for them an Off#enders original song called 'Addicted to Me' at the end of my talk. Or maybe the standing ovation was simply because I had stopped fuckin' talking! They were a very intelligent and welcoming bunch of lads, and I am so grateful for the time and respect they afforded me.

The Midlands

The last stop on this whistle-stop tour of some of Ireland's jails came after I received a phone call from none other than Mrs. Gavin, the lady who was the Governor during my stay in Loughan House. Governor Gavin is now the Governor of the entire Portlaoise campus, which includes The Midlands Prison. I think she knew I would do almost anything for her, but when she told me that it was actually the men serving life that wanted to hear me talk I froze. I know this sounds stupid, but I felt my approach of 'work hard and keep fighting' was more suited to men who were nearing their release. I suppose I felt I had nothing to offer these men. But Governor Gavin told me not to be so foolish. And I always listen to her.

I was brought to the corridor that houses the Governor's office, and as I put my hand on the handle, the door opens and there stands Governor Gavin. We embrace and both shed a tear.

There was a mix-up that day so the lads in attendance now consisted of half who were serving life, and half who had various different sentences. Again, I was escorted to the prison's school and the room they had chosen for the talk actually reminded me of my old classroom from sixth class. It was a long, wide room, and all its walls were lined with shelves holding books and copybooks. The lads start to arrive in, and again I am shocked at how many have decided to come. I gave another rousing speech, similar to the one I gave in Portlaoise, but it was a comment from one of the prisoners that really struck a chord with me.

I was in the middle of telling the lads that, yes, it is really difficult to get a job, but that they must never give up. One of the lads raises his hand and patiently waits for me to get to him. When I do, he says the following:

'Would you put your clothes into a broken washing machine? And if you did, would you expect your clothes to come out okay?'

Of course my answer was no.

'So how do people out there expect us to come out okay, when the process of rehabilitation in our jails is broken?' Powerful. And I fully agree with this man. The current system of rehabilitation in our jails could be vastly improved. Of course it won't be a perfect fit for all as there are those who couldn't care less about rehabilitation or reform. But the majority of prisoners do, and I am a strong believer in highlighting this issue on behalf of them, and on behalf of myself too.

Another moving talk with a really good bunch of men, although I did have one embarrassing moment. A real 'Gary' moment. As I was leaving, each prisoner came up to me, gave me a hug, thanked me, and wished me all the best. It was very touching. So when this man with glasses was standing there waiting for me, I assumed he was a prisoner. 'How long did ya get pal?' I ask.

'Oh ... em, no Gary. I am actually the English teacher here. I was just wondering if you could sign this for me.' He hands me a copy of my book just as my cheeks turn bright red.

Before I move on to the last group I gave a talk to, I want to leave you with this English teacher's parting words to me. I'm sure you can guess what state these words left me in:

> I just wanted to thank you for writing such an incredible book Gary. It really struck a chord with me. And I love how passionate you are about education being the key to reforming prisoners. I couldn't agree more. In fact, your story had such an impact on me that I turned down the chance of becoming a primary school teacher, and instead I applied for a position here in the Midlands prison, in the hope that I can make even a small bit of a difference. This is only my third week, but I feel I am making some headway already. So, thank you Gary.

Wow...

Youthreach Dundalk

Before I sign off on this chapter, I would like to take a moment to praise these young adults. This last section is not about my talks, or how I approach them, but about a very impressive bunch of young men and women who are at a difficult junction in their lives. There is peer pressure and temptation all around them, and it is exactly this type of group that I long to give talks to. I would tell them all the stuff I purposely left out of *Joys of Joy* – all the violence, fear, loneliness and depression that goes hand in hand with being a prisoner.

I was invited to this particular Youthreach in Dundalk by a lovely guy named Paul. The time, energy and dedication that Paul and his fellow colleagues give to these young adults is to be commended. I was looking forward to chatting to these young men and women, but I foolishly assumed, because I was dealing with mostly late teens, that I would have a few 'messers' or 'class clowns' to handle. Yet again, I was wrong.

They were so respectful and sat in total silence as I talked about the horrors of prison life. If they wanted to address something, they would raise their hand and wait until they were asked. And their questions were excellent. They craved knowledge. I was so impressed with this group, with their impeccable manners and how they seemed to absorb my story. At the end of my talk, one of the group's leaders addressed both myself and the group at the same time.

'Incredible talk Gary. You're a natural. And the way we gauge how interesting our guest speakers are is by how many get up to use the toilet during the talk.' Only one girl got up to use the toilet during my talk, and when she came back in she asked what she had missed.

I enjoyed every one of the talks from this chapter. Never in a million years did I think I would be standing in front of a group of people discussing how I turned my life around. I got so much out of each talk, and I came away from them feeling like I had learned something new. I really hope they got something out of it from me too.

And people say I talk too much!

Chapter 36

'CHARLIE CHAPLAIN'
AND THE BISHOP

One of the (many) perks of writing my book was being forwarded letters sent to my publisher that were addressed to me. One such letter was actually handwritten by a really friendly lady by the name of Aideen, who resides in County Offaly. She congratulated me on the writing of my story. She also mirrored what I seemed to be hearing from others who were good enough to finish my tale, when she told me that she 'laughed, cried, got angry, cried some more, and laughed some more'. We still keep in touch, although I type my letters to her. I do this because my handwriting is deplorable. I am lucky that books are not published in the handwriting of the author or not one person would be able to read my ramblings.

My publisher David, who was recovering from hip surgery at the time, asked me to come to his home one day. He said that he had a surprise for me. When I arrived at his house, he and his wife Darina could not have done more to make me feel welcome. Darina wanted to feckin' cook for me at one stage. The fact that these two people are now what I would consider close friends plasters a permanent smile across my face.

The sun was shining this day, so David suggested we sit out in his back garden and make the most of its harmful UV rays. We talked business – book sales, future marketing plans etc. – and then he told me of his surprise. He had received an email from Charlie Chaplain. I was shocked. In fact, I was feckin' convinced he had long passed away! David clears things up.

'So, I got this email, which has a letter addressed to you attached to it. In the body of the email, this man Charlie explains that he is a chaplain in a prison in the English Midlands – hence Charlie Chaplain.'

I have to admit I was a little disappointed. Although, hoping the actual Charlie Chaplin had been reincarnated and handed a copy of my book, which in turn he loved, was probably wishful thinking!

David explains to me that Charlie had mentioned something in this email that kind of blew him away. He explains that Charlie (who's second name was actually Sweeney) had said that *Joys of Joy* was one of the best books he had ever read. There was an English phone number in this email, so David decided to give him a ring. And when he spoke to Charlie on the phone, Charlie reiterated that same point. I was stuck to my chair. I could never have imagined anyone making a comment like that about anything I had done. Charlie made sure to say to David that he felt it was imperative that he and I meet, and he asked for me to give him a call. And once I read the letter that he had sent me, I had absolutely no problem making that call!

In this letter, after he complimented me on telling my story, Charlie explained his idea. And here is this idea, in Charlie's own words:

> I have a vision of setting up a real coherent residential community style to support the young and the not-so-young who have nowhere else to go after leaving prison. I was wondering if you

would be interested in meeting up with me in a few weeks' time when I am next in Dublin. In your book you say that you are searching for something, that would give your life a sense of fulfilment and meaning. This project might be what you are looking for where you could combine all your talents and skills into one, supporting a section of our society that are very vulnerable and often ostracised by society as losers and no hoppers etc. Your achievements throughout your time on the inside were next to none. If you can achieve so much on the inside, think what you can do on the outside, if you keep your head. The name I have chosen for my project is the Dawnbreakers Community, more information on that later. Remember Gary, you can't go forward if you keep looking back – the future is now. Thanks for the book. I am going to get a few copies and give it to the lads in the prison who want to change their lives for the better.

Yours Sincerely

Charlie Sweeney (known on the prison landings as Charlie Chaplain).

I was very impressed with this Dawnbreakers idea. I am firmly of the belief that we need to try something new with the men and women who are released from our jails, and I felt Charlie's idea might be a good starting point. We spoke on the phone, and I found him to be quite a character, with his booming Donegal tone almost deafening me. I told him I loved his idea, and I shared with him the story of how a young student by the name of Nela had recently reached out to me. Nela was doing her Masters thesis on the 'Reintegration of Prisoners Back into Our Society,' and she asked if I would take part. I was only too happy to. Nela handed me a disposable camera and asked me to tell my story of reintegration through my eyes, by taking as many photos as I could. Nela would then interview me as we both looked at the photos I took, and I would explain to her why I had taken them. For photo one, I lay on my stomach and took a picture from the bottom of a hill, with the camera aimed at the hilltop. My idea with this picture was, 'It can feel like an uphill struggle trying to fit in after you are released.' For photo two, I walked to the top of this hill, and snapped a picture once I got there. My idea here was, 'But once you reach the top, there is so much beauty to take in, and you feel like the struggle was worth it.' Nela loved the pictures I took. I just hope they helped her get the marks she was looking for.

Charlie was impressed by Nela too, adding that he would love to meet her at some stage. He made that trip to Dublin, and we met for coffee and a chat. We are currently in the process of trying to make Charlie's *Dawnbreakers* dream become a reality, although it is a tough process. I find you can't mention giving someone who deserves it a second chance without being labeled a 'bleeding-heart liberal'. But, as I have said to Charlie, I am used to knock backs and rejections and they don't stop me, especially if I believe in something.

But it seemed the church wasn't finished with me just yet.

I'll never forget that phone call from David. 'Gary! There was a letter addressed to me, but once I opened it, I quickly noted it was actually for you. Gary? It's from a bishop!'

I actually burst out laughing. What? A feckin' *bishop*? But my question to David was one of genuine concern. 'Am I in trouble boss ('boss' has become my nickname for David)? Am I being excommunicated?'

This makes David laugh. 'Quite the opposite Gary,' he says, 'in fact, this letter is something else. I'll send you a picture of it now, and I'll give it to you when I see you next.' Here is what The Bishop (Bishop John Kirby) had to say:

Dear Mr. Cunningham

Looking for something to read while on holiday, I bought your book, *Joys of Joy*, on Sat 5th of August. I finished it five days later. It was 'un-put-downable' and I enjoyed every page and every chapter. I have rarely come across anything as fresh or as positive as this account of your personal growth and development during your 2.75 years of incarceration in Mountjoy and Loughan House. Your acknowledgement of your own issues was brilliant.

I have no great interest in rock music and I probably will not be a listener to The Off#enders, but I was still fascinated by the story of its beginnings and performances. Well done on the band and on your account of it.

Most of all I was 'blown away' (*I'm sure this was a little dig at yours truly, as this is a statement I find very appropriate these days*) by your accounts of your relationships with your mother, your girlfriend Antoinette, with Fitzer, Cunny, No. 2 and many of your former colleagues in both institutions. I also liked the positive way you presented so many of the prison staff in Mountjoy. It would have been easier to be negative when it came to this.

Críost Linn,

Bishop John Kirby.

Jaysis! What a letter to receive. I emailed the bishop back and thanked him from the bottom of my heart. We agreed to meet for coffee the next time he was in Dublin.

So, between 'Charlie Chaplain' and The Bishop, I have received holy blessings from servants of 'The Big Man' himself.

Yes Bishop, you're right. I am *blown away*!

Chapter 37

LILY

'*Families are like branches on a tree. They grow in different directions, yet their roots remain as one.*'

I came across the above statement one day somewhere on the internet. There was no name attached to it, just these simple yet powerful words. So of course I grabbed a pen, jotted it down and thought to myself, *damn − I wish I had come up with that!* My relationship with my family has improved tenfold since my release from prison. If truth be known, I had an almost nonexistent relationship with them before I entered the massive blue gates of Mountjoy, but that is a reflection on me and not them.

In my brothers, Gerry, Noel and Jason, I have three ready-made role models. They each improved the Cunningham family by marrying three beautiful and strong women, Barbara, Bernadette, and Niamh. Each of these couples have gifted the Cunningham clan with fantastic children, each one special and unique in their own way. And yet, I was nothing but a gobshite to all of them before I got sent away. But they never turned their backs to me...

One of the best things I have done with my life since my release is show these people how sorry I am through my actions. I didn't make them false promises, I just knuckled down and worked as hard as I could so they could see the changes for themselves. And now, our personal relationships have vastly improved. Take my eldest brother Gerry. Before I ended up in prison, all I ever did was let this man down. In the past, if my phone rang and I saw Gerry's name on the screen, I knew I was in trouble. But today, Gerry rings me just for a chat and some gossip, and every time he does I am left with a massive lump in my throat. All I ever wanted was the closeness of a brotherly relationship, and it was always on offer to me by all of my brothers. I was just too selfish to see it. But today we're like the four musketeers. Yes there are arguments and falling out to beat the band. But this is real life. We are the Cunninghams, not the feckin' Waltons.

And sitting proudly at the top of our particular family tree is the root of all our branches, our mam, Lily. I've been told that my mam fell quite ill when she was pregnant with me and spent a number of weeks in hospital before and after my birth. So literally, from day one, I've been hard work for this lady. And yet, all she has ever done is to love me unconditionally. Through my teens I was a little fucker. I drank from a young age. I gave cheek and caused rows. I brought embarrassment to my family home with dreadful behaviour and the telling of lies. Nobody could tell *me* what to do, because I knew *everything*. Still, my Mam loved and protected me. It took me being ripped from her loving grasp and thrown into prison to make me realise just how special she truly was. How pathetic is that? I always loved her but I was too wrapped up in my own bullshit to show her.

My mam needed a new hip, and just after I got sent down her condition deteriorated. Seeing her struggle up to see me every Monday in Mountjoy soon put manners on me. I hated myself for making my mam enter that kip of a building, for putting her through searches and the embarrassment of having to visit her youngest behind bars. But it didn't faze her one bit. I saw my mother's love in all its glory during the darkest time of my life. So I made a promise to myself: *Once you get home Gary, mam and her happiness is your number one priority.*

And that is exactly what I have done. You could say I am just making up for lost time and you would be correct. You could also say that all the time I now spend with my mam is born out of guilt and shame and regret, and again you would be spot on. But better late than never. I am so lucky to still have my mam by my side. So I make sure that every day she spends on this earth, she is filled to the brim with love and care. And she is so easy to please. She doesn't want gifts, in fact she is impossible to buy for. If you do get her something, she runs straight out and buys *you* a gift in return, even on her feckin' birthday! Material things mean nothing to her. All she wants is your time. She has a beautiful saying, one which sums her up perfectly: 'Your presence is my favourite present.'

With my health in the toilet (literally), I needed to turn the negative fact that I was out of work into something more positive. So I focused on my mam. I would turn up uninvited and sit in her kitchen in the home where she reared me, and listen to her talk about the love she has for her sisters and brothers, and for her own mammy and daddy. I get lost in time, hanging on her words as she relives her youth for me. I am, and forever will be, in total awe of her.

I had the brainwave of bringing her out once a week for breakfast, and this has become one of my better decisions. Every Wednesday, myself and 'me ma' head off to Blanchardstown Shopping Centre in order to mill a hearty breakfast. Every Wednesday morning feels like the first time we've ever done this. My mam has a wonderful, mischievous way about her and is a fantastic storyteller (I am learning from the best). She also became a bit of a celeb thanks to *The Late Late Show*. While I sat there with Ryan Tubridy, sobbing like a feckin' eejit, the camera would go to my mam sitting in the audience. She looked perfect.

My mam is proud of me. Even writing those words creates tears in my eyes. She loved *Joys of Joy* on a level I never saw coming. I thought it might be a difficult read for her, seeing how I struggled without her and so on. But no, she absolutely loves it. And she tells everyone she meets about it, and almost insists they go buy a copy. In fact, I reckon my mam has been responsible for the majority of its feckin' sales. One funny story came about when my mam was renewing her house insurance on the phone.

'So, there I am Gary, trying to get the best deal – your Antoinette has been soooo helpful – when I get this lovely man on the phone. He starts giving me quotes and what have you, when I interrupt him and say, 'My son wrote a book you know.'

'Oh really missus? How wonderful. So, I think this particular package suits...'

'Yes, it's a bestseller – *and* he was on *The Late Late Show*' (you've gotta love Lily's persistence).

'Oh really missus? How wonderful. So, I can email you the...'

'I don't have a feckin' email or Gmail or feckin Bmail, but do you have a pen? Write this down. *Joys of Joy...*'

Yet another sale for this shark of a saleswoman.

So I hope I have shown others that it is never too late to have a relationship with anyone. It could be your mam or dad, brother or sister, dog or parrot, it's *never* too late. I was such a prick to this woman in the past. But I have chosen not to live in that past, feeling sorry for myself. Instead I will make sure my actions show her just how much she means to me. I will never stop doing all I can to make her happy.

I'll leave you with the words my mam says to me every evening as we say our goodbyes on the phone:

'I'm so proud of you Gary, and I love you – I love the two of you. Goodnight and God bless.'

Goodnight Elizabeth Carmel Mary Conway (Cunningham). I love you too – with all I've got.

Chapter 38

THE INSPIRE SERIES

As mentioned previously, I was shocked by the amount of people who deemed *Joys of Joy* 'too positive'. And with this follow-up volume, I am again faced with this dilemma. I started this story with brutal honesty. I have publicly declared that I was, as they would say in Mountjoy, 'fuckin' major balls rough' when I was initially released. I was down and very depressed. I have given you an insight into my battle with alcohol. I have laid bare the truth of what a bastard I was to Antoinette. I wanted you to see how bad it got. I wanted to bring you down, and then shoot you back up with the stories that changed my life. I could write ten books on the depression, isolation and frustration I have faced. Instead, I have chosen to describe 'the lows', but quickly followed by an outpouring of 'the highs'. We live in a world filled with hate, violence, sadness and loss, all of which can be difficult to hide away from. But we can choose to try our damnedest to fill our days with as much positive energy as possible. And that is the route I chose. So, I'm sorry if you find these short stories 'too positive'. I'm sorry if you long for more sadness and strife. That's just not me anymore.

Here is an example of how I almost slipped again and how a positive mind (and Antoinette of course) helped me to keep my head above water.

It's Monday morning, but it could be any day. I am awake since are-ya-havin'-a-laugh-o'clock. I was woken from my sleep the same way I have been for the past few months, with shooting pains in my stomach and a soreness in my derrière that I wouldn't wish on anyone. I slink my body out of bed and creep out the door, not wanting to wake up Antoinette. I limp up the stairs and head for the bathroom, noting I have tears of sheer agony forming already. I am then forced to use the toilet. I'm sure if my neighbours are awake at this silly time as well they are probably thinking it's '50 Shades of Annie' going on in our place, and that our bathroom is her 'Red Room of Pain'. I have no choice but to spend at *least* thirty minutes on the loo, my feet falling asleep as pins and needles begin to formulate. Once that ordeal is over, I head into my man-cave as quiet as I can, and cry my eyes out. When Antoinette gets up and readies herself for work, work that is putting food on our table and (barely) keeping a roof over our heads, I don't want her to see me in this state. So I get as much out of my system as I can. And no matter what day it is, no matter what season we are in, that is how my day has started for *way* too long now. This surgery I need can't come quick enough.

I find that most days I am housebound. It's almost like I am incarcerated again. I try my best to fill my days being as creative as I can. I write, both songs and stories, in order to fill the hours. My OCD means that I clean our apartment from top to bottom, do the washing, and cook the dinner like an overly-zealous madman. And I do all of this whilst experiencing pain and discomfort that is so very distracting. But I need to do these chores for Antoinette. She doesn't ask me to, but I am already struggling with the fact that I am not working and therefore not contributing financially as much as I could. So I need to feel I am pulling my weight in some way. Yet every day, Antoinette comes home and makes me feel so good, just because I washed her clothes or made the bed. She makes me feel like I've done something amazing every day. But still, on occasion, I would be so low that I would lash out at her. For reasons that escape me, I would sometimes take my terrible moods out on the one person who was supporting me.

This next line scares me half to death, but I need to be honest: We almost broke up for good.

And who could blame her for wanting to leave me? I was feeling sorry for myself ... *again*! I was allowing my illness to take control of my mind and I needed to snap-the-fuck out of it pronto!

So I fought back. I refused to let my health problems define me. I reached down deep and found some resolve. I would head to my gym, Flyefit on Macken Street, and I would do ... well, not a lot really. I couldn't. 'Me arse' was killing me. But I still made sure I went every day and tried to do something, anything. Again, I embraced the mighty power of the 'Placebo Effect'.

Incredibly, during this dark time I was asked if I would like to take part in a micro-documentary series, sponsored by Flyefit, entitled 'The Inspire Series'. The idea was to film some members of the many Flyefit gyms dotted across our nation's capital who would tell their inspiring stories, and intertwine these stories with how they felt that the gym was an integral part of their set-up. And they wanted me to take part. Fucking hell! Of course I said, 'Oh hell yeah!'

I was asked to be in the Tara Building, right in the heart of Dublin's bustling city, one Tuesday morning. I woke up and went through my usual painful process, but my excitement, and slight dread, made it a lot easier. The production company tasked with creating this series is called Collective Dublin and consists of Mark Logan and Kenneth Adams, two absolute headcases, but equally two beautiful souls.

I enter the Tara Building and announce myself at the desk. 'Mark will be with you shortly,' says the lady at the reception. The room I am standing in is brilliant white from ceiling to floor. Its walls are dotted with beautiful photography depicting scenes from the Amazon Rain Forest. Soon I hear my name and I turn to see 'yer man' James Franco, the famous Hollywood actor, calling me in a Dublin accent. *Christ*, I think to myself, *he's bloody good at accents isn't he? Great actor too.* Of course, it wasn't James Franco but at least now you now know what Mark looks like. He is, in my humble opinion, the double of Mr. Franco, which I immediately tell him.

'Yeah, I kinda get that a lot,' laughs Mark. I know I am going to get on with this lad just fine. 'Ken, the cameraman, will join us shortly Gar,' Mark says, 'but I wanna show you something, up on the roof, before we start. And I'll try to walk you through the vision of what myself and Ken have planned for you. But before we go any further I need to give ya one of these.' Mark comes closer and gives me a hug. He knows me too well. I'm a 'hugger' folks. 'Your book is amazing Gary,' says Mark. 'You are perfect for this project, man. So inspiring.'

As we head for the stairs, Mark tells me that the photos in the large white room are all his own work. And just before we get to the stairs, he points at two that are side by side and says, 'That moment is you and Antoinette, that's love.' The first of these beautifully shot photographs is of a naked older gentleman (none of his 'bits' are on display) standing on the edge of a massive cliff in the Amazon Rain Forest, which has a beautiful dark blue pool of water below. The next picture is him leaping – his leap of faith. Just like the leap myself and Antoinette took. What a lovely thing for Mark to say.

We head up one flight of stairs and enter a room that is a hive of activity with young, creative men and women working away. Mark heads for a large, old fashioned, brown wardrobe. He steps into it – and simply disappears. I shit you not. One minute he is opening the wardrobe, I assumed to hang up my jacket, and next thing he's fuckin' gone! I am left standing there, looking like a massive eejit. The guys and girls in the office begin giggling. I'm sure I'm not the first one to be stunned by Mark's magician act.

'Head into the wardrobe,' shouts one of them.

'I will in me arse,' comes my reply. 'My mama didn't raise no fool...'

This brings a few more giggles, but then I hear Mark's voice coming from the wardrobe. 'Are ya coming Gar?' WTF!

I cautiously open the door and see that the back of the wardrobe has a massive hole in it that leads to another hole in the wall. And once you step through these holes, you are brought onto the roof of this building. It was brilliant! Mark is standing on the other side, smiling. 'Good, isn't it Gar? And wait until you see the view from up here,' he says.

And he wasn't lying. The view of Dublin was breathtaking. We were facing Liberty Hall and Dublin was alive and kicking below us. Mark sits me down on a wooden bench and explains how the process will work. Today will consist of me being interviewed about my story (who I am, why I am here, and so on). We would then meet a couple of days later at my home, and the lads would film me getting ready for the gym, and then working out. Mark also suggested we head to Mountjoy to get some shots there too. I was happy to do whatever they wanted. Soon we are joined by Ken, and it's very clear that he is the yin to Mark's yang. A tall lad, sporting a beard, Ken is the quiet one of this dynamic duo. He is also the cameraman and a bloody good one too. Ken has a way about him that made me feel completely at ease. I'm really going to enjoy this. I did my interview that day, and again was as honest as I could be whilst telling my story. Mark and Ken loved it. We arrange to meet in my apartment in a couple of days, and I leave them feeling very excited.

When the lads arrived at my apartment a couple of days later, I made them an omelette which they really appreciated. Ken got straight to work shooting various footage of me, all the time being directed by Mark. We then piled into Ken's silver Toyota Yaris and head for Mountjoy, but as soon as we walk up to the gate I freeze. I realise this is the closest I have been to this building since my release. Instantly, my mind is bombarded with haunting memories. It's funny. I didn't think of Fitzer or The Off#enders; instead, all I could think about were the horrible things I had witnessed almost daily. The two lads were so supportive as they could clearly see I was getting upset, but we soldiered on and got some cracking footage. Still, I was glad when we were finished and we could walk away.

Next, the lads filmed me walking to the Flyefit gym on Macken Street and then me 'training' once we got there. I have put inverted commas around the word training because this is a good example of how I refused to let negativity and pain control my life. I was in agony whilst the lads filmed me but I kept this to myself as I knew these two would insist that we just leave it. But they only had this day to get the footage done as they were on a strict timetable with this project, so I gritted my teeth and got on with it. Ken's footage was still amazing and I am so very proud of myself that I pushed through it.

After the lads filmed the other participants of this series, they got to work on their edits. I got a phone call from Mark one day inviting me to Collective Dublin's new office, just off Dame Street. 'Your story is ready for your eyes Gar, and it's special,' says Mark. And God, was he right. As I sat and watched the short video in their office, I was an emotional wreck. I felt proud of how I told my story and I am in awe of the standard of work that these two lads had produced.

The video got over 23,000 views, and the feedback and comments I received still blow me away to this day. It can be seen on Flyefit's Facebook page, my own Facebook page, or by searching, 'Gary Cunningham Flyefit Inspire Series' on YouTube. And I urge you to watch the other short films in the series too. Each one stars an incredibly inspiring person, and their stories will touch you – and hopefully inspire you too.

So there you have it. Of course my life is not a bed of roses, in fact with my health the way it is, it can be quite a struggle. But I don't want you to read this book and come away feeling down or sad. I want you to come away with a smile and some joy in your heart.

Is that such a bad thing?

Chapter 39

'GOOD EVENING DUBLIN. WE ARE THE OFF#ENDERS'

'Hi Gary, I'm arranging a gig in aid of Pieta House (an organisation that helps people who are in suicidal distress or who self-harm), and I want The Off#enders to play at it.' These are the words I hear from Shireen one day on the telephone.

'What? *Really?*' I ask stunned.

'Too right Gary,' starts Shireen, 'you guys will be amazing, and people need to hear Fitzer's voice in all its glory.'

I am rooted to the spot. The Off#enders playing a gig, and not just in front of prisoners. The Off#enders playing a gig as free men. Is this really happening? I shamefully don't consider the opinions of Fitzer, Sweeny-Todd or Cunny as I say to Shireen, 'Yep, count us in.'

Shireen was delighted. She then said, 'Ask Antoinette if she will perform at the event too. She will be amazing Gary.' I'm sure Shireen was suggesting that Antoinette performed on her own, but I had other ideas.

I waited until Antoinette came home from work that day. The second she walked in the door, I hit her with Shireen's news.

'That is fantastic Gary. Imagine, The Off#enders playing live in Dublin,' she said smiling.

'It's great all right Annie,' I start, 'but what would make it even better is if you jammed with us. Shireen wants you to perform on the night anyway, so I just thought The Off#enders could be the band backing you.'

Antoinette is stunned into silence. I can see worry and self-doubt toying with her, and I feared these emotions would prevent her from saying yes. She walked away from me for a second, but suddenly she spun around and said, 'I would absolutely love that Gar. I would fuckin' love to get on a stage with you and the lads.'

I'm sure the smile on my face told Antoinette everything she wanted to know. I was so happy. 'We'll pick a couple of songs just for you to do, and you can join in on The Off#enders' songs harmonising Fitzer's vocals,' I say.

'Oh wow, Gary. I'm so excited,' beamed Antoinette.

'It's going to be amazing, *you're* going to be amazing,' I reply. My head was doing loop the loops. *The woman I met in prison was going to perform live with the band I formed in prison*, I thought happily, until suddenly these happy thoughts came to a screeching halt. I still hadn't asked the rest of the The Off#enders if they wanted to do the gig. Shit. What if they said no?

I remember ringing Cunny to tell him the news, and his reaction still upsets me to this day. 'Ah Gar, maybe you should get a real drummer to do this gig. Sure, I'm shite.'

I have always hated when Cunny did this to himself. He is known for making comments like, 'I'm such an idiot/fool/dickhead' and so on. He would always feel that he wasn't good enough. And nothing could be further from the truth. But this self-berating is a sad result of the damage caused by his addiction to cocaine – an addiction I can proudly declare that he has well and truly kicked. When his addiction left, it took with it the remainder of Cunny's self-worth. But there was no way I was going to stand by and let these dark thoughts manifest any further.

'Fuck off ya gobshite,' I eloquently start, 'you blew away the toughest of crowds when you played in front of a bunch of prisoners, so this will be a walk in the park for you.' Cunny wasn't convinced, but he also knew how stubborn I was, so he knew not to fight back. 'This Thursday, 7.00 pm at the rehearsal room. Be there ... or I'll burst ya!' I say.

'Right ya are boss,' laughs Cunny followed by, 'and Antoinette is jamming with us? Ah Gar. That is going to be fucking unreal man.'

'It sure will be Cunny,' I say smiling.

Sweeny-Todd was next. I have chosen not to disclose as much about Sweeny-Todd in either this book or *Joys of Joy* because, even in prison, he was a very private guy. I respect that about him. I watched with admiration as he changed his ways whilst we were locked up together. And my admiration rose even higher when I saw his progress on the guitar and heard him sing as we served out our sentences. He has become an extremely successful businessman and is also the most giving and charitable person I have ever met. But it's his laid-back attitude that I love the most. When I told him of the impending gig, and the fact that Antoinette was going to jam with us, he simply answered, 'Fuck it Gar. Count me in pal.' Brilliant.

Lastly, I had Fitzer to deal with, and this one worried me. As I'm sure is clear, Fitzer is not his real name, nor is it close to his real name, just like with Sweeny-Todd and Cunny. I have no right to disclose their true identities and never would. Cunny and Sweeny-Todd wouldn't mind if I did, but Fitzer's anonymity is paramount to him. And I love the bloke too much to ever ruin what we have by giving out his name, or posting pictures of him on social media. But when I told him about this gig, he jumped at it.

'For Pieta House is it Gar? Well, count me in so.' And I knew why. During our time in prison, Fitzer lost someone very close to him in Mountjoy through suicide. It had such an effect on him and The Off#enders that when we recorded our album, with the intention of selling it internally in every prison in Ireland, we wanted the money to go to three charities, one of which was SOSAD, an Irish organisation helping those dealing with suicide.

'What about your anonymity Fitzer?' I ask.

'I'll wear a bleedin' crash-helmet Gar, just like Daft Punk,' says Fitzer. This makes us both laugh as we picture Fitzer's incredible voice being sung through a motorbike helmet. 'And Annie is gonna jam with us Gar?' says Fitzer smiling, followed by, 'this is going to be fuckin' brilliant Gary. Jaysis. I can't wait now.'

So The Off#enders, now featuring Antoinette, got back to work. I was struggling health-wise, but my determination got me through it. We worked so hard on constructing a set-list, which included a mix of original material and covers of songs that inspired us to be in a band in the first place, like Pink Floyd's 'Coming Back to Life'. We recorded a version of this song for our album, and hearing Fitzer sing the opening bars whilst only an organ holds a chord in the background is something truly special:

> And where were you? When I was burned, and broken. While the day slips by, from my window, watching. And where were you? When I was hurt, and I was helpless. Because the things you say, and the things you do, surround me. While you were hanging yourself, off someone else's words. Dying to believe what you heard. I was staring straight, into the shining sun.

But to hear him sing the same lines live is truly something to behold.

Cunny's playing was getting better and better. I remember watching him as we jammed the thunderous, non-stop track I wrote entitled 'Can You Hear Me', and I feel my levels of pride about to burst out of the top of my head. He inserted his own, very impressive, fills into this track, and to watch him get lost in the song, whilst terrified he was making a mistake, was truly something I'll never forget. Similarly with Sweeny-Todd's haunting song that he penned in prison, 'In My Dreams', one of my favourite tracks from our album. The reaction we received once it was put out there confirmed to me just how good it is.

But it was the addition of Antoinette that brought smiles to the all our faces as we jammed. Once she took to the mic there was no stopping her. From providing perfect harmonies for Fitzer's vocals to belting out songs on her own like Jefferson Airplane's 'Don't You Want Somebody to Love' while The Off#enders rocked behind her. I remember one moment when we were in the middle of 'Scream My Name', a song penned by Fitzer for his wife. When Antoinette joined Fitzer in perfect harmony, I was so overcome with feelings of pride and happiness. All the people I loved so much standing in a room together making music. I was stunned. And with each jam, we got better and better.

'Tighter than a Cavan man's grip around a fiver,' Fitzer would say.

This gig was to be held in The Academy on Dublin's Abbey Street, which for a band that was used to having no equipment, sometimes not even a stage to perform on, was a really big deal.

Let's do this! 'Ladies and Gentlemen, *The Off#enders, Featuring Antoinette*' (the crowd goes wild...)

If only. You didn't actually think it was going to be *that* easy did you? Oh God no. It was time for another, rather large spanner, to be lobbed into the works.

Chapter 40

A CLOSE CALL...

About two months before the Pieta House gig, and with The Off#enders rehearsals becoming more and more enjoyable, I got word from my surgeon, Mr. Mulsow, that I was next on his list for surgery. He asked if I minded going to Our Lady's Hospital in Navan to have the procedure done. I would have gone to Timbuktu, so of course this wasn't a problem for me. Everyone in my life was so happy for me at this time. They saw daily how much I was struggling and they knew this would be a massive relief for me.

And so, on the fateful morning of my operation, myself, Antoinette and my mam all piled into Antoinette's car and made the trip to Navan. The mood in the car was really upbeat, considering we had to be on the road for 6.00 am. My mam and Antoinette were having great craic at my expense, but I cared not. I had waited a very long time for this. After today? Well, I'd have my life back. But there was one 'minor' issue that was niggling away at me. In fact, it had been annoying me for the last couple of days.

Two days before the surgery, I was heading down the stairs in my apartment when I got this shooting pain in my right calf. When I looked at it, the calf was roaring red and had a lump sticking out of it. *It's nothing – no need for alarm, and no need to tell anyone, sure it might prevent me from getting my surgery*. This was the stupid thought I had once I saw my leg. I had what some might call a 'typical man's reaction' – I said nothing to anyone about my leg and hoped it would just go away. But, of course, it didn't. And if it wasn't for my mam, there is a very real chance I wouldn't be here telling this story.

As we pulled up to Our Lady's Hospital, Antoinette dropped myself and my mam at the main entrance and headed off to park the car. As soon as I put my right leg out of the car, I let out a whimper. My mam is looking at me the whole time and says, 'Are you okay Gary? What's wrong with your leg?'

'Ahh nothin' ma,' I start, 'I just went over on my ankle. Don't be making a fuss now okay?' I felt like a shithead lying to her, but I was not letting anything get in the way of this surgery. Then I take a step away from the car and almost collapse into my mother's arms. The pain in my leg was getting worse. Again, I try to brush it off, but like all 'Irish mammies' nothing gets past her. And to this day, I thank God for that fact.

We make our way to the ward and luckily for me it is only a stone's throw from the hospital's main entrance. I had been to this hospital a couple of weeks beforehand, in order to get my bloods done, and I had met some of the staff who worked in this particular ward. In fact, most of them had read my feckin' book and loved it. And the nurses and staff I encountered in Our Lady's Hospital in Navan could not have done enough for me.

We enter the ward and I am met with the nurse who will be tending to me. My Asian 'Florence Nightingale', this nurse deserves an award simply because of the attention she shows to all her patients. I wasn't the only one she had to tend to that morning, and yet she made me feel like I was. Antoinette joined us, and she too notes my newly acquired limp. 'Are you okay baby?' she asks worryingly.

'Ahh, I'm bleedin' grand. I went over on me ankle. No big deal. Stop goin' on about it.' I bark all of this at Antoinette. What a fool I can be. My mam is very worried, so she becomes my next target. 'Look, will you stop going on about my leg mam, please. I'm grand.' Thankfully, my mam very rarely listens to me.

I put on my surgery garments, which consisted of paper thin underwear, a gown and a silly hat to put on my head. I was seconds away from being wheeled down to have my surgery, when my mam says to the nurse, 'Will you please take a look at his leg.' I was fuming. But once the nurse saw my leg, she immediately cancelled my surgery so that my leg could be looked at by a doctor, which it was moments later. It is suggested that I have an ultrasound done, and before I know it I am in a wheelchair headed for the x-ray department. The lady tasked with doing this ultrasound was great craic. She compliments me on my appearance on *The Late Late Show* and says she is halfway through my book.

'Jesus Gary. I've laughed and cried and laughed again whilst reading your tale. Great work. Now, let's rule out any shite here, and get you that surgery you tell me you need so badly.'

I get some form of jelly rubbed on my right leg, and the nurse starts the scan at the top of my groin. But as soon as she comes to the back of my knee, and then moves on to my calf, her mood changes notably. After lingering around my calf and the back of my knee, she says the words I really was *not* expecting.

'Gary, you have two rather large clots in your right leg. One on your calf, and one behind your knee. Gary, it's a miracle we found them. Today could have gone a lot differently for you.'

And I knew how right she was. I might not have survived surgery as clots and anaesthetics don't mix, and the results can be fatal. I was asked by someone that morning if I believed in miracles or guardian angels. I told them my daughter had passed away and that I like to think she looks after me. 'Well, she most certainly did today Gary,' came their reply.

Mr Mulsow came to see me after I came back from the ultrasound. My head was spinning and he picked up on that. He explained the gravity of the situation and told me that my surgery was now cancelled for the foreseeable future. This was a crushing blow. I knew I was fortunate to have discovered 'me two clots' (or 'Madge' and 'Franny' as I like to call them) and how serious all of that was, but my other problems were still ever present too. And now I was looking at a minimum of six months to a year before Mr Mulsow could perform the surgery that would give me some sort of life back. I was distraught. My mam was so upset, and she kept crying beside me whilst holding on to my hand for dear life. Antoinette was stunned too as she knew how much I was crushed by this news. Please don't think I was ungrateful, but I had put all my eggs into the one basket that morning and just wanted the surgery I desperately needed. But, at the same time, I knew I had just dodged a huge bullet. I knew how lucky I was.

The staff in Our Lady's treated me so well, and as I was discharged later that morning they almost walked me out to Antoinette's car. I didn't speak much on the way home – or for the next couple of days.

The Off#enders gig had to be cancelled! I couldn't rehearse anymore, and I wasn't sure if I'd be ready on the night. I was feeling so low. The lads all supported me as best they could. Just like back when we were in prison, they rallied around me. I was so grateful for them. As I was for the love and care being bestowed on me from Antoinette. She knew I was taking this news badly. But she also knew how lucky I was, and I think she got a fright herself.

'Imagine if I lost you Gary. Jesus. I don't even want to think about it.'

I'd try to make silly jokes like, 'Ahh, ya can't kill a bad thing,' or 'ya won't be gettin' rid of me that easily baby.' But I didn't find jokes that easy to come by at that time. What the fuck was I going to do now? I've been put on tablets that I must take every morning for the foreseeable future to control these clots. But I now also faced the prospect of having to start my day the way I described in a previous chapter. Nothing has changed, except I now had 'me two clots' sharing my days with me. The alcoholic in me would pop into my mind around this time too. *Sure, after a few pints, all the pain will slowly dissolve,* I would foolishly think. But thankfully, I had absolutely no desire to ever see that gobshite again.

So yet again, I needed to dig deep and shift my focus. I will admit to feeling quite sorry for myself for a bit, but I soon snapped out of that thinking. There was nothing I could do about the fact I now had clots. There was nothing I could do about the fact I must wait for the all clear before I can have my surgery. I must do what we all have to do in times of crisis. I must learn, change and adapt.

At the time of writing, I am still waiting to be seen by a hematologist so they can give Mr. Mulsow the green light to proceed with my surgery. Some days are good, although when I say good I mean less bad than other days! Sadly, though, most days are dreadful. I'm still out of work, and believe it or not, that is the heaviest cross for me to bear. But this is the hand I've been dealt – for now. And every day I am grateful for all I have and for all the people who share my life with me.

So 'me two clots' are a 'pain in the arse'. Literally.

But I am surrounded by incredible people. Antoinette is so supportive and she knows I appreciate her more than I can articulate. As does Fitzer. He may not do 'soppy', he may hate public displays of affection, but when his mates are down he does all he can to make sure they're okay.

And that's just what he did with me...

Chapter 41

FITZER'S FRIENDSHIP

'Howya Ted. What's the story? How are ya today? Are ya still balls rough or wha'?' This is how the first phone call of the day from Fitzer usually starts. But I know what he's up to. I know he is doing all he can to lift my spirits, and I love him for that. He rings me several times a day, and each call lasts about an hour! Ash and Antoinette both have the same reaction. 'Ahh, you're not on the phone to *him* again are ya?' they would laugh. But these calls give me a boost every day.

I suppose I did worry that once Fitzer was released he would immerse himself back into his life and I would become nothing more than a fond memory. But thankfully, he had other ideas. I was brought even further into his world and introduced to his mam, dad and two sisters. And I became even closer to his wife Ash. She too has become one of the people who brightens up my darker days. They have been together 17 years, 17 years of highs and lows, of separation and reunion. And nothing ever seems to come between them. They have always wanted a full wedding, having only had a quick registry office blessing before Fitzer went inside, and I know how important it would be to Fitzer.

'She is my best friend Gar ... after you of course buddy,' he would say to me.

'Ash will box the ears off ya if she hears ya saying that me aul' flower,' I would laugh back.

I got to spend more time with Cian, their beautiful son. He is great craic altogether, and he is the double of Fitzer. Watching Fitzer become the father he feared might allude him is something else. As tough as Fitzer is, he still harbours doubts and fears just like the rest of us. But he had no need for fear when it came to his son. They adore each other. And when Ash and Fitzer announced they were going to have another child, everyone who knew them was over the moon for them both, myself included.

Fitzer's relationship with my mam is brilliant. A little awkward sometimes, but brilliant. I say awkward because they flirt with each other constantly. My mam is mad about him. And Fitzer loves to wind me up with this.

'It won't be long now Gar,' he would start. 'Soon, you'll have to address me as dad. And I'll be havin' none of your shite. Once you're under *my* roof, you live by *my* rules!' But the joy he brings to my mam is there for all to see, and my entire family is so grateful to him for that.

Behind Fitzer's tough exterior lies the most giving, thoughtful and generous man you could meet. Take my birthday one year. Fitzer had only been released a couple of months, and he was facing the same challenges I had in trying to obtain work. But his attitude never allowed him to feel down. He would take every rejection on the chin, but with another baby on the way, I knew he was anxious to get working. So when he arrives outside of my apartment one evening and calls my phone to tell me to come outside, I'm intrigued. But when I open my front door, my intrigue soon turns into tears. There is the first true friend I have ever had, standing in front of me with his son Cian standing beside him. Cian is holding a birthday card and singing happy birthday at the top of his voice, while Fitzer is holding a red Fender

Squire Strat, the same model guitar I had used in prison to record our album.

'Happy birthday buddy. Look, I'll never forget all you did for me inside Gar. So this is our little thank you from myself, Ash and Cian here. But no fuckin' cryin' now, do ya hear me?' He hands me this beautiful guitar.

No crying? Is he fucking insane? I was sobbing! I have never had a friend in my life do something as thoughtful as this for me. I knew money was tight for him at that time, and yet here he was handing me the most perfect of gifts. And little did I know, but Antoinette and Fitzer were in cahoots. Antoinette appears at the door holding a huge Fender amp, and wearing the most beautiful smile on her face. 'We love ya baby,' she says. I almost fall to my knees and cry, like a really bad actor in a B-movie, which just makes Antoinette, Fitzer and Cian laugh at my expense. What an amazing and thoughtful thing for them to do for me.

But Fitzer wasn't finished yet...

I was loving the craic we were all having about the impending arrival of Fitzer and Ash's new bundle of joy. We would take turns winding Ash up, but she was well able for anything we threw at her. Fitzer had just purchased his first iPhone, and watching him come to terms with it was hilarious. Not being overly tech savvy, he would mock himself daily as he tried to learn all about apps and what have you. He quickly became a fan of WhatsApp, and the laugh we both share through this particular form of social media is incredible. Not for public consumption most of the time, but very funny.

One Saturday evening as I am sitting on my sofa on my own, I see a WhatsApp video call coming in from Fitzer. I think to myself, *look at this gobshite ... video calling me. He must've made a mistake.* I answer and am met by the sight of Fitzer's big mug smiling back at me through the screen on my phone. I don't give him a chance to speak.

'Ya gobshite. Did ya video call me by accident yeah? Ya *gobshite!*'

'Ehhh, no Gar, I haven't made a mistake. I just thought you might wanna say hello to *your new godson!*'

What?!? *Godson?* What is he talking about? But before I can ask, he has turned the phone around and there is Ash holding their brand new baby boy. 'He's perfect Gar, and he needs a godfather. So, what do ya say?' asks Ash.

I couldn't really say anything. My lips moved, but nothing came out. Of course I started crying, and Ash can be heard laughing to Fitzer, 'Ahh Jaysis, here we go. He's bleedin' off.'

Fitzer's head reappears on my phone's screen. 'Give it bleedin' over will ya? Pull yourself together and say hello to your godson, Calum.'

Calum ... my godson. I was completely and utterly blown away.

But, again, Fitzer wasn't finished yet...

It's Christmas day, and myself and Antoinette were sitting around the table in my brother Gerry's home, surrounded by my mam and Gerry and Barbara's beautiful family. We had just devoured Barbara's award winning feast when my niece Jennifer comes running into the kitchen and says to me, 'Have you seen what Ash's mam and dad have done for her and Fitzer? They have booked their wedding for them, so they can have their special day at last.'

I immediately take out my phone, and soon I am confirming Jennifer's story. I see Ash has posted a video one of her sisters took of her, as she read out what the gift was that her mam and dad had just given to her and Fitzer. And as my family all huddled around my phone, we all shared that warm feeling. A real Christmas miracle. Not long after, Fitzer rings me. I ask everyone to be quiet. I answer my phone to him, put him on speakerphone, and then get everyone to sing, 'We Wish You a Merry Christmas' and 'Congratulations' down the phone to him. He remains quiet, but as soon as the last note is sung he says, 'Am I still on speaker pal, yeah?'

'Ya are buddy,' I reply.

'And is Antoinette and all your family still there too?' he asks.

'They surely are Fitzer,' I answer.

'Good. I want them to see your bleedin' reaction. Here, Gar? Do ya wanna be my best man at my wedding?'

Barbara and Gerry's kitchen falls silent, as does Fitzer. We all know what happened to me next, but that bollox Fitzer can be heard shouting, 'Is he crying folks yeah? Bleedin' gobshite!' Of course I was crying. But I was so happy, and so very proud. 'There is only one man that could be my best man pal, and that's you. We've had some journey, haven't we? So this, to me, is full circle,' he said to me once my tears subsided.

And so I am to be the best man at the wedding of my first true friend. Wait 'til Fitzer gets a load of my speech. Oh, revenge shall be sweet!

Through every dark moment I encountered from the second I walked into Mountjoy to the moment my clots were discovered, Fitzer has been there for me and done all he could to help and protect me. When I'm down he lifts me up, and when I'm up he lifts me higher. To this day he remains anonymous in the public eye. But every single person who read *Joys of Joy* has taken him into their hearts. And it has started a really funny trend called 'Who's Fitzer?' He came to a surprise birthday party we had for my mam. Ash took our photo, but Fitzer held a pint glass in front of his face. We shared it on Facebook and the reaction was hilarious. Everyone wants to put a face to his singing voice. Maybe in time Fitzer will drop his mask. But that will always be his decision.

Fitzer is truly greatest male friend I have ever had. Even if he does take the piss out of me – constantly!

Chapter 42

DO I DESERVE THIS?

We are nearing the end of my story ('thanks-be-to-Jaysis' says you), and as we do I find myself reflecting on what has been an unbelievable rollercoaster of a ride. I can never run away from the fact that I broke the law and went to prison. I served my full sentence and changed in there, but I still felt so much shame and regret that I ended up incarcerated in the first place. I hurt so many people, and though most have forgiven me there are some who find forgiveness a bridge too far. The bastard I was is still ever present in their minds, and I can't blame them for that. So, just because I have become a better man doesn't mean I can expect these people to dive straight in and forgive the horrendous things I had done.

When I was on *The Late Late Show*, these particular people were weighing heavily on my mind. On the one hand, I hoped they would see how much I had changed, but on the other hand, I hoped they weren't annoyed by seeing my stupid gob on their TV screen. I had the same feelings when my book was published. I wanted them to read it and see how much I regret all the nasty things I had done, but I was also fearful they would be hurt or insulted by what I wrote. I have written letters to these people since my release explaining these fears and much more, but I have heard nothing back. But until my dying day, my door will forever remain open to them in the

252

hope that a conversation can begin, in the hope that I can show them that the Gary they knew from seven years ago is well and truly gone.

Joys of Joy became a best seller ... a *best seller!* Amazingly, I have been told by countless people that it actually helped them with their own struggles. I have no words. But with the book's success came an abundance of attention. I was asked on to many radio and TV shows – all of which was incredible – but I have always been mindful that I was being asked on these shows to talk about one of the most shameful times in my life. Which is why I refuse to play the 'poor me' card. I refuse to offer any excuses as to why my life ended up the way it did. It was all my own selfish doing, plain and simple. And when I combine the people who can't forgive me with the fact that I am now receiving a lot of attention, I ask myself the question, 'Do you really deserve this Gary?'

And one moment in my life asked and answered that question for me.

I had been invited on to the first episode of Baz Ashmawy's weekly show on RTÉ Radio 1 entitled 'That Baz Thing'. I have always been a fan of Baz, and once again, after meeting him, I came away an even bigger fan. They really seem to produce good 'un's in those Donnybrook studios. I was being joined by two others, and the topic of the night was 'The Power of Change'. The other two guests were Simone George and Michael Downey. This is when I began questioning myself. This is when I questioned everything, if I'm honest.

Simone George is married to the most incredible and bravest man to ever grace this planet, Mark Pollock. Mark is blind and as a result of a spinal cord injury is also confined to a wheelchair. But none of this prevents him from achieving things almost all of us would find too difficult. He got himself into extreme and endurance sports, and went on to compete in ultra-endurance races across deserts, mountains and the polar ice caps. He became the first blind person to race to the South Pole and ran 'The Race of No Return' across the Gobi desert, which involved six marathons in seven days. He is also a renowned public speaker. Wow. And you would be forgiven for thinking that this man was the reason Simone was invited onto Baz's show. But no. Simone is a tour de force herself. She is a consultant litigator and a human rights lawyer. And although their story is one of utter love and devotion, Simone stands proudly on her own as one very inspiring woman.

Michael Downey is a rising star on the comedy circuit, and I can confirm he is extremely funny. He had me in feckin' stitches from the moment I met him. And his story is so inspiring too. On his way to perform a gig in Dublin one evening, Michael was involved in a serious car crash, which left him with a lot of physical injuries such as an Achilles tendon which had exploded, a laceration of the knee, his hip broken in four places, his sternum broken in three places, and his right shoulder broken too. But what was even more worrying was that the crash had left Michael with a brain injury as well. He spent months in rehabilitation. Here is his description of what his brain injury did to him:

> It changes your drive and your memory from being hugely enthusiastic about everything to not being terribly enthusiastic about anything. You just have to relearn how to live life again, to be excited about things again.

And that is exactly what he did. He is now back out on the circuit, which is simply remarkable.

Myself and Antoinette were sitting in one of the staff eating areas of Radio 1, and we were joined by Simone, Michael and his partner, while we waited to be brought to the studio for the show. The conversation was one filled with wonder, as we were to be the first guests on this particular radio show.

But once Simone started talking about her husband Mark, or Michael began describing how he had to adapt to life with a brain injury, I began sinking further into myself. Suddenly, the very spacious eating area became as small as my cell on C Wing back in The Joy. *What am I doing here?* I thought to myself.

Antoinette cops it. 'What's wrong baby? Are you okay?' she asks, worryingly.

'I'm far from okay Annie,' I whisper, not wanting Simone or Michael to hear my petty worries. 'These two people are beyond inspiring. I'm just some prick who went to prison and wrote a book.' And there it was. The last statement was the one causing my doubts and fears. I was too caught up in the bad things I had done, and wasn't allowing myself to embrace the changes I had made or the impact my story was having on others. I was always my own worst enemy. I just felt like an imposter or a fraud, Here I was, about to go on the radio with two of the most inspiring people you could ever meet, to tell the listeners how I served my time in prison. Hardly earth shattering now is it? And yet, it was the two other guests who came to my rescue.

Michael had overheard my conversation with Antoinette, and he spent the next couple of minutes, along with Simone, quashing my fears entirely. Together they showed me how my story of personal change was indeed inspiring. I still felt embarrassed and told them so, but they were so very good to me, and we ended up having a moving, funny and honest chat with Baz live on-air. And after the show, Baz too instilled in me some confidence.

'What a great story Gary. Be proud of yourself man.' I thanked him from the bottom of my heart and handed him a copy of my book. I hope he liked it.

I learned two valuable lessons that night. One was to swallow my own medicine. I was forever telling others to believe in themselves, and yet here I was without a shred of self-belief. And two, and this one is even hard to write down, I do deserve all that is happening to me, just like I deserved to be sent to prison for breaking the law. My actions, and my treatment of others back then, meant I deserved everything I got. But equally, my actions today and how I now treat people means that I do deserve these goods things that are happening. We all deserve to be happy. No matter what you have done, you deserve to be happy. If you find yourself in the same situation as I did, own your problems and shortcomings. Admit your mistakes and accept full responsibility. You will be amazed at how quickly people can start forgiving you when they see you are not offering excuses. Speak well of people and refrain from putting others down. And always remember this crucial fact: Someone else's opinion of you is none of *your* business. So leave them to it. If someone wants to run you down, let them at it. They can only hurt you if you allow them to.

That's how I do things, anyway. Every day, from the moment I wake up, I strive to be a better man. I am still under construction, and I may remain that way until my dying day. But I will forever put in the work so that maybe, one day, the people who currently won't talk to me will see the changes for themselves.

And I owe it to Antoinette too. She stands by me no matter what the drama and no matter what the problem. 'Of course you deserve this Gary. Look at all you have done, both inside prison and out here. And remember, once you continue to work on yourself, I will never leave your side.'

I promise to never stop trying to for you Antoinette ... never.

Chapter 43

THE BEAUTIFUL SIDE OF HUMANITY

As you've shared my journey from the gates of Loughan House to the publishing of my first book and all that came with it, I have tried to introduce you to the many people who have made such an impact in my life. From my publisher David and his wife Darina, to Frank, Maggie, Dee, Eilish, Deborah ... the list goes on and on. And as I've brought you into their world, I hope I have painted each of them in the light they truly deserve. But these next two chapters are for an army of people who I am quite frankly crazy about. I want to introduce you to my friends' list.

Let me explain...

Before prison, I had very few friends on Facebook. I was just an overweight alcoholic with the most negative outlook on life. So I was hardly friend material. Then I come out of prison, tell my story, publish a book, and bang! I've got a big ol' bunch of new friends to share this journey with me, and some old friends too. Added to this friends' list were people I knew most of my life, yet we had never really interacted. Two of my favourites are my GP's secretary Collette and a lady who runs a shop in St. Stephens Green Shopping Centre, Sophia. Collette is a lady I only ever said hello to when I paid my doctor a visit. But after she read *Joys of Joy* she almost became my counsellor! The help and advice Collette provides me is something that, quite simply, blows me away. Sophia is a lady I have known almost my entire life, yet our only interaction would come when, as a teenager, I purchased a Metallica T-shirt from her shop. Again, Sophia read my book, and one day while I was in her shop she asked me to go for a coffee. Sophia displayed incredible honesty that day, as she openly admitted to having had a very dim view of all ex-prisoners. But, incredibly, my book changed her mind entirely, and today I am honored to call this lady my friend. These beautifully strong women, like the rest of my new friends, are now sharing my life with me. And that is what I love about these people. They are not afraid to share with me. I have been inundated with reviews, photos and love pertaining to *Joys of Joy*. I have been reduced to tears on many occasions after reading how my story helped some of these people. These days, helping others is far more addictive in my life than alcohol ever was. In fact, it was the main reason I decided to write this book.

I couldn't believe what was happening and, again, questioned if I really deserved it. But each and every one of these people made sure I knew that I did. And it is the most moving and humbling thing I have ever experienced. Social media can be a truly wonderful tool if it is used for the right reasons. I have great banter with these new friends. I have never actually met the majority of them, but we still have a great laugh. There is one guy, Stephen Gleeson, who I am convinced is somehow tracking my moods because when I'm feeling down it's like he can sense it. He will send me jokes, funny videos or simply a few lines of text asking if I am okay. Such a good man.

I have been very lucky to have met some of these people though, like my neighbour and fellow Dubs fanatic, Debbie, or my other neighbour, and fellow positive thinker, Shell. But the majority of my interactions happen on a screen. Every Monday, when I'm not under attack from 'me two clots' and 'me arse', I take to Facebook and try as hard as I can to put up a post filled with humour and positivity, a 'fuck Monday and all it stands for and be happy' post if you will. And it seems to do the trick. I always offer my ear to those who feel alone, and sadly, I have had so many reach out to me just for a chat. And I always make sure I'm there to listen.

Then I started to receive gifts, feckin' presents from these crazy new mates of mine. They wanted to express their gratitude for my book in this way. I was mortified, but two stories are very special to me.

Tony and the Most Thoughtful Gift Ever

I'm heading home on the bus and my head is racing. I have just given my first ever talk in a prison, the story I spoke of earlier about Wheatfield.

I turn on my phone and receive a Facebook mail from a guy named Tony who had added me as a friend a few weeks earlier. The mail was so moving, and although its contents are private to the two of us, I can tell you it contained an outpouring of gratitude for *Joys of Joy*. He tells me that his favourite character is Cunny, who he feels he can relate to the most. Tony also informed me how, after reading the book, it helped him right a wrong he felt he needed to address. I was stunned. He ended the mail by asking for my address. He reassured me he wasn't a psycho, and told me that since through my book and Facebook I am always giving to others he wanted to give something to me. I told him there is absolutely no need for that, but he insists. So I give him my mam's address and thank him from the bottom of my heart.

Three days later, myself, Antoinette, and her (very funny) friend Mary are having a laugh in our kitchen. My phone rings and it's Cunny.

'Howya. I'm around in your ma's here, and there was a knock at the door. It was some bloke. He handed me a black bag and said, "Give that to Gary for me will ya? It's from Tony, he'll know what it's about." And then he just walked off, lookin' kinda nervous if I'm honest. I thought those days were over Gar, wha'?' Cunny has begun laughing.

'Long gone, ya gobshite.' I told Cunny that I knew what it's about and say goodbye.

I then explained to Antoinette what just happened. Mary looks at me as if I am actually the thickest person she has ever laid her eyes upon and says, 'Eh ... like, what's in the bag? Don't you want to know? Ring Cunny back for God's sake man!'

Myself and Antoinette are in stitches. 'Yep. That's a good point Mary. I'll do that now,' I sheepishly reply. I ring Cunny and ask him to tell me what is in the bag.

'Hang on ... ehh, wow. Gary? It's you and Antoinette. It's a fucking beautiful, and really big, photo of you and Antoinette.' I have Cunny on speaker, and we are all united in silence.

Mary breaks it. 'Send a picture Cunny. Gary will probably forget to ask.'

Again we're laughing. But when Cunny sends the picture we are blown away. Tony had taken a picture of myself and Antoinette from my public Facebook page, blown it up and mounted it on a canvas for us. It hangs on the wall in my man-cave to this day. I laugh when I think how Tony had no idea that he had handed it to the character he felt he most related to from *Joys of Joy*, Cunny. But it was after I put the story of what Tony did on Facebook that the real worth of this man was shown to me. Complete strangers were leaving comments of how he helped them raise money for the sick or terminally ill, or how he was always around if they needed him.

But my good friend Deborah Blacoe summed up what Tony did for me up perfectly: 'It's like he looked into your mind and gave you the only thing you truly want, Antoinette.' What an amazing thing for Tony to do.

Karen (and how she saved the day)

Karen was one of the first on this newly acquired friends' list I was so lucky to be a part of. She would take to my page and openly discuss chapters from my book, and how they were making her either, quote, 'Laugh me bleedin' socks off, or cry me bleedin' eyes out.' Karen is a panic. But we have had many private chats, and it saddens me that I have seen the 'tears of her clown'. But we always work through our issues together and she helps me as much as I help her.

One Saturday, I was irate. The Dubs were playing a championship match, but because it fell on a Saturday it was only being shown on Sky Sports. I was fuming. I took to Facebook and did something I never do – I went off on a fuckin' mad one. I ranted 'til I had no more rant inside me. And I did this because I was struggling. I couldn't go to Hill 16 in Croke Park any more because Dublin games were a massive trigger for me when it comes to 'the drink'. If the Dubs lost? I went on the piss. If the Dubs won? I was on the lash. If the Dubs weren't playing? I was still getting pissed. So this ruled me out going to the games. And I love The Dubs, so not going to games was tough, but being sober was worth it.

Because I didn't have Sky TV, my only other option to watch the match was the pub. But as a recovering alcoholic, I was not at the stage where I could go into a pub and sip a 7-up. I would be eyeballing the Guinness taps in no time. I was so annoyed. My rant gets some feedback and soon my phone is ringing. I see it's Karen making a Facebook call.

Karen: 'Howya Gary. Listen, I'm not being a weirdo or anything ringing ya, okay?'

Gary: 'I know you're not a weirdo ... ya weirdo!'

Karen: 'Ha ha, very funny. Listen, log onto Facebook and go to my page. I'm gonna sit on the end of me bed and hold the phone to the telly so you can see the match. Now, you'll see an urn on top of the telly. That's me ma. She was a true Dub. In fact, when The Dubs were playing the neighbours used to think me da was a battered husband. Me ma would be screaming, "Ya dirty, filthy, good-for-nothing gobshite," but she'd be talking about the ref. And I too know what it's like to struggle Gary. So be proud that you're not at the game or in a pub. And anyway, you're book saved my life, Gary. Gary? Are ya there?'

Gary: (whimpers)

I was there all right, but yet again I was stunned by the thoughtfulness of someone I'd never actually met. I find I can only repeat, over and over again, the words, 'Thank you Karen.'

'Well, ya can thank me again,' she starts, 'the game is on now. Get on to my page.' I did, and Karen even added some of my friends so they could do the same. I got to see my team, and I didn't have the longing for a pint thrust in front of me. All thanks to Karen.

But there was one funny thing that Karen hadn't factored in. She was using Facebook live, which meant that she would be engaging the microphone and video camera on her phone. All that joined me on her feed were then treated to some of the funniest, foulest commentating of a GAA match ever. She was cursing and cheering to beat the band. And when Karen turned to the ref to give him a piece of her mind, I looked at the urn on the top of her telly and thought, 'Your mammy will always be alive through you Karen.'

The thoughtfulness, love and support from all these new friends has given me enough material to fill a book with stories similar to the two above. Daily, I am blessed to see the most beautiful side of humanity in all its glory, and I cannot thank them all enough for that. But I can try...

Chapter 44

AN ODE TO MY FRIENDS (LIST)

I wanted to write, a poem for my friends,
But I didn't know where to start.
Then I thought to myself, 'Use the alphabet,'
Well Jaysis – aren't I very smart?

There is Anthony C, Annmaire from Dunnes,
April M and Annmaire R too,
Alan B, Andy G, Annette from England,
Amy F and her mammy, Lou.

And one strong lady, that sits on this list,
Whose strength is so plain to see,
Is my American Hero, who never gives up,
The beautiful Andreya T.

Bernadette O'N, Bernie K,
Who has a sister named Cathy,
Christine from England, Cat D and Charmayne,
All combine to make me so happy.

Christine Fitz, Claire D,
Casey H and her Mammy Jen,
Danielle Mc D, Deborah Mc B,
Hang on ... where are all the men?

There's Deco M, Debbie D,
And of course her sister Steph,
Debbie M, Dee Ring and Dorothy,
And that is all the D's that are left.

Emma L, Emma K,
Erica B, Emer and Flo,
Big Francis W, and Gary D,
And Garrett and Helena, you already know (from
Classic Hits 4FM).

There's Geraldine, who married Roger,
And a lady named Helen C too,
Then there is, the mysterious H...
Who is this girl?
I haven't got a clue!

Jadez-annmaire, Julieanne,
Jimmy G and Jessica K,
Joanna T, Johanna C,
Every one of them brightens my day.

Juile G and her hubby Ned,
John S, John D, Jude and Anne,
There's Keith D, taking selfies in toilets,
'Here Keith? Yer some bleedin' man!'

How could I forget Kelly R,
Or Karl M, and his brother Mark?
Or Karen B, who is dating Niall,
Their love lights the way when its dark.

There's 'Limerick Liz,' Laura W,
Leanne and her friend Sarah M,
Laura and Ray, Lesley R,
And Lyndsey K, who is a little gem.

An Ode to My Friends (list)

Lauren K, and her daddy Joe,
Laura McG strutting her stuff in the gym,
Martian H, Martina K,
And the wonderful Melissa M.

There's Mary Kate, who would box your ears,
But who could also stand for you in Court,
Marykate O'B and Mary O'C
standing tall and holding the fort.

Michelle W, Michelle C,
Megan F, and Noel Fitz,
Olivia F, Paddy D,
and 'Prince Paul,' showing off his glitz.

Paula C, my Galway Girl,
Paula O'C Mc G,
Rachel L, Regina F,
not forgetting Peter O'T.

Robert S, Sabrina M,
Sarah-Jane and the Cummins Crew,
Sharon K and Sian H,
I'm really glad I know both of you.

Shauna K, Shauna L,
Shay Ryan and Stacey M,
Tom K, Tom O'D and Trevor K,
At last – a few feckin' men.

Trish M, and Trisha R,
Two ladies that mean so much to me,
Tommy W, Trevor Gib,
And of course, Tori D.

Then there are groups, like the Bookstation,
and all they did for me,
Alison, Lyndsey, Nicola, and Tammy,
LEGENDS the four of ye.

Or Erins Isle, my parish club,
I couldn't name every feckin' team,
Tracy F, Elaine, Yvonne Mark and Andy,
You and the club, helped me chase my dream
(HON THE PARISH).

The lads that go to Hill 16,
Paddy, Eamo and Davey,
And Pat, Des, Donal and Barry,
And Darragh – jaysis – there's too many.

So that is my little thank you,
To my social media friends,
And please don't worry if I forgot you,
Writing this poem drove me 'round the bend.

So I may have forgotten many,
But that is not a reflection on you,
I still think you are 'deadly',
And I thank you, for all that you do.

Chapter 45

THE JOYS OF FILMING

A comment I often heard from people when they had finished reading *Joys of Joy* was that they thought it would make a great film. A feckin' film! Of course, I didn't share this view; in fact, I thought they were off their heads if I'm honest. But even my publisher shared the views of many. 'Brian Langan even mentioned it to you in his first email Gary,' he reminded me one day. He also gave me some sound advice. 'If anyone ever approaches you about wanting to turn *Joys* into a film, I recommend you keep Frank in mind. He knows his way around these kind of things, so his advice would be very valuable.' And I could not have agreed with David more. But bringing up Frank's name also gave me an idea.

I remember ringing Frank and feeling very nervous. Frank doesn't make me nervous, but the question I wanted to ask him did.

'Ah, howya Gar, how's things man?' came the chirpy voice of Frank down my phone.

'Yeah, yeah, all is good Frank,' I begin. 'I do have something I would like to ask you though.'

'Fire away Gar,' replies Frank.

'Well, I have had an approach, albeit on Twitter, from a guy who loved my book and said he would love to meet me and chat about adapting it for the big screen.'

'Wow Gar, that is great news man,' starts Frank, 'just tread carefully Gar.'

'Well, that's one of the reasons I'm ringing you actually...'

I didn't have a chance to finish my sentence when Frank interrupts with, 'Of course Gar. I will give you all the advice I can.'

'Yeah,' I start, 'that's great Frank, and very much appreciated, but I wanted to ask you how you'd feel about writing the adaptation yourself? You know how much I valued your input into the book in the first place. And I know, from listening to David, what a good playwright you are. So, I would be honoured if you felt like this was a good fit for you.'

There is silence on the phone for about twenty seconds, which for myself and Frank is a record. Then he says, 'Jesus Gar. Eh, I mean, well, I'd love to if I'm honest. Jesus man, thank you for even thinking of me.'

'You can thank David and Darina,' I reply, 'they are the ones who sold you to me. And, like I said, I know you know what you're doing. I trust you.' And when it came to something as serious as turning *Joys* into a film, trust was paramount to me. I knew I could trust Frank with my life, so I had no worries when it came to him. It was putting my trust in others that sadly backfired on me.

I met with the man who had reached out to me on Twitter and instantly liked him. He told me he conducts his work with another colleague, and we arranged to meet a few days later to discuss the idea of turning my book into a film. I was on cloud nine, but it can be dangerous when you are up that high. If you are not careful, you can fall. And sadly, I did.

I am not going to go into the 'ins and outs' of what happened between myself and these two men. All I will say is that I really liked both of them. They treated me so well and I enjoyed listening to their ideas for the film. We were even invited to my publisher's house so we could all sit down and have a chat. Frank was there, and I was really impressed with how he presented himself. At this stage, Frank had kindly agreed to take hold of the reins when it came to adapting my story. We became a team, and it's a team I am so grateful to be a part of. But, unfortunately, the two lads didn't seem to share my view. Something happened, and I was left feeling hurt and let down so myself and the two lads parted ways, though I wish both men success in all they do.

The one good thing from my parting with the two lads was that it actually pushed myself and Frank closer together. He told me one day that he had begun a synopsis of sorts, a rough guide, and asked if I would like to read it. I loved that Frank still wanted to work on the project, even though there were no offers on the table at the time. But if you believe in something, you never give up on it. And Frank and I really believed in this. In fact, I became a true believer once I had read the first rough draft that Frank had drawn up. It was only a page or so, but I loved it. He had created new names for each of the characters and was flexing his creative muscle.

'That is fuckin' quality Frank,' I almost shot at him.

'Ah, it's not Gar. It's only a start. And this is just what is coming out of me from reading your book. But I hope this synopsis of sorts might be good enough to catch the eye of potential filmmakers.'

'Well, I love it Frank. So, if you want to put it out there and see what happens? I'm good with that.'

And so he did. We were presenting ourselves as a team. And there was no way I was giving away the rights to my book if Frank wasn't part of the deal. So, we plugged away, but nothing major happened.

Then life took over. My health was still deplorable and I was struggling daily. So as much as these dreams of turning my book into a film were exciting, the realisation that I was suffering from delusions of grandeur soon made me cop on a bit. *A feckin' film – who was I kidding?* were the thoughts that went through my mind. I gave up on the idea and returned my focus to getting better, and getting back to work.

But Frank never gave up.

One day, Antoinette and I were out with both of our mams. We were sitting in a coffee shop, and I find I am the butt of my mam and Antoinette's jokes. They enjoy teaming up and attacking me, and they're both very funny at doing it. And if I dared to answer Antoinette back, my mam would jump to her defense. Even if Antoinette was completely in the wrong! I loved it. In fact, when the two of them gang up on me, I can honestly tell you I feel nothing but happiness. At least Antoinette's mammy is always on my side.

So, there I am, getting slagged by two head cases, when my phone rings. It's Frank. He seemed a little out of breath, and I tell him to calm down. I was worried. I thought something had happened. It takes Frank a further fifteen seconds to gather himself before he says, 'Sorry man. I'm just a bit excited. Are you out and about there?'

'I am Frank,' I respond, 'I'm just out having coffee with two slagging feckers, and Annie's ma.'

Frank seems completely uninterested in my joke, but what he says next explained everything to me.

'Great. You're with your mam and Antoinette, *and* Antoinette's mam, that's great. Okay man, are you sitting down?'

I was about to fuckin' pass out with the excitement and I barked back, 'Of course I'm bleedin' sitting down. What in God's name is going on with ya buddy?'

'Well, I got an email this morning Gar...' Then nothing. He just stops talking. Is he taking the piss?

'Frank?!? Are you there?' I shout. Another slight pause, followed by Frank's unmistakable laugh.

'Of course I'm here, ya eejit, I was just trying to build suspense.'

'Come on Franky-Boy, spit it out...'

What Frank did eventually spit out rocked me to my very core, as it did the three beautiful ladies sitting next to me. But, if I was to tell you every last detail now, well, where would the suspense be? This is the end of my story, for now. So I must end on a cliffhanger. That seems like the right thing to do.

So, here is the first thing Frank said to me that day:

'Gar? Have you ever heard the names Juanita Wilson and James Flynn before, or Metropolitan Films?'

Chapter 46

A Time to Reflect...

As I write the final words of this story, I am filled with so many mixed emotions. The writing of this tale brought with it the same feelings I had when I was experiencing these events in real life. I have smiled, even laughed, whilst remembering the good times. I have felt shame and regret as I relived the darker times. I've gone up and down like a fuckin' yoyo, but the one feeling that seems stronger than the rest is the feeling of pride that now engulfs me. I knew from the start I had to be as honest as I could while I wrote this story. Believe it or not, I could have elaborated more on the darker times. I could have brought you on a much more depressing journey. But that was never my intention. Instead, I wanted to show how much can be achieved when you embrace a positive lifestyle, when you believe in yourself. I wanted to show the importance of family and friends, and how it is imperative that you reach out if you find yourself down or lost. And, above all, I wanted to show you that anyone can change.

My change from idiotic Gary to a slightly less idiotic Gary was hampered at every turn by all the rejections and knock backs I was receiving. But then I would find myself thinking of other men and women who weren't as lucky as I was. Who had no family or friends. Who did not have one person believing in them. I imagined them trying to find work and facing the same rejections I had. I remember one lad coming up to talk to me.

'Gar, I just can't get a job anywhere! I'd pick shit up off the street if they would pay me to do it, but I can't get work. I need money Gar, and if something doesn't happen soon, well, I know how to make money.'

His last statement made my blood run cold. I lit on him, and explained that that shouldn't even be an option. Imagine, after serving your time, changing your life, trying to go on the straight and narrow, but with all the rejections, thinking, *ah, sure I'll just go back to doing what I was doing that landed me in prison in the first place.* Insanity. Thankfully, this man didn't go down that road and he is doing really well now. But what about the ones who did choose that path?

I have stated already that there are men and women who have no longing for change, who are happy living their life in an illegal way, no matter what you or I think. But there is an army of men and women just like me who fucked up royally, but who want nothing more than to change and reform. The reoffending rate in this country sits somewhere around an alarming 65%. Yes, some may be 'scumbags', but how many tried and tried but got sick of being rejected for the same reason: 'You were in prison, you're damaged goods.'

I had the honour of writing an article in *The Irish Times* last year. In it, I spoke of these fears I have just laid out for you, and the reaction to it was very positive. And this left me feeling somewhat optimistic. I suppose I expected a backlash along the lines of, *Look at yer man, stickin' up for prisoners. Bleedin' gobshite!* But I really feel that something needs to change. It would take a lot of work, a lot of trust and a lot of risk to bring it about, but it would benefit us all.

With this book, my hope was to highlight that not everyone who walks out of the gates of a prison is bad. If they are capable of showing you how sorry they are, how much they have changed, and how much they long for some sort of normality, should they not be given a chance? Maybe if they got one that reoffending rate might start to decrease.

I have had the chance to meet all the fantastic people who have graced the pages of this book. I even got to have coffee with an idol of mine, and I wanted to share the story of this man's generosity with you at the end. Saving the best for last, so to speak.

Thanks to Maggie, I got to hand a copy of my book to the author and playwright Peter Sheridan. As I did so I said that it felt like a football player from the local pub team handing his boots to Pelé, which made Peter laugh. He ended up loving my book. I find the tears are coming, so I'll pause and let Peter tell you, in his own words, how much he enjoyed it:

> Many people thought that Brendan Behan had given us the definitive Mountjoy story in his play, *The Quare Fellow*. Then along comes Gary Cunningham, and he gives us another unforgettable experience in the history of this infamous Gaol. *Joys of Joy* just teems with life and it is both heart-breaking and hilarious. At the heart of it all, is an author who is not afraid to reveal his vulnerability and the book, in the end, becomes a spiritual reflection on the themes of love, life and loss. I wholeheartedly recommend it.
>
> Peter Sheridan

All I can say is, thank you Mr. Sheridan.

So, I keep going. My health is just as bad today, in fact it's slightly worse than it was when I first started experiencing these difficulties. But my family are so supportive, especially my mam, and so are the friends I now share my days with. There is one part of my life that, somehow, gets better with every passing second – my relationship with Antoinette. I would not be where I am today without her, and I love her with everything I've got. I have shown how hard things have been for us, but we never complain. We've got each other, and that's all that matters. And as I say my goodbye to you, I will now walk down the stairs into my living room, take Antoinette by the hands, look into her magnificent eyes and say: 'Thank you baby. Thank you for being my everything. I love you Antoinette.'

ACKNOWLEDGEMENTS

This book is filled with acknowledgments, which makes me feel so proud, as that was a primary goal in writing it. I would still like to take a short moment to thank the following people, without whom I wouldn't be where I am today:

My entire family: For everything you have done and continue to do for me, with a special mention going out to my nephews and nieces, Mark, Alan, Jennifer, Leah, Cian, Calvin, Séan, Sarah, Conor, Luke, Adam and Dylan. And, of course, my brothers and sister-in-law. Each of you owns a very large piece of my heart, and I love you all so very much.

Antoinette's family: I just want to say I love you all so much (even you David). You have all made me feel like the luckiest man alive.

My mam and Antoinette: Without you I wouldn't be where I am today. My love for the two of you cannot be measured. Sure didn't I dedicate this book to you both? Knowing I have the two of you by my side makes me feel like I can take on any of life's challenges, and win. I, quite simply, adore you both with all I've got.

David and Darina: Where do I start? Never in a million years did I think I would be lucky enough to call such beautiful people my friends. Darina, you encapsulate perfectly all the good in this world. I love you so very much. And as for you

David (boss), I know you are similar to Fitzer when it comes to 'all that soppy shite', but I need you to know, that I am *blown away* and I think you're *amazing* (lol)!! All joking aside, I am in awe of your work, and moved by your friendship, and I will never be able to repay you for how you singlehandedly changed my whole life for the better.

Frank: 'Me aul' buddy wha'?' What can I say Frank? I hated you before we met (lol), I was wary of you for the first five minutes of our first meeting, and now I think the sun shines out of your arse! Since day one, you have done nothing but been a really good friend to me, and you have offered me incredible advice when I needed it most. And as for our future? It's looking bright buddy. I am just so sorry to Rachel for all the time I am stealing you away from her. Just one thing needs to change between us Franky-Boy – It begins with an M, ends with an O, and there is an A and a Y in the middle. *Hon the Dubs!*

James and Juanita: I am, quite simply, blown away by the both of you, in fact, I can't stop smiling. Here's to a very successful future together.

The Irish Prison Service: When I was under your care, you assisted me in changing my whole life around, and the support you have shown me since my release has knocked me off my feet. From prison officers to ACOs, Chiefs and Governors, I shall remain forever grateful for all you did for me.

To all the staff from the different radio shows I was so lucky to be invited onto, and to the crew from *The Late Late Show*, from the bottom of my heart ... *thank you all so very much*. The way you all treated me has left me with the most beautiful of memories.

Niall and Karen: Thanks for being my friend. Thanks for caring for me. And most importantly, thank you for showing this world that true love really does exist.

To all the lads I did me whack with ... cheers for the friendship, both in there and out here. I hope each and every one of you is living a life that you truly deserve.

Mark and Kenneth: 'I fuckin' love the pair of yiz.'

And to all my friends on Facebook. A big beautiful bunch that have assisted in making me who I am today. I love you all so very much.

To Robert and all the staff at Anderson and Gallagher Solicitors. You all helped me during a very dark and painful time in my life, and I will always remain grateful for that, and for all the work you have done for me.

Fitzer, Ash, Cian, and Calum: Fitzer, you can feck off. But Ash, Cian and Calum, I really want you to know that I am just crazy about you all. From videos of Cian singing to the most adorable photos of my godson Calum, I find I am topped up daily with love. And you know how much I love you Ash. You mean the world to me. Thank you for being my friend. And I suppose you are all right too Fitzer (ya know I love ya, me aul' mucker)!

My last thanks go to you, the person good enough to be holding this book in your hands. I hope you have enjoyed my story, and I hope you come away from it clear in the knowledge that, with the right attitude, you can achieve anything. That is my dream anyway...

And if you want to hear some of The Off#enders songs, head over to YouTube and search Gary Cunningham, The Offenders.